PENNANT RACE

Jim Brosnan was born in Cincinnati, Ohio, and grew up there. After graduating high school he was signed to a minor league contract by the Chicago Cubs, and later played major league baseball for the Cubs, the St. Louis Cardinals, the Cincinnati Reds, and the Chicago White Sox. In eight and a half major league seasons as a pitcher, he won 55 games, lost 47, and had an earned run average of 3.54. His book *The Long Season* is often called the best baseball book ever written by a player.

PENNANT RACE

by JIM BROSNAN

IVAN R. DEE   CHICAGO

Library of Congress Cataloging-in-Publication Data:
Brosnan, Jim.
    Pennant race / Jim Brosnan.
      p. cm.
   Reprint. Originally published: New York : Harper, 1962.
    ISBN 1-56663-549-7 (alk. paper)
   1. Cincinnati Reds (Baseball team) I. Title.
GV875.C65B7 2004
796.357'64'0977178—dc22   2003062732

Introduction

Critics of major league baseball claim it is a dull game. "Nothing ever happens," they say. "There's nothing new in baseball. You see one game you've seen them all."

Major league ballplayers claim that theirs is a tough, challenging profession, for: "You learn something new every day."

The fan's-eye view is limited; yet he always thinks he knows what's going on. (If he's not sure, he tunes in on a broadcaster or telecaster who is positive that *he* knows what's going on.)

The veteran professional ballplayer is never sure of what will happen in any given play on any given day. When he's wrong he desperately calls it "percentage" or "the breaks"; when he's right he modestly calls it "experience." His life is extremely rewarding when he wins, extremely frustrating if he loses. On and off the field he finds that every day has its moments if he swings with it. The pleasant, and unpleasant, nuances are carefully treasured, not easily forgotten.

This journal is my attempt to record the daily, game-by-game lives of the Cincinnati Reds during 1961. Some of it was written under the influence of success. Never taken seriously as pennant contenders, the Reds found ways and means to win often enough in the season of '61. *How* and *why* they won the pennant is the subject of my book.

Pennants are won as games are played, but baseball life stands out in a series of episodes, or recollections of the scheduled series as they succeed each other during the season. There are varying degrees of disappointment in the life of a ballplayer, for even on a pennant winner he must lose 35 percent of the time. Each game has its moments and a pennant-winning seasonful presents a memorable kaleidoscope.

This journal is as accurate as I could make it, using daily notes and my own fallible observations. Myopia and a begrudging cynicism may have obscured the flag from my sight until the last out of the final, pennant-clinching game. It was really there then; and it is really here now, dedicated to the men who made it worthwhile.

Cincinnati — April 11

LIKE most baseball seasons in Cincinnati the 1961 National League schedule opened to the optimistic applause of a packed house at Crosley Field. The encouraging shouts of the Red bench echoed throughout the stands as eight white-uniformed Reds rushed onto the field, followed more leisurely by the pitcher starting the first game of the year. For all of us, as hopefully expectant as the crowd, the symbolic opening bell rang loud and clear.

Earlier in the day the pregame clubhouse meeting had been postponed till one o'clock—"after we hit," said Fred Hutchinson. Gave him more time to think of something to say. Hutch, in the throes of uplifting oratory, tends to mumble, verbally. His gestures are vehement, his hands gripping the tension and flexing the atmosphere almost tangibly. His eyes urgently seek and push. His words seep through clenched teeth, baffling the avidly attentive ear.

He'd made one dramatic appeal, as forcefully pleading as he can get, during the "Meet The Reds" luncheon the day before. Hutch concluded his analysis of the club's hopes by saying, "I'm putting the burden on our young pitchers. Of course they can take it, I think. They've got great arms, great desire, great potential. We'll go as far as they can take us."

In the clubhouse before the game he said, simply, "This is it. *You* know it. Wish you all a good year. Let's go get 'em."

Ask a pro how he feels on Opening Day, he'll say, "I feel . . . uh, great. Why not? Great day for a ball game." Then he'll rush around the clubhouse shaking hands, urging each teammate to "Have a good season!"

Six weeks of spring training had given little indication that a good season was in prospect. After one particularly inept performance in mid-March the new general manager, Bill DeWitt, had said, "If I'd seen some of these guys play before they talked contract with me, I might have signed them for less money!"

Hot, sunny days and balmy nights in Tampa may have contributed to the miasma that affected the Reds in the first twenty games of the spring training schedule. Florida weather is not usually so pleasant—spring training, 1961, had elements of a vacation, even for ballplayers.

After we broke camp on April 4, and headed north, the weather turned bad and the Reds started to play well. The starting pitchers, especially Jim O'Toole, shook the soreness from their arms, lengthened their strides, and jammed the ball down the Milwaukee batters' throats. Bill Henry, the skinny left-hander from Texas, threw as hard as anyone could expect and encouraged Hutchinson to predict we'd have the strongest bullpen in the league.

We had a four-game winning streak when we arrived in Cincinnati to open the season, and even DeWitt was convinced that the Reds not only would show up for every scheduled game but would even win a few before October.

Young O'Toole shouldered the load for the first of the 154 steps along the 1961 National League tour. Jim's a bit too cocky to be nervous, you'd say; but he had failed to hit a ball out of the cage during his batting practice, causing Bill Henry to yell at him from center field, "Put the bat down, O'Toole. You're making me sick!"

O'Toole looked better with the warm-up ball in his hands, kneading it quietly while one hundred and one photographers bustled about the dugout snapping pictures of other photographers taking pictures of ballplayers smiling slightly green smiles. As we lined up along the third base line for the pre-game introduction, O'Toole stared at the minute hand of the scoreboard clock and asked me, "Don't you think I should warm up? You didn't wait for all this crap to finish, did ya?"

"Go ahead, I guess," I urged him. "Get hot. And try to go farther than I did last year." (Although I'd thrown the first pitch of the 1960 season I watched most of that Opening Day game on TV, after the second inning. Nerves, of course. *I'm* only *half*-Irish.)

O'Toole is as brash as Brendan Behan himself and he brushed the Chicago Cub batters aside as if they were teetotaling drama critics. The season was hardly an hour old before Robinson and Post had hit home runs for us. O'Toole himself had lined two singles over shortstop and Henry's sarcasm had turned to chuckles. It isn't every day that a bull-penner gets a chance to laugh. Most days we work, running down to the bullpen mound, hushing stomach butterflies, and cursing the "lousy starting pitchers who get four days' rest between assignments and can't go five innings without getting into trouble."

In the sixth inning O'Toole had a six-run lead to go with his self-confidence. It was hardly necessary for Henry and me to warm up in the ninth inning.

"You should hit so well as Tootie this year," I said to Henry.

"You should pitch so good," he retorted.

All in all, it was a pretty dull Opening Day game. Don't know why O'Toole was so excited after the ninth inning had ended. He damn near kissed Post in the clubhouse, where two celebrations were carried on simultaneously, one for the win, and another, even more pleasant: we would be allowed beer in the clubhouse during the 1961 season!

Even the peanut vendors, wearing stovepipe hats and pushing their dilapidated carts down Dalton Street couldn't have sung happier work songs.

Elvin Tappe, the Cubs' coach, had one sharp comment on the game:

"———!" (He said it quietly, though.)

The only good thing about a cold spring day at the ball park is the pitcher's heart-warming sight of the flag blowing in from center field. Takes a brisk wind to hold today's lively ball inside the park. So, blow, nor'easter, blow.

On the other hand, cold days usually follow or concur with rain showers, and the soggy, spring-green grass of the outfield makes pregame practice gingerly distasteful footwise. Extra-thick inner soles plus two pair of socks can't keep the damp cold out. The clubhouse consensus is usually, and was on this, our second, day, "They can't be serious, can they, about playing this contest?"

3

"Forget it!" said Lew Crosley, scion of the Cincinnati club owners and for the apprentice-time, novice ticket salesman. "We have ten thousand coming for Safety Patrol Day and the game's being televised. We'll play."

Crosley waved at the TV cameras behind home plate, pointing with a legal-sized memo pad containing "Bills, bills. The creditors are after us. Expensive spring training, you know."

I shivered sympathetically. "But, Lew," I said, "you made a fortune on concessions on Opening Day! It was in the paper." Sportservice, Inc., claimed that 300 vendors had sold 24,000 hot dogs, 350 pounds of hamburgers, 300 pounds of fish, 1,200 pounds of popcorn—"and that ain't peanuts, Lew."

"We sold twenty thousand bags of them, too. Go get warmed up, Brosnan!"

It was too finger-stiffening cold for cowhide gloves by Wilson, a conclusion of mine soon confirmed by Vada Pinson, who donned woolen mittens before taking his batting practice.

Marshall Bridges and I shivered uncomfortably in the outfield as Pinson swung weakly at four pitches and ran back to the warm-heated dugout. Bridges, a colored left-hander from Jackson, Mississippi, who had several nicknames like "The Fox" and "The Sheriff," threw his glove on the ground, put his hands in his jacket pockets, and stamped up and down.

"Did you know," I asked Bridges, "there's a hot prospect at the University of Cincinnati who puts on golf gloves before he hits so he won't bruise his pitching hand? He's a left-hander, of course."

"Sho' nuff?" said Bridges. "How much he want to sign?"

"Fifty thousand dollars, of course," I said. "A year. For life, or thereabouts. Great prospect."

"Guess we'll get to hit off'n him then, I guess," Bridges said, shaking his head sadly.

It is the temper-straining responsibility of major league pitchers to suffer wishful-dreaming amateurs to throw batting practice at, toward, and around the plate three hours before the game in the home park. Pitchers are allowed to hit just forty hours a season, half of which time seems to be spent in helpless, disapproving audience of semi-pro deliveries. I

4

joined Bridges in a pitcher-pitying groan, then ran across the field twenty times to stir my blood before the game.

Although the weather was as cold as the seat of a gravedigger's consciousness, our Florida-conditioned bats were still hot and we had ten hits by the end of the fourth inning. So curiously timed or placed were they, however, that we had managed just two runs, or enough to tie the score. This frustrating bounce of the old ball added further warmth to the old bullpen, where an election was taking place.

"Who's to be Captain of the Bullpen?"

The question raised a noisy wrangle, for the two catchers, natural nominees, declined the job because of inexperience. Since Pitching Coach Jim Turner had decided to stay on the bench with the rest of the brains, it was necessary to elect, or appoint, a man in charge—of answering the telephone, ordering hot dogs and peanuts, guarding the warm-up balls, and alerting all sleeping or relaxing pitchers on hot Saturday afternoons. There had to be a man of authority in the bullpen. Anarchy will never lead to a championship.

Jim Turner, who had been pitching coach for the New York Yankees for ten years, was an ex-Cincinnati Red pitcher. He had played with the last pennant-winning Cincinnati team, in 1940. As a starting pitcher he had spent most of his time then in the dugout, and apparently he had no more desire now to enjoy the home games from our bullpen.

Turner, known as "The Colonel," had taken a somewhat unorthodox position, at least for National League pitching coaches. Most of them lived in the bullpen with the relief pitchers, who often need more help than the starters—or so it says in the Book.

Jerry Lynch, the Reds'—and the world's—No. 1 pinch-hitter, explained Turner's stand.

"The Colonel wants to watch all his troops work on the mound. You guys in the bullpen will have to take care of yourselves until you come in to pitch during a game. Who wants to be Captain?"

"I do," I said. "Besides, somebody wrote my name all over the bullpen wall: 'Brosnan, Captain.'"

"Looks like you're it then, Broz," said Lynch.

In the sixth inning the Cubs threatened to score. From then on both catchers warmed up the pitching staff—for exercise mostly, and, in the eighth, to good purpose. *We* threatened to score, necessitating the possible use of a pinch-hitter for the pitcher. Bill Henry and I heated our little dabs and Jerry Lynch batted for Jim Baumer, the eighth man in the order.

"What's the odds he swings at the first pitch?" asked Henry.

"Even," I said.

The Cubs changed pitchers, bringing in a left-hander, Jim Brewer. "Bet he takes one pitch now," I said.

"Never happen," Henry insisted. "Lynch came to swing."

He swung. First pitch. Home run. Ball game.

We'd taken the first two games of the season and left home in first place. That's the only way to start the year.

St. Louis — April 14

As we rode the bus to Busch Stadium for our first road game of the year Jay Hook, his attitude anxiously sincere, asked me, "What do you think of the academic quality of the Engineering School at the University of Cincinnati?"

I no more knew the answer to that question than a girl hop-scotch player would know how to handle Warren Spahn's curve, so I paused, pseudo-sagely, and said, "One of the best in the country."

Hook nodded, saying, "I've got to start a lab project somewhere. My whole summer is just about wasted, don't you see? Research-wise, that is."

"Sorry baseball's interfering with your career," I mumbled.

Hook, who has earned a B.S. in mechanical engineering and intends to pitch in the major leagues each summer while studying winters for his Master's and his doctorate, was scheduled to start against the St. Louis Cardinals in their home opener. In four years as a professional Hook had shown the kind of ability that brands young pitchers as "potentially great."

"How about researching twenty-seven hitters for tonight's

6

game," I thought to ask, but held my tongue, foregoing such mundane matters. Maybe Hook relaxes before a game by planning his future.

Nearly ten thousand fans decided to miss the game and its festivities, which included five pretty girls smiling in convertibles as they rode round the park playing "Redbird Queen." Not a princess in the bunch.

Hook ignored the parade. As it passed by he tightened his belt, fingered the ball, and walked out to warm up. His first fifty pitches were thrown side-arm instead of overhand.

"Somebody better tell him to get on top of the ball," I said to Bridges as we sat down in the bullpen.

No one did.

"He'll walk five men in the first three innings," I predicted. "He's got to get on top of his pitches to have good stuff."

"No, he won't," said Jim Maloney. "He'll be all right." (Those young kids stick together.)

Hook did walk two. He also hit two, was wildly and generally ineffective, and disgusted himself as well as Hutch, who got him out of there in the fifth.

I ran up to the dugout for a drink of water and a fresh chew of tobacco. Hook was still in the anteroom behind our dugout, pacing back and forth, back and forth, dragging his windbreaker over the wet, muddy concrete floor. His cap was pulled down tight over his forehead, his face drawn upward into the cap, his cheeks pinched in and flushed with an awesome, extreme anger. Self-hate.

You can't say a word that will help.

I patted him gingerly on his ass and walked out to the bench just in time to see Wally Post hit a tremendous drive off the big neon sign atop the Busch Stadium scoreboard. The neon eagle flapped as it does after all home runs there, but it looked rightfully scared. That's about as high and hard as a ball can be batted by a human being.

And suddenly, we were back in the game, goaded by the unprofessional, almost obscenely optimistic cheers of Otis Douglas, our physical training instructor. Curt Simmons, the Cardinal pitcher, had had just the one ball hit well off him in six innings, but Otis shouted, sneeringly, to the world, "We'll get him yet. You'll see." He roared at the Cardinals, the echo of his voice forcing similar bellows from the other bench-warmers in our dugout. The noise, unexpected but welcome, made the bats in the bat rack jump. In fifteen years as a professional ballplayer I'd never heard anything like it. If spirited enthusiasm could help win a pennant, we were loaded.

Before our half of the ninth was over we had five more runs, the Cardinals had used three more pitchers, and Hemus, the Cardinal manager, was flinching from the boos of nineteen thousand irritated fans. Since it was my job to get the last three outs I silently prayed for just one more run. You can't have too many.

In this, my first game of 1961, I felt as nervous as a doubt-ridden rookie. "Where, oh, where has my slider ball gone?" I hummed to myself as I walked out to the mound. My name, announced over the P.A. system, drew a few expected boos. One loud-mouth cried, "Go write a book, you hamburger!" (Well, now. Is it better to be a "hamburger" than a "hot dog"?) Distracted by the semantics of the insult I warmed up leisurely.

Red Schoendienst bounced a slow ground ball down the first base line and off I went after it with somebody yelling, "Get off that goddamn mound!" Probably Douglas, incited by Hutchinson. Hutch jeers at my graceless attempts to field ground balls.

The second bounce came up knee-high and into my lunging glove hand, surprising me and Gordon Coleman, the first baseman, who let me take the tag myself. Extraordinary play for me, but then, with such a lousy slider, I had to contribute something like a winning effort.

"Like a big cat you looked," said Coleman. "Now, get us two more outs."

I did. Three wins, no losses. Good God! We might never lose a game all year!

The beer was cold, gorgeously, tastefully cold. It always is after you win. So was the shower water. Somebody had used up a tankful of hot water.

(Had Hook tried drowning?)

Should the child of a major league pitcher be forced to attend school?

The question is not academic in some cases. In mine, for instance, it becomes a living aggravation when the National League schedule separates father and family for most parts of a six-month season. My wife and children must remain in our home in Morton Grove, a suburb of Chicago, until the school session ends in June. Meanwhile I run around the country playing games instead of being a parent.

I lay in bed pondering this irritating fact of major league life, waiting, bitterly sleepless, for the Sunday morning wake-up phone call from the Hotel Chase switchboard. The telephone rang.

"Hi, honey," she said. "Are you still in bed?"

That slightly husky bedroom voice could belong only to my wife, thank God. Three hundred miles away, though, goddamn it!

"What's the matter?" I said. "Anything wrong?"

"No, no," she said. "It's snowing! Two inches or more here in Chicago. So I crawled back into bed with the kids and thought I'd call you and hear you wake up. Jamie and Tim want to say hello, too. Here's Tim."

"Hi, Daddy. You know what? Jamie's got the day off from school. We're gonna play." (Poor kid must think he can have a family only at the whim of the weather.)

"That's good, Tim. Daddy'll be home next week."

"If it snows you won't have to go to the ball park, will you, Daddy?"

"As NBC decrees, son," I thought to myself, as bitter recollections of our first loss the day before returned to my mind.

Ordinarily the major league ballplayer looks at the question of nationwide television through rose-tinted glasses. Certain profits from TV sponsorship have enabled us to share in an attractive pension plan. And security is what we're all playing for, isn't it?

9

The reflective eye of the TV camera could hardly hurt a numbered back on the diamond, but the hands of Big Business behind that camera certainly can shape the pennant race and shake up the ballplayers. Consider Busch Stadium on April 15, 1961, a day dedicated to our fighting leeches of the Internal Revenue Service. Natural elements of rain, wind, and cold make the playing field suitable for sowing rice, perhaps, but not for playing major league baseball. In the heated press box high above the mortal fans and players sits Arthur Routzong, business manager of the Cardinals. His eyes closed as he surveys the nationwide audience about to view the game on NBC-TV, Routzong parries a reporter's question with a ready-made policy answer: "Yes, it looks bad down there, but don't you think NBC would be very unhappy if we didn't play this game?"

Amen.

And, with a stiff bow to the TV director, Chief Umpire Dusty Boggess started the game . . . in the rain . . . in the cold, persistent rain.

As a championship exhibition of professional baseball the game could have pleased only a well-soaked TV addict and bar patron. Our outfielders slipped and flopped twice while gloving fly balls. Their infielders couldn't pick up two wet ground balls which went for errors. And it wasn't lack of talent that caused Plate Umpire Vinnie Smith to make some apparent bad calls.

"I may have missed eight or eighteen pitches. I just couldn't see," Vinnie said.

The gloom was even more irritating in our dugout because the Cardinals scored two runs in the first inning and Ernie Broglio, their pitcher, looked unbeatable, weather or no. Dusty Boggess, umpiring at first base, stared straight ahead, refusing to look up at the sky or to the left at our dugout where cries were heard:

"Who in hell's running the league this year, Boggess—NBC?" And: "Why don't you call Sarnoff, Dusty, and see if it's all right to call the damn game?"

By the end of the fourth inning the outfield was a dank

green morass through which both teams' outfielders trudged, bitching loudly. The pitcher's mound, muddy and slippery, became increasingly dangerous. Broglio, an outstanding star and valuable Cardinal property, seemed likely to pull a leg muscle or strain his back as he delivered the ball. In the batter's box Cincinnati hitters backed and filled, hoping Broglio's arm might stiffen from the cold or melt in the rain. Finally Broglio called time and asked the groundskeeper to blot some of the puddles with sand. Two hours had dripped by.

Umpire Boggess supervised the hopeless task of drying the muddy mound with sand, then halted play for thirty minutes. His blue suit sopping wet, he suffered the insults from our bench with bedraggled dignity. Finally he called the game. Five innings had been completed, an official game, as any TV fan in sunny Florida could attest, and we had lost our first game of '61, 4-0. The fine blue smoke that rose from our dugout at the end was a vehement, profane blast, a lightning bolt of protest aimed at the fat wet head of Dusty Boggess as he walked off the field.

You wouldn't think they'd allow such language on TV.

The snow that my wife reported in Chicago hadn't hit St. Louis, although it would have been much better for us if it had. It was cold enough for the TV technicians to work, furred and parkaed in their perches above Busch Stadium. On the field officials of the Cardinals huddled by the batting cage, drinking hot coffee and chuckling merrily at the discomfiture of all the ballplayers in sight. There were a few fans in the stands, too, and Reggie Otero, our Cuban coach, stared at them in frozen-faced bewilderment.

"If I were a psychiatrist now," Otero said, "I'd go through those stands today and hand out one of my cards to each fan. And I'd tell them to stop in my office as soon as possible next week. 'Cause they must all be nuts!"

The temperature reached thirty-nine degrees as the game started. Batters, wearing leather golf gloves or woolen mittens, swung stiffly, striving desperately to avoid being jammed by a fast ball.

"Hit one on your fists today," said Gene Freese, "and you'll be numb to your armpits."

Clad in hooded, wool-lined overcoats, our bullpen crouched about a charcoal grille, graciously provided by the Cardinals for our comfort. In the third inning St. Louis threatened to score and Hutch signaled for me to warm up. Ha!

"What the hell," I said to Henry, grumbling as I peeled off layers of heavy clothing. "Do I look like a cold-weather pitcher?"

"It's warm in here," Henry said, smiling. "Go get naked!"

By the time I reached the bullpen and threw ten pitches O'Toole had weathered that Cardinal rally, and I ran back to the dugout, poured another bag of charcoal briquettes on the grille, and relaxed, stiffly. Getting up again in the fifth, seventh, and eighth, running down to the bullpen and throwing a few more pitches helped me pass the afternoon. The exercise was body-warming, and each appearance probably went out on the national TV network. To any pro, exposure is important, I suppose.

Hal Bevan greeted me in the eighth as I returned to the bench. Bevan, a veteran minor league ballplayer, getting one final shot at a major league job, looked at life with the special irony and humor-filled detachment of all well-traveled, aging pros. "You back here again?" he asked. "You sure spend a lotta time getting up and down, don't you, Broz."

"That's why I hired out. To go up and down."

I never did get into the game, but we lost anyway. Which made the few frozen fans happy. Nutty, but happy.

San Francisco — April 18

THE Sheraton-Palace Hotel is a huge, baroque boardinghouse on Market Street in San Francisco. It has a small side entrance on New Montgomery Street through which transient guests are more or less welcome if they don't mind the condescending greeting of those rejected members of Marin Peninsula aristocracy who work behind the front desk. Major league ballplayers are accepted, conditionally, with serious (money in advance) reservations, and we had checked in the night before.

The Garden Court, a quasi-open-air restaurant off the main lobby of the hotel, is not open to ballplayers for luncheon. One can get breakfast if he's properly attired, but coffee is forty-five cents a cup. In plain china cups.

Self-styled "Most Beautiful Dining Room in the World," the Garden Court once refused to serve the owner and general manager of the Cincinnati Reds although five unreserved, empty tables were evident. "We are saving them for Important People," said the maître d', a silver-haired greeter who could use a couple of fast sprints around the outfield to get into shape.

The Sheraton-Palace does not have automatic elevators, and as I stumbled self-consciously past the liveried official elevator starter I saw Bill Henry heading for the bus chartered to take us to the ball park for the night's work.

"Gabby!" I said. "You're still with us, ol' hoss! When they going to announce the trade?"

"Hutch is holding out," said Henry. "He wants the martini concession at the Stadium Club."

(Paired in the paper with the ninety-seventh printed rumor of a Henry-for-Blasingame trade between Cincinnati and the Giants was a note that three thousand martinis had been served on Opening Day to those elite fans at Candlestick Park who belonged to the exclusive Stadium Club.)

"I can't afford the trade anyway," Henry continued later as we settled down beneath blankets in the wind-swept right-field bullpen. "I'd have to have my car shipped out here, and the Air Freight would kill me. Forty cents a pound, four thousand pound car. You know? And besides, if this club trades me they'd take my suitcase back they gave me. I'd have to check out of the hotel carryin' my clothes in paper bags. They'd never let me outa the elevator in the lobby."

Henry, called "Gabby" because he usually treats the spoken word with the considered dignity of a Delphic oracle, grinned nervously. Any ballplayer who is publicly acknowledged as trade bait by his own club is entitled to be jumpy. He doesn't know from day to day where his season-long loyalty will lie.

"Who you rootin' for tonight, Gab?" asked Maloney.

"I'm with you, babe," Henry said.

We scored three first-inning runs and Henry said, "Look at that Loes now. Who's he think he's playin'—a bunch of kids? You gotta get naked out there if you wanna win in this league!"

Batted balls bounced around us as Giant Right-Fielder Cepeda chased them down. Loes, the Giant starter, took an early shower as we scored nine runs in three innings.

"Might as well go sit in the clubhouse," said Henry. "Ain't no need for us tonight."

The visitors' bullpen bench lies just outside the tunnel to the clubhouse. Good idea. Allows us access to the water cooler, smoking lounge, and rubbing table, where dull games are best enjoyed via radio, lying down. The Giant announcer gloomily described the action as I sat in the training room paring my nails.

"You guys in the bullpen got it made," said the clubhouse boy. "You know, when Pittsburgh was here, that Elroy Face spent six innings every game layin' on that table. Sleepin'!"

"Sure," said Henry, grumpily. "Why not? Don't think they'd trade him, do ya?"

Next morning's papers had us listed at the top of the National League, a fact which amused no less a baseball expert than the hotel barber, who breathed down my neck, "Well, it's a long season, isn't it?"

Cynical son-of-a-bitch.

The bus outside the barbershop loaded ballplayers fresh from breakfast, where they'd taken a lingering look at our No. 1 position, standing-wise. Made for jaunty steps, cocky walks. Down the sidewalk at that moment came an under-dressed, overbuilt young woman hardly unmindful of a bus-length gantlet of appraising eyes.

"Top-heavy."

"Double dribble."

"Choice wheels . . . but, ooh, a bad head!"

Sounds of a *winning* ball club. Truthfully critical. Blatant sexuality has less attraction than first place in the National League. In the morning, anyway.

"Did you win your first game in the majors?" Henry asked me.

Ken Hunt, a Young Phenom, was making his first start for Cincinnati. Hunt, a big twenty-two-year-old right-hander, hadn't even been on the Red roster when spring training started. He had had just one good minor league season, but he could "throw BB's," as all young men should. When he proved, in Florida, that he could throw them through the strike zone, Hutch signed him to a major league contract.

Hunt was not unduly impressed with his good fortune, nor did he appear to quake at the sight of the Giants as he warmed up for the game. He was an extra man in the bullpen, crowding the bench a bit, although we were anxious to give the kid all the help he'd need to win. That first one is a big one.

"Matter of fact I did, Gabby," I said to Henry as Hunt walked the first batter. "We won, 23-10."

Hunt walked two more hitters and a run was scored. Maloney heated up.

"Beat St. Louis," I went on. "Didn't know what I was doing."

Hunt retired the side; only one run scored.

"Almost tied a record that day," I mused. "Second time I hit in the same inning I just missed my second base-hit with the bases loaded."

"You always were a good hitter," Henry admitted, graciously. Pitchers love to butter up other pitchers about their hitting.

"Forget it!" said Hal Bevan. "Brosnan couldn't hit me with a broken finger." Bevan held up his splint and waved it at us. The white bandage covering Bevan's broken finger had a certain pathetic tone, even if Bevan laughed about it. Some years before, Bevan had been a Young Phenom himself, as a third baseman with the old Philadelphia Athletics. Sliding into a base he had broken his ankle so severely that he never could move well again, and had to return to the minors to learn how to be a catcher. Had he slid safely that day *he* would have had seniority in our bullpen—and been named Captain instead of me.

"Shut up, Sergeant," I said to Bevan. "As a matter of fact, I think I'll demote you to PFC. Move down the bench."

"You're taking this 'Captain of the Bullpen' a bit too seriously, Broz," said Maloney.

"And why not? I got seniority. Nineteen more days in the pension plan than anybody else."

Hunt and Sanford, of the Giants, dueled for six innings, tied up 2-2. Mays tried to steal second in the sixth, spikes up, cutting Elio Chacon, our Venezuelan second baseman, as he tagged Mays out.

"Mays slid a little high, didn't he?" asked Bevan. Chacon was carried past our bench to the clubhouse, his sliced thigh visible, bleeding from three spike wounds.

"Somebody'll have to knock Mays down now," I pointed out. "Can't have any rough stuff this early in the year."

"Did you know," said Bevan, "Chacon's brother cut *me* up just like that? In Venezuela one winter. I was playin' second then. See this scar on my hand? Well, he rips me real good, see. My leg, too. So they carry me off the field, take me to this, uh—well, *garage* practically, you'd call it. And they start sewing me up. Seven stitches. And I'm tryin' to tell them to give me a tetanus shot first. Y'know? But I can't speak any Spanish! You're lucky I'm here today, agitatin' ya."

I nodded, sympathetically, as Zimmerman, Bevan's roomie, said, "Jesus, will you shut up so I can watch the game!"

Jerry Zimmerman, a one-time bonus baby with the Boston Red Sox, had spent almost as many years in the minor leagues enjoying his good fortune as Hal Bevan had spent regretting his bad break. Although he had never quite justified the $75,000 that the Red Sox had given him for being a good-looking prospect, Zimmerman had developed a sense of humor that made him sound like a veteran old pro. He and Bevan had roomed together at Seattle in 1960 and reminded each other constantly that each had heard the other's stories before.

Tied 2-2 we went to the ninth with Hunt scheduled to hit third.

"Somebody's gonna have to heat up," Zimmerman pointed out. "Hutch'll use a hitter for sure."

I peeled off my jacket and looked around for my glove. We scored two runs to make my job look easier as I trudged out to the mound. Nine pitches were all I needed for three outs and an official save. (If a relief pitcher faces the tying run and finishes the ball game he receives a special credit—*a save*—to be used as a valuable argument at contract time.)

"You threw nothin' but fast balls, didn't ya?" said Bevan in the clubhouse as we drank beer. "Your slider wasn't worth a damn when you were warmin' up."

"Sure. They got one hit. On the only fast ball I threw," I said.

What I like is a bullpen catcher who has faith in my best pitch.

Before the game the next day I had my eyes peeled for two special fans. A local State Department representative had arranged to have a couple of V.I.P.'s from Venezuela sit in a box behind the Red dugout and (as he had said over the phone), "You can do your citizen's duty to promote inter-American friendship by talking with them for a few minutes. Okay?"

Why not? Anything for JFK.

Venezuelans, like most Latin Americans, seem to prefer vigorous, bloody revolutions to the dull peace and platitudes of U.S.-style democracy, but they do love baseball. Ergo, they can't be all bad.

Our two visitors from Caracas were smiling and friendly as we stared at each other before the game. My Spanish couldn't get me a passing grade in a freshman course in high school, and their Venezuelan made pleasant sounds without making any sense at all. Desperately I called Reggie Otero, who greeted the Venezuelans as long-lost *compadres*. Seems Otero had once managed a ball club in Caracas, where one of our two guests was a radio broadcaster. Which explained his mellifluous tone of voice but hardly helped us to exchange goodwill messages.

Finally I asked Otero if the Venezuelan government wouldn't consider sponsoring another postseason tour of major league players to Caracas, Maracaibo, and points south. Meanwhile I'd study Spanish or Portuguese or whatever they spoke and could oblige the State Department in proper manner. (Besides, having already traveled on baseball tours to Europe and the Far East I needed the South American trip to complete the baseball world circuit.) Otero's translation of my request evoked an apparently approving Venezuelan smile so I ran back to the outfield. If I hadn't made it for the State Department I'd gotten in a possible bid for me. Let us waste no pitches.

Alvin Dark, the Giant manager, took batting practice with his players, slapping the ball about the park just as he had done for ten years as an active player. Dark was a "scientific" hitter who always studied a pitched ball carefully, measuring its plateward movement with delicate optical precision, and striking at it with calculated force. At least 70 percent of the time all this concentrated coordination netted him a big, fat A.B. and a trip back to the dugout. The frustration tore at his soul, and Alvin, who eschews profanity, often released his pent-up self-torment by slinging his batting helmet around the dugout. (The helmet, constructed to protect the head from a loose fast ball, is of durable plastic. Occasionally unwary benchwarmers are bruised by helmet-slingers.)

Dark, according to the clubhouse grapevine, this year had kept his hands off the hats, although the frustrations of managing must be equally as intense as those of batting. Perhaps helmet-tossing lost its appeal one day several seasons ago. Dark, after a series of depressing trips to and from the batter's box, had finally smashed a line drive—right at an infielder.

"Look out now!" whispered the bench as Alvin ran back to the dugout, both hands gripping the helmet, his teeth grinding. Stopping still at the bat rack he carefully set the helmet down, half-turned to sit himself down on the bench, then wheeled about and leaped into the air, jumping onto his helmet and crunching it with the weight of his raging, spike-shod body.

18

The ball club made him pay for the helmet, of course.

As this day's game began and O'Toole and McCormick started what was to become a swift, classy pitching duel, bets were placed in our bullpen.

"There's too damn much noise down here," said Bevan. "A guy can't even think. Let's the three of us shut up for once—me, you, and Zimmerman."

I was more than willing. Conversation sharpens the ache of a hangover. "First guy to say anything buys the beer after the game," I said.

Silence reigned. Uneasily. "Gabby" Henry wouldn't join the bet and it amazed me how loud his few comments on life and the game could sound.

Late in the game, a fly ball was hit toward us. Harvey Kuenn, playing right field for the Giants, came running for it. Apparently Kuenn was going to have to run right into the wall to get to the ball, but no word of warning was sounded. The ball drifted back into the field and Kuenn, stumbling in front of our bench, caught it.

"Christ, let a guy know somethin'!" he yelled at us. No one said a word.

"That's sickening!" said Henry, shaking his head. "You three guys'd let a man get killed just so you could win a bet!"

Three grinning faces nodded in agreement.

There was little to say about the game either. The Giants won 2-1 in an hour and fifty minutes. O'Toole, shaking his head sadly as he dropped his spikes to the clubhouse floor, mumbled, "Three games I've pitched in this park. Two to one, two to one, and one to nothing. Enough to make a guy take the pipe."

Whoa now, boy. Rather have you sling helmets.

Los Angeles—April 21

THE baseball fan comes in every emotional size and shape. It is not surprising that in Los Angeles, where religious sects of outrageous and neurotic extremes are embarrassingly common,

19

some baseball fans go batty. One kook, not even lovably harmless, sends a mimeographed letter to visiting major league clubs, analyzing the Los Angeles Dodger ballplayers for all us stupid professionals. Convinced by his own wild imagination that, after just one year as Self-Appointed Super-Scout and Instructor, he is "now revolutionizing our National Game," he advertises his "Method Laboratory" as the "Home of Baseball's 'Orbit Swing' and 'Astronaut Pitch,' developments [how could you doubt it?] of 'Gyroscopic Space Age Balance.' "

Presumably this guy lost a lot of his marbles betting against the Dodgers in the '59 World Series. He's *against* the Dodgers anyway, "for the sake of science and the Future Instructional Purposes." Particularly, he hates Duke Snider. His "method" for pitching Snider is to "waste all pitches but the fast ball and use it to jam him with 'chin-skinners.' This will force him to hit your pitch" (on his back?) "or walk. *And he can't make* any money walking." End of Instruction.

Hoo boy. The mail you get some days.

At the Coliseum as we gathered for our usual pregame meeting on the hitters, our self-appointed adviser's instruction drew a giggle or two, as Hutchinson read from it to warm up, or relax, his audience.

"Now," Hutch said, turning to the score card, "about Moon. He's been hitting the ——— out of the ball!"

Wally Moon is a medium-sized, slightly bowlegged, left-handed-hitting outfielder. He doesn't look like an athlete particularly. He looks more like a skinny, beat-up cowboy, wiry but tired of the horse—game. (As a contrasting matter of fact, he has a Master's degree, is a clever guy despite all that, and uses his brain to make good money playing baseball.)

In the first ten games of the 1961 season Moon had hit six home runs over the left field screen at the Coliseum. That screen is just a few steps behind shortstop so that Moon's feat raised some cynical eyebrows as well as the admiration of the press, which proclaimed Moon a "Dodger Hero." (Our aforementioned adviser and some other sportswriters had originally recommended that all National League left-handers do as

Moon was doing when the Coliseum was adapted for baseball. Few pros paid much attention to this simple advice; those that did usually hit themselves into a slump. It isn't as easy as it looks.)

"Moon's always been a good fast hitter," said Hutchinson. "Now he's slicing pitches over that screen. Inside pitches. Fast balls as well as other stuff." Hutchinson paused, pursing his mouth in proper salute to Moon's accomplishments. "He's dangerous, real dangerous right now. Don't let him beat you."

That's not a hell of a lot of help, Hutch! Presumably one had to learn how to pitch to Moon by pitching to Moon. Still, he can't hit the inside fast ball and the outside fast ball the same way, with the same stroke. Suppose we make him hit nothing but fast balls away from him. Low fast balls. Perfect pitches right on the black edge of the plate. Or walk him. He can't be a Dodger hero walking all the time.

Moon hit a high outside fast ball over the screen in the second inning, a run that didn't beat us but which received a grudging acknowledgment from the bullpen.

"He's changed his style of hitting," I said.

"Yeah," said Henry. "Sure. You're real smart, aren't you?"

"*I'm* not smart," said Bevan, buttoning his parka over his windbreaker.

"You're stupid," said Zimmerman.

"You just wanta be as dumb as I am," Bevan retorted. "I'm so dumb I thought it would be as cold here as it was in Frisco so I brought this big coat out with me."

"Did you bring one for me?" I asked. "I'm Captain down here, ain't I?"

"Freeze, you smart bastard!" said Bevan, pulling the parka hood up over his head.

The Dodgers won, 5-3, and as the two clubs trudged up the long ramp to the clubhouse I walked along next to Wally Moon.

"Enjoyed your book," Moon said. "You doing any more writing?"

"As a matter of fact, yes," I said. And, like a typical writer, asked, "What are you doing different this year?"

"Nothing," Moon said, shrugging his shoulders. "Just a hot streak."

"Beautiful stroke you got, though," I said as we reached the locker room doors.

"Why don't you catch pneumonia for the weekend?" I added to myself.

"Did you know," asked Hal Bevan the next night, "Johnny Podres is the greatest left-hander I ever saw?"

I kicked open a folding metal chair, planted its legs in the bullpen gravel, and shivered uncomfortably in the smoggy, damp, chilly Coliseum air. Podres, pitching for the Dodgers, dazzled our troops, giving them lots of motion but very little baseball to hit at in the first inning of our second game with L.A. for 1961.

"One man's stupid opinion," I said to Bevan for the sake of a warming argument. "You ever seen Whitey Ford pitch?"

"Podres is the best I ever *hit* against then, you smart bastard!" Bevan said. "Listen to me now. I just get back from winter ball, see—couple years ago—and I'm having a good spring. Two hits every day in exhibition games. You know? I got a hot bat. So we play the Dodgers. Podres pitchin'. I ain't hit the ball yet off him! I *see* it. Like a big balloon. But I swing, it ain't there! All motion. I go back to the bench talkin' to myself."

"What did you say?" I asked, fascinated.

" 'Podres is the best left-hander I ever saw,' of course," said Bevan. "I'm through. I'm not talkin' to you no more."

Fortunately a fan sitting just behind us had brought a transistor radio along to hear Vin Scully broadcast the ball game. Scully is the best of baseball's broadcasters, a redhead with a wry twist of humor. Scully's gentle witticisms send titters of amusement throughout the Coliseum crowd as he describes the game. Seems like half the fans bring radios along to hear Scully tell them what is going on right before their eyes.

"One to Nothing" is as close to perfection as a game can be pitched. Podres, for L.A., and Joey Jay, for us, cut and polished a little gem for Scully and the fans. Jay, after giving up a run in the first inning, pitched even better than Podres, who needed a driving catch by Willie Davis of a line drive hit by Jay in order to stop one Red rally.

"Willie Davis will lead off the next inning," announced Scully as the Dodgers ran to their bench, where Davis was applauded. "Naturally."

Scully meant this as an aside, probably, but it's eerily true that a man, after he's made an outstanding defensive play, will often bat first in the next inning, earning fresh, loud applause. (Abner Doubleday and Destiny apparently agreed on this matter when they formulated the rules of baseball.)

In the ninth inning Bevan and I went through the unnecessary gestures of warming up in case we tied the score. "Best I ever saw," Bevan grumbled as Podres prepared to pitch. "Didn't I tell ya?"

"He's the best tonight anyway," I agreed, sadly watching as Jay climbed from our dugout and headed for the clubhouse. He could stand it no longer. The tension of the Perfectly Pitched Game is unique. Neither pitcher wants to lose; yet he must admire the other guy, too. Jay was not far ahead of the rest of us heading for the showers.

"They oughta win the pennant by twenty games," I said.

"Best I've seen so far in this league," Bevan agreed.

Making the Hollywood scene is a natural postgame pastime for any visiting major-leaguer earning over fifteen grand a year. It has something to do with Acting the Role of Celebrity. By one definition a celebrity is anybody who hogs headlines or otherwise impinges on the conscious mind of newspaper readers. (By definition in the bullpen such a print collector is known as an Ink Hound, and is as much suspect as he is read.)

Just before we had left San Francisco for Los Angeles Jim Murray, the *Times* columnist, called me from his Malibu home and suggested that I "play the role."

"We'll dine at Scandia, have a drink at Romanoff's—you'll like Mike—and catch the show at the Crescendo. Don Rickles is there. He likes baseball. Probably give you a plug. Now. I need a column for Sunday. The *Times* has a million circulation on that day and I'll mention your book. What do you think?"

With his expense account and my big mouth we might even get a good story out of one night's play. Murray had met the plane and, though I'm not good at playing that scene my role read swift, loud and funny—and so did his column two days later.

Willie Jones was reading it to several players huddled around him by the rubbing table as I came in to have my arm oiled before the Sunday game, the fifth and last of our Western trip. Murray had asked me sometime during the night to analyze the Dodgers. His interpretations of my comments (half me, half Murray) were short of calumny but as sensationally ego-destroying as an ex-*Time* magazine staffer could make them.

"Best column I ever saw on that sports page," I said to Jones, defensively.

"If you pitch today, they're li'ble to come to the plate throwin' bats at you," Willie warned me.

"Why don't you read the nice things in there?" I asked.

"They ain't so funny!" said Jones, grinning.

"We'll just call you 'The Ripper' from now on," said Zimmerman.

Apprehension bubbled in my stomach as I walked down the tunnel to the field, but aside from six boos from the stands and a hurt look on Don Drysdale's face I noticed little reaction. I ran five extra laps to get my legs in shape in case there were a fight during the game.

Seventeen thousand more boos, plus a few hisses, greeted me when I got into the game in the eighth inning. Vin Scully announced to his radio listeners (among whom were Mr. and Mrs. Jim Murray on the road to Palm Springs): "This guy Brosnan has to be the bravest man in Los Angeles. Here he's just written exactly what he's going to do to the Dodgers. Now he's gotta go out there and do it!"

Weak-kneed but strong-armed I picked up the ball, worried less about Dodger ire over my remarks (which didn't seem so funny in the daylight, come to think of it) than I was that I'd let what I said about them affect the way I pitched to them. Pitchers cannot afford to change their successful pitching pattern for any reason.

Four pitches earned me two outs, but Wally Moon ran the count to 3-2 and then persistently fouled off my best stuff. Murray (his wife attested) screamed every time Moon fouled off a pitch.

"I thought he was going to drive the car off the road," she commented. (She's not really a baseball fan or she'd never have noticed.)

Moon finally struck out, but the game was gone already. In four games we'd scored just five runs, wasting some pretty good pitching. After winning three straight games to start the season we'd lost six out of eight games to put us under .500, a percentage all professionals hope to attain at least, if not exceed. At this early stage of the season the pennant race was barely starting, but our performance as possible contenders had already nauseated Hutchinson. He invited us to stay dressed after the game for a little batting practice.

"Good," I said, lying to myself. Batting practice is pretty much of a drag any time. After a ball game . . . ugh!

Fortunately Hutch allowed those pitchers who threw to the hitters to shower and dress immediately. Jay Hook and I were shaving long before the bitching in the batting cage had ceased.

"They're really griping out there," said Hook. "Maybe I *wasn't* getting the ball over the plate all the time, but I wanted to work on my pitches."

"Forget it," I reminded him. Hitters have been criticizing batting practice pitchers since 1839. "Your job is to get your work in. Their job is to hit the ball. Christ, they got us into this, didn't they?"

Someday I must sit down with Murray and go over *our* club.

Chicago — April 24

"THE champagne is chilled," said my wife when she met our jet at the O'Hare Airport. "I'm in the mood. Let's celebrate something. It's going to rain tomorrow. You won't play."

"That's right, Daddy," echoed Jamie, solemnly. "I've been watching the Weather-Clock on TV. Vari-uh-ble showers and colder . . . uh . . . temperchurs."

"Is that what they teach you in school?" I asked her. "How to watch TV?"

"Oh, no," she laughed. "We just have fun in school. Playing games and stuff."

"Jamie, let me talk to your father," my wife said, pushing her into the back seat and snuggling up to me.

"Meat," she said, smiling. "I feel just like a bride every time I pick you up at the airport. All those ballplayers staring at me. Just like the wedding reception. Waiting for the car. Even Hutch leered at me while you were getting your luggage."

"That was his smile," I said. "Did it look a little sick? We haven't been hitting worth a damn. Can you hit?"

"Later, Daddy-o, later," she promised.

By the time the next game started two days later I'd given up tobacco, exercise, and even my part of bullpen conversation. Hal Bevan jumped at the chance to tell a long, uninterrupted, rambling tale of his boyhood in New Orleans. Bevan illustrated certain points with gestures of his right hand, which still had a broken, splinted middle finger and a nicotine-stained thumb that looked like the subject for a study of external skin cancer.

"Why don't you at least give up smoking with your right hand?" I mumbled. "Tobacco shortens your time, you know."

"So," Bevan said, frowning at my interruption, "we lived in this shotgun house, see. . . ."

I really didn't know what a "shotgun" house was but I was too tired, or slow, to insert the proper needling comment that would have covered up my ignorance and evoked an explanation. Bevan's monologue had a pleasant, lulling effect that soon put me in reverie. (Since the Cubs were considered lower than us even by Chicago writers we hoped to end our losing streak.)

Hutchinson simultaneously astonished me, O'Toole (our pitcher), and Hobbie (the Cubs' pitcher) by pinch-hitting Lynch for O'Toole in the seventh. O'Toole was down 1-0, but the one run came on the only hit Chicago had had. I had to warm up in a hurry. Ha!

Lynch relaxed at the plate, knowing that with two out, a man on second, and Cardenas the next hitter, Hobbie would not throw him a strike.

Hobbie (as I learned later) was thinking the same thing. Only: "Lynch can hit anything near the plate so I thought I'd fool him and throw a change-up! In the dirt, of course."

Hobbie's pitch never made the dirt. It hit a fan in the right-field bleachers and we were ahead 2-1. I was the pitcher. Sort of.

Santo hit my first pitch (a fast ball meant for his hands but thrown over the plate) into the right field corner for a double.

Frank Thomas hit my third pitch (a hanging slider) against the center field fence for another double.

Rodgers walked; and I was knocked out of there in two minutes and eighteen seconds. (My wife, alerted by Jamie while she was ironing my shirts, had said, "I'll be right there, honey," and missed the whole thing on television.)

That night I helped a couple of friends help me drink a quart of gin. For medicinal purposes, of course.

"Where in hell's the Dexamyl, Doc?" I yelled at the trainer, rooting about in his leather valise. "There's nothing in here but phenobarbital and that kind of crap."

"I don't have any more," said Rohde. "Gave out the last one yesterday. Get more when we get home."

"Been a rough road trip, huh, Doc?" I said. "How'm I to get through the day then? Order some more, Doc. It looks like a long season."

"Try one of these," he said.

"Jesus, that's got opium in it! Whaddya think I am, an addict or something?"

Ken Hunt started for us in our second game with Chicago, anxious to pitch a shutout and give us a chance to win. The momentum of losing a series of games creates a mental force against which a superhuman effort seems called for.

Don Cardwell started for the Cubs and hit a two-run homer in the second, adding despair to the cold in the bullpen. An attitude of let's-get-it-over-with prevailed as Cardwell pitched as well as he had swung the bat.

"Watch your hat after the game," said Henry. "The kids steal 'em here in this park."

"Game's not over yet, Gab," said Hook.

"Keep you eye on 'em," Henry warned.

Frank Robinson hit a hanging curve for a home run in the sixth but Thomas hit one for them in their half. The wind was off Lake Michigan, blowing into the plate; but a pitcher still cannot hang curve balls! I pulled my cap down over my eyes.

Hunt was relieved by Nunn in the seventh but Howie couldn't get the third Cub out in the eighth so Hutch asked me to. Banks hit my first pitch to Pinson and I hustled into the clubhouse.

"One pitch!" I smiled to myself in the shaving mirror. "One pitch a game. That's the way to work!"

"Congratulations," Bevan whispered. "You looked great. Listen. Guess was happened to Henry. All that jazz about kids stealing hats here? Well, some little brat reached over the screen—six feet at least—and took Gabby's! How about that?"

"Crazy. Some kid lifted mine in L.A., you know. Hazards of the profession."

The long bus ride to Midway Airport and the bumpy plane ride to Cincinnati were equally depressing. After winning four of six games to start the season we'd stumbled down the long road trip and returned home just one step out of the cellar. Where we looked like we belonged, to tell the truth.

Hutchinson was paged in the lobby of the Greater Cincinnati Airport just after our plane landed. Both sportswriters dashed for the phone booths.

28

"Somethin's happened," said Zimmerman. "Look at 'em go. Bet somebody's been traded."

Ed Bailey, his face white, rushed into the baggage room, where most of the club had gathered. "Boys," he said, "I'll see ya. I'm goin' to Frisco."

"Forget it, Gar," said Robinson. "You ain't goin' anywhere."

"Believe me, now! Hutch just told me! I gotta be in Milwaukee tomorrow." Bailey started to shake hands right and left. "My wife's just driven in from Knoxville today," he added. "Can you imagine that?"

"Well," said Robinson, "since it's you that's been traded we won't have to change our signs!"

Bailey didn't join in the laughter. "It's rough on a guy's family."

"The first time's always the hardest, Ed," I assured him. "You've been with this club too long anyway."

"Yeah. Ever since '53," Bailey said. He paused and shook his head. He started to say something, then stopped, and remained silent for several minutes. (A shocking feat in itself. I once thought his nickname "Gar" stemmed from "garrulous.") Finally he said in a low voice, "It's a funny feeling, you know?"

Baseball is not the career for a man who needs security.

Cincinnati — April 29

FROM my window on the twenty-seventh floor of the Netherland Hilton the panoramic vista of smoggy Cincinnati includes a miniaturized glimpse of the left field grandstand at Crosley Field. Below those rows of empty green chairs lies the bullpen, not visible from my room, but consciously sensed. I can't seem to get away from my work. I *liked* my room; liked to look at the horizon up the Millcreek Valley, to look down on Cincinnati. The other side of the hotel afforded a view of the Ohio River. Looking down at rivers gives me the blues.

To get to Crosley Field I usually take a bus through the old, crumbling streets of the Bottoms. Negroes stand on the corners watching their homes fall down. The insecurity of being in the second division of the National League—in the cellar even—leaves me. For twenty-five cents the daily bus ride gives me enough humility to get me through any baseball game, or season.

Occasionally the bus, as it rumbles toward the ball park, is stalled in traffic by the peanut vendor's cart. Wobbly-wheeled and groaning under a crazily tilted, six-foot-high stovepipe, the cart is pushed by a tall Negro in a shining, black-silk top hat. Undisturbed by the noise of the air-braking bus behind him the vendor waves traffic around him, the fingertips of his big hand poked through an old glove, charcoal-white, I'd guess. I'm a little color-blind.

The vendor fascinates me. He's not as old as he looks when he's roasting peanuts in front of the ball park gates. (I've seen his friend add gray to that black head with a piece of chalk.) The peanut vendor neither cries nor sings about his wares, but he's inevitably there, roasting his peanuts in what must be an original method.

Once after a night game, I saw him cheated of a bag of peanuts by one beer-happy passenger of a bus loaded with fans noisily irritated because we'd lost a game. I stared at the peanut vendor, who stood in the street empty-handed of the dime unreasonably withheld by the raucous peanut-eater, who slowly crept away in the back of the bus.

It was only peanuts but it looked as if it might have been a day's work for the vendor. He blinked his eyes—once, I think—then assumed his expression of melancholy resignation. I thought to myself, "Why don't I buy a bag of peanuts?" But:

I don't like peanuts.

I like pathos.

Joey Jay started for us against the Pirates. He had been shut out twice in two starts so all of us pitchers were extra-vehement in our cries to "get some goddamn runs." It's human nature to sympathize with the victim of nonsupport.

Unfortunately there's a peculiar fact of professional life among starting pitchers. There must be, on each club, some guy who seldom gets runs, just as there is one who almost always gets a bunch. Jay left in the sixth inning, down 5-0. We'd given the Pirates three runs; we had one more to give. They earned two.

At 9:24 P.M. our bats exploded—briefly. Freese homered, Post walked, Robinson homered, and Coleman tripled to left. The fans roared, phones rang in the bullpen, relief pitchers rushed back and forth, pinch-hitters swung bats . . . and the Pirates brought in Elroy Face to relieve Vernon Law. That brought some order to the situation.

We'd scored three runs, all on home runs. In seven games we'd scored just eleven runs, ten of them on home runs. That's because we were a power club. It said so in the papers.

Three runs were insufficient. We gave Pittsburgh four. A typical Pirate victory. They won the 1960 championship that way.

We might do well to try it. Try something, anyway. Losing seven games in a row is no way to win fans *or* pennants.

"Let's get up a pool for the bullpen," I suggested as I walked into the trainer's room at ten-fifteen the next day. "I'll bet we don't get away from here till seven o'clock tonight." We were scheduled for our first double-header of the season.

Bill Henry stood by the pill table, rubbing a salve on his lips. "Wind's blowin' in. We'll be eatin' supper at six."

"Hook's pitching," I reminded him. "There's a three-hour game right there."

"Paper says it's gonna rain," said Bevan. "I'll say we're outa here by three-thirty."

"How stupid can one guy get," scoffed Zimmerman. "Let's go, Gab!"

"Doc," said Henry. "Better get more of this salve. My lips have never been so sore as they have this season."

"You're talking too much, Henry, that's why," I said, and he grinned as if it were possible.

Hook rattled off three innings in fifty-nine minutes, which made my prediction look good, but put Bevan to sleep on a pile of seat cushions in the bullpen. We scored our daily quota of three runs early but Hook soon departed after Pittsburgh scored five; and I relieved him with an assortment of the lousiest pitches I'd seen from either the mound or the plate. Mediocre fast balls, hanging curves, a flat slider, and everything high! Anxiously, too anxiously, the Pirate batters swung, and squealed when they failed to hit the ball well. Outraged profanity covered the first base line down which most of them trotted in vain. I used up a month's worth of luck but they failed to score. We lost, 6-3, in two hours, twenty-one minutes.

Between games I stuffed myself at the clubhouse lunch table. Two roast beef sandwiches, two cups of soup, a bottle of grape soda, three dill pickles, one olive, and a bar of ice cream. Then, plugging a chew of tobacco into my mouth I went, burping, to the bullpen, comfortable in the knowledge that if I had to pitch in the second game I'd die with a full stomach.

Bob Schmidt, the catcher who had come from the Giants in the Bailey trade, joined the bullpen for the first time. I introduced myself, explained that I was the Captain, and gave him a corporal's rating because he had three years in the pension plan. Schmidt had once made the All-Star team and was a valuable receiver even if he didn't hit much.

"Did you ever see worse pitching than mine last game?" I asked him.

"No," he said.

I took away one of his stripes.

"You threw strikes, though," Schmidt added. "Took guts, but you got the ball over the plate. That's all you pitchers gotta do."

Bob Purkey got the first pitch of the second game over, and Virdon hit it off the center field fence. He scored three minutes later.

"Man, man!" cried Bridges. "Heah we go agin!"

"Tell us some lies, Fox," Maloney urged him. "I can't stand any more of this."

Bridges cleared his throat, spat out his chew, and we

gathered around. Bridges has a sense of the ridiculous as broad as his grinning face, and he was in rare form. For forty-five minutes while Purkey pitched well enough to keep our phone from ringing and we managed to score four (4!) runs, Bridges regaled us with tall tales about:

His hitting: "You can b'lieve this. The Fox can buggy-whip dat ball! Why, when ah hit a line drive the sho'tstop he jumps foh it, the centah fieldah he jumps foh it, then it cleahs the fence and dey go get the tape measurah."

His hunting: "One time I borrows me a ol' shotgun. It's a mess! Wires holdin' it together an' everythin'. So I spies me a rabbit. De rabbit sees me. He stops. I shoots. BWHAM! The barrel goes one way. The handle goes de othah way. Ah's scared ah broke mah hand! But de rabbit drops. So ah walks ovah, picks him up. Not a mark on him. Broz, now b'lieve me. Dat rabbit had a heart attackt!"

His hustling: "So ah says to this cute lil ol' fox—dis is *befoh* ah's married, yuh understand—ah says, 'Honey, let's me and you make a little happiness.' She . . . just . . . smiles! Ooh-eee!"

The phone rang in the seventh inning. Claude Osteen, the young left-hander from Reading, Ohio, answered it. "Yeah. Yeah. Okay." And he hung up.

"Hold it! Hold it, Claude!" I said. "That's no way to answer the phone. When the Colonel calls down here, you say, 'Yes, sah!' and then you repeat what he wants so there's no mistake. Now, what did he want?"

"He says for you and the Fox to stay loose."

"He's out of his cotton-pickin' mind," I mumbled.

Purkey was just six outs away from a 4-2 win and a welcome end to an eight-game losing streak that had dropped us into the National League cellar. The way I had pitched in the first game could hardly have inspired confidence in anyone that I could be a "stopper." Purkey, perhaps, sensed this. He breezed through the eighth and ninth, needing no help whatsoever.

I glanced at the clock just before Clemente grounded to Cardenas for the third out.

33

"Not quite six, 'Fess," said Bridges. "Pretty good day."

"You were great, Fox," I agreed.

The Philadelphia Phillies followed the Pirates into Cincinnati, a prospect that should have encouraged the most pessimistic Red fan. As bad as we had looked for two weeks, the Phillies had looked worse. We welcomed them.

Three hours before they showed up for the game we pitchers had already played one game. On our first day of batting practice we renewed a traditional rivalry—Bullpen vs. Starting Pitchers. As Captain of the Bullpen I had had to trade off one of our long men, since there were just four starters and six relievers at the batting cage. Unfortunately I made a bad deal, giving them Osteen and keeping Maloney. Osteen hit two out, Maloney one, and that was the score, 2-1. The wind, blowing in from left field, hampered our right-handed power. The Fox had forgotten his buggy whip.

"One more trade like that, Brosnan," said Henry, "and we're gonna have to court-martial you."

"Hit one out of the cage," I snarled, "before you pop off."

Those friendly games cause more dissension than they do good.

In the clubhouse the rumor circulated that Otis Douglas would give exercises in the gym—a small room attached to the trainer's room—"for all those that need it."

Sucking in my stomach I looked about the clubhouse, where some players cast furtive glances at their mirror reflections. Joey Jay frowned at his figure.

"Looks like you're about sixty-seven-laps-around-the-field overweight, Jumbo," I laughed.

"No, no," he said. "But I am about twelve jelly rolls and fifteen cream puffs too heavy tonight. I buy 'em for the kids, then eat 'em myself."

Hal Bevan groaned as Douglas tapped him on the shoulder and said, "You're first, Hal. Come on, let's do some sit-ups."

"But I might hurt my finger, Otis! Doc just took the splint off today!"

Douglas snickered, menacingly. (I had thought Otis was

34

supposed to be in charge of morale. Nothing deflates a ball-player's spirits more than exercise.)

On this cold Monday night with Philadelphia in town and the game being televised locally, nobody expected a crowd. Gene Mauch, the Phillies' manager, claimed he had a young, exciting ball club, but only two thousand people cared enough to come see them.

"Did I ever tell you about the time Mauch hung 'em up?" Zimmerman asked me in the bullpen.

Teeth chattering, I shook my head. "No," I said. "Don't tell me. I don't want to hear it. Every time you open your mouth you obscure the field with your breath."

"I'll tell you anyway," he said. "Mauch's the playing manager at Minneapolis, see. So he goes two-for-fifty-six or some-thin', and finally he asks the clubhouse man for a hammer and some nails, and he nails his shoes—right through the soles—into the wall behind his locker. That was a couple of years ago. Now, look where he is—in the majors."

"Barefoot?" I wondered.

He was with the right club.

The major league ballplayer is paid twice monthly, on the first and fifteenth—which accounted for the tranquil facial glow that lit up the clubhouse after the game. We won the game, 3-2, extending our winning streak to two straight, which made the beer taste better. And the beer, we learned, was *free*, courtesy of the brewery sponsoring the broadcasts of the games.

Beer makes some players happy. Winning ball games makes some players happy. Cashing checks makes me delirious with joy.

I opened my envelope to look at the deductions. I'd swear sometimes that I'm working for the government! Two weeks of hard labor—rapidly I calculated my time-on-the-mound in five games between April 15 and May 1; I'd actually toiled a total of ten minutes and thirteen seconds—and here I had seven columns full of deductions: F.I.C.A., City Tax, Withholding Tax, Pension Plan, Accounts Receivable, Advances, Fines, and

Net Amount. Damn good thing the beer *was* free.

"What should a starting pitcher in the majors make per year, Broz?" Maloney asked me in the Barn, a restaurant where we ate dinner after the game.

"If he starts thirty games he should make at least fifteen grand, no matter how young he is," I said.

"That should stir up the troops," I thought to myself. The Cincinnati Reds of 1961 obviously had the youngest, lowest-paid starting staff in the league: Hunt, Maloney, Hook, O'Toole, and Joey Jay. Maloney forked a sauce-covered spare rib into his mouth, swallowed some beer, and frowned. "I'm worth more money," he said. Maloney, a big, blond, young kid, not yet twenty-one, had already made enough money out of baseball to buy an apartment building. His $100,000 bonus had made him the biggest bonus baby on the team and stamped him as money-oriented.

"Do you think if I pitched tomorrow night like, say, Robin Roberts," Maloney went on, "that they'd give me a raise?"

"Roberts is 0-4 this year so far," I said. "You pitch like him and they'll send you to Indianapolis."

"He was a helluva pitcher, though, Broz."

"You're damn right. Some days he still is. But you're not him. Don't try to imitate him. Or anybody else. When you go out there you pitch like yourself, not like Jim Maloney imitating Robin Roberts . . . imitating Robin Roberts. Ol' Robby ain't what he used to be."

"Bet he's makin' over fifteen thousand," Maloney muttered.

The next night Ken Hunt, not Maloney, started the game, and threw 158 pitches in the first eight innings—which is a tough way to make a living. Still, he had a 3-2 lead when we came to bat in the bottom of the eighth. The bullpen phone rang.

"Tell Brosnan he's gonna finish up," said Hutchinson.

"Good God!" I grumbled. "He's mollycoddlin' the kid! Just 'cause he's underpaid doesn't mean he shouldn't try for nine innings!"

"Get naked!" said Henry.

I rushed up to the dugout to relieve myself before I took the mound to relieve Hunt. Seventeen pitches later Hutchinson shook my hand and said, "All right. You needed the work."

"Why did you bitch on that curve?" asked Willie Jones. "You know that just makes Barlick mad behind the plate."

"I was crying for later," I said. "Y'know that last pitch? It was a slider, three inches inside. But Barlick gives it to me. I *did* think he missed the curve earlier. It was right on the black. So I bitched a little. Not too much. Just enough. And he gives me the third strike a couple minutes later."

Lynch laughed. "That's our Broz. The Ol' Prof's always thinkin'."

What do you think I'm overpaid for?

The warm glow that I felt from our quick ascent from the cellar to seventh place was somewhat chilled the following morning when I opened my paper and read: "RICH REDS OVERWEIGHT!"

That headline on the sports page would be enough to scare a big league trainer into a diet. So it should have been no surprise to me to find myself nude on the clubhouse scale, trembling around the abdomen after a heavy Dago meal at Caproni's, where I'd read a news squib about Soviet aristocracy.

"What's the story, Doc?" I asked, whirling the weights back and forth on the scale and giving him a fast reading. "Two-thirteen, Doc. That includes veal parmigian', tortoni, and spaghetti on the side. Who wants to know?"

"Otis," said Doc Rohde. "He's gonna work some of that flab off your fat asses."

"Be discreet, Doc," I whispered. "Tell him I have gland trouble or something. I want no part of those exercises."

Hal Bevan tottered from the gym room, where the snapping of Douglas's commands and the moaning of mature male athletes was enough to make me cry. Bevan groaned, gripping the rubbing table with one hand while he massaged his stomach with the other. "I can't straighten up!" he yelped. "Otis is killin' me. I wanna go home to N'Orleans and die."

"Batting practice in ten minutes!" yelled Dick Sisler. "Hey,

37

Bevan! We need a catcher."

"Oh, God!" Bevan moaned. "Guess I'll hafta die with my shin guards on."

Otis Douglas played professional football until he was forty-four years old, and his tales of the mayhem and violence that pass for sport on the pro gridiron are enough to make my blood turn and run the other way. He sneers at the plaintive cries of baseball's babied batters who are afraid of a pitched ball.

"You got to learn to take care of yourself in this life," says Douglas. "If people know you'll run, they'll get their kicks chasin' you."

Big Otis (the name, coincidentally, of a cartoon character my boy, Tim, uses to intimidate *me*) has a rib cage like an aluminum washboard. He invites experimental punches. "Come on," he says. "Hit me in the stomach. Hard as you can."

The fat, rich Reds (who can get rich in Crosley Field? It seats only thirty thousand customers!) were convinced that Otis believed a pennant winner gets there on a solid stomach. His exercises caused several players to assume a constant crouching position like a partially deflated accordion. The sounds they made were inhuman.

For the moment pitchers are excluded.

Makes sense. We're underpaid. Can't be fat.

Maloney pitched as well as could be expected against the Phillies. He looked like Hunt as much as anyone, but we scored nine runs and Maloney made his way triumphantly to the shower—in the eighth inning. Henry had to pitch the ninth.

"We had a six-run lead so I couldn't hardly get a save even," said Henry. "And it was too cold to break a sweat. Waste of my time."

But it's great to be on a winner.

Whichever gods determine the fates of other players in the baseball world, there is a simple, unimaginative destiny controlling the fateful hand from which pitchers dance their roles, half-willingly. Coincidental pitching patterns seem to be established early in the season and nothing short of monsoon rains can change them.

Certain relief pitchers soon become attached to certain starters, making a tandem entry in the late-season gambling market, where the day's line is made up on the basis of who's pitching the day's game.

Bad weather plagues the appearances of one starter. He's a rainmaker. Another starting pitcher is an automatic run-maker, and his appearance on the mound makes his team's bats jump.

Conversely, another poor slob is doomed to draw an unbeatable opponent most of the time. If he's lucky he can count on two runs to work with.

Joey Jay looked more resigned than nervous as he waited for Doc Rohde to give his arm a massage before the final game of our series with the Phillies. In three starts he'd pitched well enough, but we hadn't scored a single run for him! That's a worse fate than being sent to Coventry by the union.

"Listen, Joe," I said, "if we get you a couple runs in the first, will you go nine?"

"It'll be a pleasure," he said.

"Okay, we'll root for you tonight in the bullpen," I said. Not that we don't support all starters, but in most cases it's covert, subconscious sympathizing, that doesn't interfere with the latest Fox tale.

". . . so ah start in to sweet-talkin' this lil ol' fox, y'see," Bridges went on . . . and on . . . and on.

"And you mean she put you down? That's hard to believe," said Nunn. "In fact, I believe that's the first time that's ever happened. At least in this bullpen."

"It's mah story, Nunn," said Bridges. "You gotta story? You jest wait. Now, y'see, ah figgah ah made a wrong move. Ah started scufflin' too soon."

"*Scufflin'!*" cried Nunn. "What the hell kinda language is that? Try and talk English, why don't ya?"

Bridges spat tobacco on the floor of the bullpen, stood up, buttoned his jacket, and said, "That does it. Ah'm leavin'. Goin' up on the bench where ah's 'preciated. And where it's warm."

39

The weather suited Joey Jay. He smiled briefly when we got him two runs in the first inning. Then he went to work, retiring twenty-four of the next twenty-five batters he faced.

In the ninth he threw two pitches over Amaro's head in retaliation for a knockdown pitch that had bounced off Frank Robinson's helmet in the eighth. Ed Vargo, the plate umpire, ran out to the mound to warn Jay not to throw at another hitter. And Hutchinson ran out to tell Vargo that he, Hutch, had told Jay to knock some Philly hitter down because "I'm not gonna stand by and see my boys hit in the head. I'll do something about it. You umpires don't seem to be able to!"

Hutch told Vargo to throw *him* out, not Jay, and when Vargo did just that, Hutch told him where he could stick the automatic fine that results from an umpire's eviction order. (What's more, a question was raised as to Vargo's parentage, which hadn't been at issue during the entire game. Vargo had called a remarkably good ball game behind the plate.)

Jay threw a third strike past the last Philly hitter, jumped off the mound, and danced a little happy jig, pounding his glove.

Shut 'em out and you're bound to get that first win.

Milwaukee — May 5

THE thing I like best about the Milwaukee Braves' ball park is its location, a ninety-minute drive from my home. I can hustle down there to play with the kids, or my wife can hustle north—"to get away from the little monsters for a while."

She brightened the empty rows of third-base-line boxes forty-five minutes before the game started. Her mink stole seemed hardly enough to keep her warm and I was afraid that she might, like a welcome spring flower, wilt before morning.

"Your wife looks mighty good to *me*, Broz," said Wally Post. "That is a pretty color mink."

"Isn't it, though? Elizabeth Taylor gets her furs at the same place, y'know."

"Wholesaled it, did you? That figures."

"You want the name? Evans. State Street, Chicago."

"I can't afford it. I don't write books."

Having wrapped a warm towel around my neck I donned a wool-lined parka, its pockets full of candy bars, and set out on the long trek to the right center field bullpen. The southeast wind, cold and damp from Lake Michigan, blew toward home plate, hardly an ill wind, from a pitcher's viewpoint.

Bob Purkey, our starting pitcher, was invariably described by a Cincinnati writer as "the handsome, clever change-up artist." As a matter of fact, Purkey *is* smart and good-looking (though his hairline is receding rapidly). But he uses a change-of-pace less than most pitchers, and likes to think of himself as a fast ball, sinker ball pitcher with a pretty good slider and an excellent—on some days—knuckle ball.

Purkey and Burdette, the Braves' pitcher, got right down to it, in a business-like way. Purkey, after two runs had scored in the first, knocked Aaron and Adcock down to show that he wasn't about to retreat under fire. Burdette, in retaliation, hit Purkey with a fast ball and it looked like it might be a warm night after all.

The fight never got off the mound, however, and we went into the ninth, down three runs. Burdette couldn't make it though, and before the Braves returned to their bench we were ahead 5-4 on Post's three-run, pinch-hit home run.

Hutch called me in to protect the lead and pick up a save for myself. Since my bread is earned with saves as well as wins, my wife led the scattered applause. (Purkey's brother, Don, sitting in the same box with my wife, added a hopeful cheer. Purkey stood to win the game since Post had hit for him.)

Spangler, the Braves' first hitter, missed my first two pitches, giving me confidence. It was too much. I hung him a curve ball. (Jerry Lynch said afterward, "I could have wrung your neck for throwin' him that lousy curve") and Spangler dropped it into left center for a double.

McMillan bunted and I threw the ball past first, allowing the tying run to score. My wife shuddered in the cold; and I didn't feel so damn hot either.

Blasingame had thoughtfully backed up first on the bunt,

catching my overthrow and preventing McMillan from taking second. So Lau had to bunt Mac over. And I finally had retired a batter.

Crandall batted for the pitcher, and I yelled at myself: "Let out a little shaft now." And: "Reach back for a little extra." And: "Bow your neck, Brosnan."

If I'd said those things to myself while I had two strikes on Spangler I wouldn't have been in this position!

Crandall grounded out to first, Maye bounced to second, and we were still in the game. We stayed there, tied, till the twelfth inning, when we scored one run. As I left the bench Hutch urged me, "Let out a little shaft now."

Truth is, I don't have a hell of a lot. That's why I'm a relief pitcher. But Lau hit the first pitch to Blasingame, encouraging me. Before the inning ended Logan and Bolling had fouled off twenty-one pitches between them; and eventually they both reached base, Logan on a walk and Bolling on an infield single. Hutch came out to get me and Bill Henry came in to save me.

I couldn't watch it. By the time Henry had thrown a third strike past Mathews I was opening a can of beer in the clubhouse. The taste of victory is the taste of Schlitz!

My wife, frozen as I had feared, grinned stiffly until after the third martini. "Why do I always get these extra-inning games?" she groaned. "God, I didn't think we'd ever get it over with."

Ray Jackson, whose restaurant fascinates her, finally bought her a Drambuie and got her mind off the field and back into the stands where it belongs.

". . . and this little boy comes up to us and says, 'Can I sit here with you?' and, Meat, believe me, he looked like a poster for CARE! You know? A waif! He had red hair and corduroy pants, and a *T-shirt* with just a blue-jean jacket over it. He must have been freezing. Purkey's brother asks him, 'Are you going to root for the Braves or the Reds?' and he says 'Sure!' and sits down and stares at me. Then he says, 'Lady, is that mink?'

42

" 'Yes,' I said. I had the damn thing over my head, my ears were so cold.

" 'Well, why are you so cold then?' he asks!

"Oh, he was so filthy and shivering I wanted to wrap my stole around him!"

She shook her head, reminiscing. She gets more out of sitting in the stands than I do pitching on the mound.

The Sunday morning sports page pompously proclaimed: "Mr. Wonderful will pitch the first game of the doubleheader. Warren Spahn, the great Milwaukee southpaw, will oppose Jimmy O'Toole, who has never beaten the Braves."

Such gloomy news seemed to doom our chances of extending our six-game winning streak. We were just two games out of the first division and close enough to first place to smell the Giants. Hutchinson switched his pitchers, sending O'Toole back to bed until the second game. Modern managerial strategy says there is no point in throwing your best against theirs. Play for one well-pitched game and hope their ace has a bad day.

Spahn, the hook-nosed left-hander, had given up just two hits in his last eighteen innings, winning both games by shutouts.

"Spahnie's due," said the hitters, hopefully.

"We'll get him today," said Jim Turner, our pitching coach. "At his age he can't pitch every fourth day and have his best stuff."

"He can't be perfect," agreed the pitchers. "Can he?"

As we came to bat in the eighth Spahn had a 4-0 lead and the admiring attention he'd received from our bullpen had given way to a diversion created by Marshall Bridges. The Fox was laughing and giggling, making fun of Howard Nunn.

Nunn is a small, slight-built right-hander who wears glasses and has a prominent, bobbing Adam's apple. To keep his glasses free from sweat Nunn wears a thick white band on his forehead. He's called "The Apache."

"You're in there, Howard," I yelled to him, relaying the word phoned from the bench.

"Now, wehr-r-k!" yelled Bridges, slapping his leg at the sight of Nunn hurriedly heating up.

Nunn, as if to compensate for his slight stature, is particularly intense in his pitching delivery. Disregarding classic, or Spalding *Guide*, form, Nunn throws all of himself into his pitches. His neck wobbles, his hips jerk, his elbows fly about, his front foot stomps the mound, and he stares, mouth agape, toward the plate after each pitch. Fortunately he gets pretty good stuff on his pitches, the sight of which is not so funny to the batter as it was to Marshall Bridges.

"Wehr-r-k! Wehr-r-k!" the Fox yelled, laughing hoarsely. "Dat's how ah'm tellin' ya, Nunn! Wehr-r-k!"

Bridges's glee had us all laughing and we hardly noticed that Spahn had walked the first man in the eighth. For most of the game Spahn had apparently been "pitching from behind," setting up the batter with one or two bad pitches in order to make him hit a precisely placed slider or screwball or change-of-pace. Actually Spahn's precision was off just a bit and he had been getting away with some bad pitches.

Now Robinson hit a hanging screwball out, and Post homered on a low, inside slider, and we were back in the game, 4-3. Nunn got them out in their half, and three minutes later Cardenas and Coleman had hit Spahn's last pitches of the day over the fence to give us the lead. Four home runs in less than ten minutes of play! Hell catches up with the best of pitchers.

It was a perfect day for the second game of a doubleheader. Sky blue, breeze balmy, temperature sixty degrees—and we were one game up on the Braves. Even O'Toole, with an 0-8 record for his career against Milwaukee, had a confident smile for everyone.

In the dugout I predicted, "We'll win this little dolly four to one. Watch and see."

"Dat's right," said Bridges. "If the 'Fess say so, we's gonna do it."

"Go take a hike, both of you," said Robinson. We walked out to the bullpen. O'Toole had his troubles at the start but he got stronger with every run we scored and it hardly was necessary for Henry and me to warm up in the eighth and

44

ninth. Turner, who had joined us for the first time in the bullpen, insisted that we get our work. "And we'll work out tomorrow, too. All you pitchers."

"What! After winning eight straight?"

"It's a long season," said Turner, explaining everything apparently.

Cincinnati — May 10

AT midnight thirty days after the season opens the major league roster is reduced to a maximum of twenty-five players. Frequently three men are cut off each squad. To each it means loss of status, sometimes loss of salary, always loss of pride. Cut-down day is a time of man-sized tears and tribulations.

The rookie, being optioned to a minor league club asks, "Do you think I really had a chance?"

The fringe player, his hopes of benchwarming all season dashed, splutters, "It's all politics!"

And the veteran, his age showing, tries to take it on the chin gracefully. He talks about the past, ignores the present, doubts his future. Any game on cut-down day has the elements of a last-chance drama.

In our bullpen Marshall Bridges dispelled the tension with a Mississippi tale of life with his wife. Supposedly, Mrs. Bridges enforces discipline with a broom, sending the Fox scurrying through the swamp making up stories on the run. He paused for breath and I jumped at the chance to sell a stolen, disguised aphorism.

Holding up one finger for extra attentiveness I declaimed: "One wife is too few, two are too many, three are not enough."

"Forget it, Brosnan," said Bevan.

"Dat's a good line, 'Fess," said Bridges. "Kin I use it?"

"Why not? I got it from James Thurber."

"Who he?"

"For Christ's sake, Bridges," said Nunn. "Everybody knows who James Thurber is!"

"Well, I ain't no college grad-jur-wate," said Bridges.

"I guess not. You can't even speak English," said Nunn.

45

"Don't get nobody out with good grammar," the Fox retorted.

Just then Jim Turner ran out from the dugout and said, "Bridges, you're in there. Get loose."

The Cardinals had threatened to score repeatedly against Joey Jay, but he took a 3-2 lead with him into the shower after the seventh inning. Bridges took over and walked the first two men he faced.

St. Louis had cut their squad before the game; and for a while it looked like twenty-five players would not be enough to finish the game. Hemus, substituting indiscriminately, now sent Ray Sadecki, a young pitcher, in to run for Musial, who had drawn Bridges's first pass. Sadecki was promptly picked off second for one out. Bridges mumbled, "Thanks, Ray, ol' buddy," then threw a hanging curve on a 3-2 pitch to Joe Cunningham. Joe lined to center and Pinson doubled Spencer off first to retire the side.

Bridges, sweating, said in the dugout, "When you's wild you gotta use them trick plays."

Hutchinson nodded, unsmiling, and called for Henry to pitch the ninth. Gabby fanned the side.

A press release was circulated throughout the clubhouse after the game. Harry Anderson, Jim Baumer, and Claude Osteen had been sent to the minors. Willie Jones got his unconditional release.

Any contract assignment depresses a ball club but "Unconditional Release" sounds so damn final. Old Willie gone!

Jones was one of the original Whiz Kids of Philadelphia. The press release said he was thirty-five. He looked forty, a happy, good-natured, well-used forty. Jones liked major league life. He treasured status symbols—Beefeater's, Early Times, any six-dollar Scotch. He liked to win so he could laugh it up.

He had a small smile left as we shook hands. "You never know when it's gonna come," he said.

It's coming, though. For all of us.

Pittsburgh—May 12

AN Eastern road trip in 1961 could be considered a drag by the National Leaguers, who once looked forward to playing games day and night in New York. (Pittsburgh and Philadelphia used to be rest havens, being alternate stops on the road to Brooklyn and the Polo Grounds—and Broadway, Greenwich Village—and like that.) Fresh, young appetites, not yet jaded by Big Town exposure, *can* be satisfied by night life as lived in Pittsburgh and Philadelphia. Even veteran players, trained in the Ebbets Field, pre-O'Malley days, learn to live it up, Pennsylvania-style.

In Pittsburgh, where the 1960 World Series ended in confetti showers, champagne parties, and victory celebrations, the professional baseball player became a celebrity. Even non-Pirates were accepted with the ego-lifting enthusiasm that makes a town a "good place to play ball in." (Spoken with zest and lust.)

In Philadelphia one learns quickly that the nightly rumbles of overt delinquents on mating drives along Market Street and in Rittenhouse Square will entertain the daring, nighttime tourist. If you want to dip an oar, the tempting Schuylkill River slinks softly through and around town.

In Pittsburgh it's tough to win a ball game, but the challenge of the World Champions stirs the blood. In Philadelphia it's tough to lose a game.

Flying from Cincinnati to Pittsburgh we encountered resistance at the Pennsylvania-Ohio border. Several large thunderheads intercepted our plane, accepted it as a plaything, and tossed it (and us) about for thirty minutes. The landing was noisier than most as the screaming of children, groaning of men, and sighing of the pilot added disharmony to the coughing of our three or four motors, all of doubtful quality, it seemed.

Hal Bevan looked greener than his years even after we'd gone to the park, where he admitted, "That woman getting sick on the plane made *me* sick."

"You never looked better, man," I assured him.

"Brosnan, you can take a flying leap at my ——," he yelled as I stumbled over the third base line on my way to the outfield. Forbes Field is supposed to have a rock infield, but it sometimes seems ridiculous. Pinson flinched as a crazily bouncing ball hit him on the chin.

"Professor, I don't know what to tell you," he said. "You see that ball jump?"

"With your speed, you'd hit .400 in this park, Vada," I said. "Just hit a ground ball, man, that's all you need to do."

"Okay, Professor, okay," he promised.

Pinson bounced a couple of hits around the infield, but it was a day for the long ball and a bad day for our winning streak. We were due to lose one after nine straight wins that had put us in fourth place. Combining that percentage with the trauma of facing the Pirates, we were odds on to lose, at least in the Oakland gambling market. In two years we'd found more ways to help Pittsburgh win than the Book calls for.

Even Dick Stuart had a friendly greeting for us as we walked up through their dugout and onto the field. Of course, he had good reason to welcome me to the game. I had once confessed that my best chance to get Stuart out was to pitch behind him.

He smiled, though warily, I thought, and said, "Broz, please don't hit me. I wanta get in your next book." Sympathizing with his ambition took some objectivity. He got in the last book by belting a home run five or six hundred feet off one of my best pitches. I nodded to him and walked out to our bullpen. Three young kids had draped a large cloth sign reading "Don't Boo Stu" over the upper grandstand railing.

"They must really be on Stuart this year," Henry said.

"He's been having his troubles, I guess," I recalled. "Hope it's nothing temporary."

Pittsburgh took a quick four-run lead off Purkey, and Bevan was asked to pinch-hit against Joe Gibbon. Hal stroked a high fast ball against the light tower in left field. The ball caromed around inside the tower and dropped behind the screen enclosing it.

"I was shakin', b'lieve me," Bevan said when he rejoined

us in the bullpen after circling the bases. "That's the first ball I've hit good all year."

"Nice way to break in," I said, shaking his hand.

Dick Stuart also hit a pinch-hit homer, off Marshall Bridges. It broke up a tie game, broke up Stuart's slump, and gave them the ball game.

"I thought you said he wasn't hitting, Broz," said Bevan. Well, at least he didn't hit it off me.

Eddie Kasko sat before his locker, puffing and sweating during the twenty-minute break we took between infield warm-up and the start of the next day's game.

"I feel just like it was spring training," he said. "Gotta get back in shape again."

Kasko had been out of the lineup for a week after bruising his foot severely with a batted ball. (Some hitters frequently strike inside pitches down, onto, and damn near through their own feet. This seemingly avoidable accident, repeated often enough, crushes the instep as well as the will to swing. Kasko's left foot looked gangrenous before he agreed to rest it.)

"My wind's gone, my legs hurt," he moaned.

"Know how you feel, Ed," I said. "I got married during the season in '52. Took an eighteen-day honeymoon. Tried to pitch on the day I got back. Hit a ground ball in the hole, saw a base hit, ran like hell to first, came up with Charley horses in both legs! How'd you spend *your* time off?" I added.

He laughed at my lack of discretion and hobbled to the trainer's table looking for a rubdown.

In the bullpen a stumpy park policeman accosted us with his inevitable request for a baseball. His annoying plea, usually addressed to a rookie, occasionally would badger the kid into giving away a ball. As if it were an apple!

"Tell you what," said Bevan. "I'll trade you a ball for a gun."

"Oh, no," said the cop, fingering his gun protectively. "This is worth a lotta dough."

"How about a couple of bullets then?" I asked. "How much are they worth?"

"About eight cents apiece," he said, frowning.

"Okay. A baseball's worth two-fifty. Give us thirty bullets, we call it even."

"You guys are just kiddin', aren't ya?"

"We're not allowed to give baseballs away this year, didn't you hear?" I said. "No bullets, no ball."

He shuffled back to his hole, muttering. It's getting harder and harder every year to wheedle baseballs out of ballplayers. You'd think they had to pay for them.

We could have used bullets, a machine gunful to stop the Pirates. They hit the ball no matter who threw it, but they liked Hook's pitches best. Apparently his fast ball was easily adapted into line drives. In the sixth inning he gave up a single, double, triple, and home run—a vicious cycle.

After the game Hook, undressing next to my locker, complained, "Jim, I didn't have my fast ball today. Anybody could see that. Why did Hutch leave me in there? I can't work without my best pitch, can I?"

"Listen, Jay," I tried to explain, "no pitcher has his best pitch every time out. That's when you learn this game. You got other pitches to throw. Use 'em when the fast ball isn't there."

"Without my fast ball I can't pitch," he mumbled.

"You can't win in this league with that alone, though. In a way Hutch was doing you a favor, letting you work. You haven't been getting much lately. I know it's embarrassing sometimes."

"You're damn right it is," he said, blushing. Hook's E.R.A. had ascended precipitously in the inning he pitched.

"Forget it. I went through it for three years when I first got into this league."

Hook slapped a towel against his leg. "It makes me mad," he said.

Being bombed should make any man mad.

There is probably less warm-up practice and fewer pepper games before Sunday ball games than on any other day. Not that anybody needs exercise less; but there is not enough time—time to read the baseball news in the papers.

For each summer Sunday's sports section the baseball writers must write not only a column of news about the Saturday game but a column of opinion, also, about baseball in general. These additional words from the baseball world are good for laughs or snorts of derision, depending on which paper one reads.

Sunday is also the day on which the *Sporting News* frequently arrives in the clubhouse. This tabloid paper contains much statistical information and a lot of gossip about baseball. Ballplayers read it weekly in order to learn what J. G. Taylor Spink says is going on in the world of professional baseball. Certain members of the Baseball Writers' Association, gratuitously known as Spink's Spies, compile résumés of the week's baseball news in every league in organized baseball. Ballplayers seldom need to correspond to learn how well their friends in the game are playing. They can read it each week in the *Sporting News*.

Bevan pointed to Jerry Zimmerman, who scanned the report from the Pacific Coast League. "How come all minor leaguers," asked Bevan, "read the *Sporting News* from back to front?"

"That's were most of my friends are playing, stupid," growled Zimmerman.

"Lemme see who got traded?" Bevan asked.

"Wait a couple weeks. You might make it," Henry said.

"Oh, shut up, you grouchy Texan," said Zimmerman. "Broz, you ever seen anybody as grump as Texans?"

"Hurry up with the paper," I said. "It's almost time to hit."

"Ain't you gotta quarter?" Henry grouched.

"No," I said. "Bad night last night."

The bleachers behind our bullpen filled rapidly. Kids too young to play little league ball advised how to lose to the Pirates. Zimmerman stumbled out to our bench in the first inning pressing an ice bag to his mouth.

"Finally said the wrong thing, I see," I said.

"Don't be wise," Zimmerman muttered. "That damn Purkey! He's gotta work on his *knuckle ball* before the game!"

He shifted the ice bag, uncovering a badly split lip.

"You're a mess," said Henry.

"You ever have a nice thing to say?" Zimmerman complained.

"Yeah. Go sit on the bench, Grumpy," said Bevan.

"Can't. I'm the long man today," Henry said.

"You and I both," I said. "We're long and short today. Everybody else gets a rest."

Ken Hunt, starting for us, had other ideas. Never having pitched against the Pirates before, he didn't know they were supposed to beat us. He refused to make the bad pitch in a jam the way Pirate batters had come to expect. In the seventh inning he held a 4-1 lead as Henry and I got up to loosen our arms in case of trouble. With one out, he walked a batter and Hutch went out to the mound.

Usually an experienced relief pitcher knows exactly when he may be called into the game. Rapport with the manager is developed over a period of games. In this case Hutch shocked me unexpectedly by removing Hunt and waving me in. "I'm not warm," I said to myself.

"You know what to do," said Hutch, handing me the ball.

The Pirate bats were cold, too, and I struggled out of the inning. In the ninth Post warmed me up while Schmidt put his catching equipment on. One of my pitches sailed past Post's glove and skittered back to the screen. Wally asked for a new ball, threw it to me, and yelled, "Cut it out!" Later Schmidt came out to the mound, rubbing up the ball.

"Post says you threw him a good spitter," Schmidt said. "You wanta use it?"

"Wish I knew how," I said.

I didn't need it. The fans groaned, got up, and left.

Philadelphia — May 16

THE epitaph on the tombstone of W. C. Fields is supposed to read: "I'd rather be here than in Philadelphia."

Mr. Fields wanted one last laugh and his declaration is not, probably, to be taken seriously—unless you have had to play

52

left field at Connie Mack Stadium. The most obnoxious fans in baseball sit in the grandstand and bleachers overlooking left field in the Phillies' park. (An obnoxious fan has a big mouth filled with penetrating sarcasm, and he is capable of projecting his voice over 212 feet. He has, usually, a bass voice, a baser personality, and would like to run ballplayers out of the park. He is quick enough on his feet never to be caught. He often leaves the park in the eighth inning, hoarse; and his absence makes the game more enjoyable.)

Joey Jay gave the Philly fans, some of whom are not obnoxious, little to cheer for or talk about. Even sharper than in his one-hit game against them, Joe threw a new pitch at their already confused lineup.

"It's a change-up screwball. I just turn it over a little. They're all young, and stride too much anyway. I've been working on it for a while. Gives me four pitches now. Two or three more and I'll be ready to win twenty," Jay said, smiling after the game.

"You win the cigar, Joe," I said. "Anybody got a cigar? Merchant, you got a cigar for a twenty-game winner?"

Larry Merchant, a bearded sportswriter, giggled and agreed that "Cincinnati has been getting good pitching. You look a lot better than you did this spring."

"Definite pennant contenders," I kidded him. "Your beard looks better than it did in Florida, too. I think all sportswriters should grow beards."

"You win the pennant and *you* can grow a beard," said Merchant.

"Hey, beatnik-lover!" said Post. "Let somebody else talk to the press."

"Go shave your head, Post," I said. "Some of us would like to get outa here sometime tonight."

Ballplayers are notoriously slow getting dressed after a ball game. Between the end of a game and the moment the bus carries us to the hotel, enough time usually elapsed to play another ball game. Or replay the one just ended over several cans of refreshing suds.

"I never saw so much beer drinking in one club," said Jim

53

Turner, staring over my third beer at my naked waistline.

Besides winning ball games what else is there to *do* in Philadelphia?

In Connie Mack Stadium the visitors' bullpen is squeezed between the left field line and the wall of the grandstand (from which pennies are thrown to the catchers who warm up relief pitchers). Just behind the catcher, abutting the left field wall is a bench. A wire gate leads back under the stands, where several benches provide room to sit and watch the game, catch a quick nap, read *Playboy*, or discuss world affairs.

"What did you do in the bullpen tonight?" Merchant asked me. The game had bored him, apparently.

"Just like any game here," I recalled. "We took turns on a crossword book, and discussed the income tax laws."

Bob Purkey had declared before the game, "I'm going all the way tonight. You guys can rest." He knew that Johnny Buzhardt, the Philly pitcher, never got any runs to work with —only one in four games so far in 1961. And we seemed to be scoring just enough every game; not scaring anybody, but winning just the same.

Bill Henry sat on the bench in front of the bullpen, shaking his head as Buzhardt pitched just badly enough to get the loss.

"My ol' roomie's gonna get mad at those Philly hitters some-day and bust all their bats so they don't have any alibi."

Buzhardt and Henry had roomed together at Chicago in 1959.

"Whose side you on, Grumpy?" asked Zimmerman, inter-rupting Maloney's complaint about the Internal Revenue Bureau.

"I don't think it's right how much money they take away from ballplayers," Jim said. "Why don't we do somethin' about it?"

"Get married," I suggested. "Marry a broad with five kids. Or build yourself a house in Fresno, rent an apartment where you play ball during the summer, and then you can write off your expenses during the season."

"They don't allow that everywhere, though, Broz," said

54

Bevan. "The tax agent in Memphis won't allow you to deduct anything!"

"They do most places," I said. "It's a good rule."

"With Maloney's money he should complain," said Zimmerman. "How much you get to sign, Tits?"

"Hundred and ten grand. And the government wants most of it," said Maloney. "They gimme ten thousand to be a pitcher, hundred thousand to be a hitter when I signed. I could really swing that stick in high school!"

"I sho' wish I had yo' problems," said Bridges. "Man, I sho' would like that kinda trouble."

"There's another one," Henry said, as a fan dropped a penny onto the bullpen plate.

"I got it!" Maloney yelled.

Figures.

Cincinnati — May 19

THE best investment a major league ballplayer can make during the baseball season is the price he pays for the daily newspaper. In the box scores of each major league game he can find more tips on how to run his business than the ads for the *Wall Street Journal* can promise would-be capitalists. The daily box score tells the baseball world which hitter has the hot bat, which club is ineffective against a certain kind of pitching, and which manager is overworking his bullpen.

The sight of the 1961 Milwaukee Braves' lineup was enough to make a pitcher's arm ache. Apparently the Braves had a mass of muscled batters, an array of graceful fielders, a staff of veteran pitchers, and enough overweening confidence to crush any impressionable spirit. The Braves also had a manager who modestly declaimed that, with a little help from his ballplayers, *he* ought to be a cinch to win the pennant. Yet at the start of our second series of the season with them we'd beaten them four straight. That *could* have made them mad.

"How we going to pitch to them?" I asked Joey Jay.

"Don't worry about 'em," he said. "Pitch a good game, they won't beat you. Sure, they'll beat the hell outa you once

55

in a while. But they don't care enough any more. Not like they used to four, five years ago."

My arm ached anyway even before the game started. For an undisclosed reason the pitchers were allowed to hit for forty minutes instead of thirty, and everybody took too many cuts. Never thought it possible for a pitcher to get too much hitting.

"Congratulations, Gabby," I said to Henry as we waited in the outfield for O'Toole to take his cuts with the regulars.

"All I needed was to get my timing down," Henry admitted. "One of these days I'll jerk one out of here during a game, too."

"Forget it. You haven't had a hit in two years, have you?" I laughed. "Save that long ball for our pregame games. You're all the power we got since Osteen left."

"Look at that O'Toole now," said Henry. "How's he get so many hits in the game? He's the worst batting practice hitter I ever saw!"

"Looks like he's using a cricket paddle," I said. "He doesn't swing at a ball; he swacks it!"

O'Toole waved at a final pitch from my brother, Pat, the batting practice pitcher. Disgustedly O'Toole threw his bat toward the bat rack and walked down the ramp to the clubhouse.

"Jimmy can't hit your brother either, see," said Jerry Lynch. "Pat's the only right-hander in baseball who can get me out regular. What's he do for a living?"

"Sells insurance," I said.

"Wasting his time," grumbled Lynch.

"You just *think* you can't hit Pat," I pointed out. "Wish more of you hitters had that kind of respect for pitchers."

Otis Douglas ambled by, herding the benchwarmers, pinch-hitters, and reserve infielders toward their running track in left field. Douglas had almost convinced the nonpitchers on the club that running was good for them during the season. As a rule they run only in spring training, and laugh as the pitching staff runs every day. Hutchinson endorsed Douglas's plan with such enthusiasm that he directed the running when

Douglas was absent.

"Post," I yelled, "you'll never make a good pitcher. You can't run ten laps without falling on your face."

"I'm saving myself for when you pitch," Post retorted, puffing. "If you can keep the ball inside the park, that is."

The big crowd that had purchased advance tickets, mostly because the Braves' Big Bats were in town, responded to O'Toole's sharp, power-muffling pitching with loud enthusiasm.

"More noise than I've heard in this park in years," I said to my wife after the game. "You think those fans are going to cheer for *us* this year for a change?"

"Betty O'Toole didn't cheer much," Anne Stewart replied. "She's so nervous when her husband is out there pitching she chatters constantly. Doesn't even look at the game except when we're hitting. She's pregnant and she couldn't get out of her seat when O'Toole got his double."

"Is that right?" I said. "Henry fell off the bench in the bullpen. Tootie's the best 'worst-looking' hitter in the game."

O'Toole's two-base hit, the key blow in our attack, was a line drive, as well placed as it was sharply struck.

"I give up," said Henry.

The Braves did, too.

"How many straight we beat them now?" asked Nunn.

"Nine in a row counting spring training," Bevan said. "They ain't gonna win the pennant if they can't beat us."

"Saturday is a bad day," I muttered first thing in the morning. "Let's order room service, have breakfast in bed, do something different to start the day off."

"What kind of 'different' you got in mind?" My wife asked, smiling. (Some women look damn good in the morning.)

"Watch it! I'm due to work today. 'Cause we're due to get ripped, and soon. We got no business beating the Braves all the time. They're liable to wake up—today."

"Order a steak then," she said. "I might as well stay in bed if you're going to the park with that attitude."

"Just a hunch," I explained.

Jerry Zimmerman added his gloomy bit to the morose pessimism that affected everyone in the bullpen. Saturday games follow Friday night wins much too closely. There's not enough time to celebrate, and if you win infrequently you *must* celebrate. Day games should start at four o'clock on Saturday afternoons.

"Hunt's wild," Zimmerman said after he'd warmed Ken up, run up to the clubhouse, changed his shirt, drank a ginger ale, and hustled, late, onto the field.

"Yeah, Zim," said Bevan. "You're right again. Hunt's already walked three guys."

"And there's the phone," Bridges noted. "Nunn! Hey, Nunn! Wake up an' answer the phone!"

"Christ. Man can't get any sleep around hyah!"

"Get naked, Nunn," Henry said as Howie grabbed his glove, tied his shoes, picked up a ball, and ran to the bullpen mound.

"Pray for rain, boys," I said as thunder rolled over the clouds behind left field.

The Braves accepted each base on balls from Hunt and gleefully ran around the bases, stealing six of them before Hutch concluded that the kid wasn't learning anything.

"Hunt looks like Bob Rush did as a rookie. Can't take that big, slow stride with men on. They're gonna steal his jockstrap pretty soon!"

"Yeah. And then you pitchers blame the catchers," said Bevan. "Only way you're gonna stop 'em running on him is to call time when you see 'em goin'."

"Boy, are you a grouch, Bevan," Henry said.

Don Nottebart, the Braves' pitcher, couldn't get the third out in the fifth inning. Dressen relieved him, and sent him to the showers, screaming. A starting pitcher has to go five innings to get credit for a win. With a big lead and three outs to go, he sometimes says to himself, "Just let me get these three, Lord," forgetting that it merely takes the same kind of pitching that got the first twelve outs. Already this season we'd seen three starters fail to get that last man in the fifth,

58

and the reliever had picked up the win.

"Pray for a thunderstorm now," I thought to myself in the bullpen. "Or a cloudburst—or an earthquake. I might get into this contest!"

"You're in there, Broz," Henry said, answering the phone. "Mop it up, will ya? We got a double-header tomorrow."

Hutch used a hitter for me, though, after I'd pitched one inning. Henry had to mop it up. I hurried through my shower, opened a beer, and took a seat behind the home plate screen, best place in the park to watch a game.

Moe Drabowsky, once my roommate at Chicago, and now an off-season neighbor there, relieved for the Braves in the ninth when we loaded the bases and excited the crowd.

"Who you rooting for, us or Moe?" I asked my wife (who likes him well enough to say, "I can see he'd make a nice roomie!").

"He's got great stuff, hasn't he?" she said.

"Always did have. That's why he got eighty grand to sign. Now watch. He'll get behind and take a little off his fast ball just to get a strike. He makes great pitches but not often enough at the right time."

"I like him anyway," she insisted.

One might doubt her ethics. Especially when Drabowsky got us out to save the Braves' win.

Charlie Dressen explained his club's unimpressive early season record, saying, "I don't have no catching."

Del Crandall, the Braves' No. 1 receiver, a technical expert who Joey Jay says was "the best thing that could ever happen to a young pitcher" when Jay joined the Braves, had a sore arm.

Crandall couldn't throw; therefore he couldn't play; therefore he couldn't run the club on the field. Ostensibly the manager's job, since Dressen took credit for it, the technical chore of directing each pitch as it comes up is handled best by the catcher. His leadership qualities often determine the club's success.

The Braves had recalled Joe Torre, a young catcher playing at Louisville as late as Saturday night, May 20. Torre spent a sleepless night hurrying up to the big leagues, and his appearance in the lineup caused the phone in our bullpen to ring. This time *we* were calling the bench to inquire, "How in hell do you pitch Torre?"

Nobody on the bench knew for sure so we paid closer attention to Torre's batting than to the other Milwaukee hitters as they faced Joey Jay.

"With my luck we won't get to pitch to him today anyway," I warned them. "Lynch and I got a bet goin'. Fifty to one that Jay and Maloney go all the way, in both games. So the bullpen doesn't have to work."

"Don't you know it's illegal to bet on ball games, Brosnan?" asked Bevan.

Major League Rule 21-d bans betting "in any form," and imposes a "one-year suspension" on players who wager for or against their own club. I couldn't have cared less whether or not I worked in either game, but I'd just as soon not lose fifty bucks just for a day of rest.

Jay went into the ninth with a 6-3 lead, thanks in part to Hank Aaron's bad memory. Aaron forgot to wear his sunglasses to center field in the fourth inning and lost a fly ball that drove Warren Spahn to distraction, Charlie Dressen to the water fountain for an aspirin, and two Red runners across the plate. Aaron called time after his *faux pas* to ask for a pair of glasses. Spahn stood on the mound, hands on hips, staring disgustedly at the tableau of Aaron and the batboy searching the sunglass case for a late, lost cause.

Torre hit a high fast ball out for a fourth run to start the ninth, and with one out and a man on first Blasingame failed to relay a perfect double play ball to first, giving Lee Maye a chance to tie the game with a home run. Maye did just that, hitting a low fast ball halfway up the bleachers in right.

Just to make Jay feel worse, we scored a run in our half of the ninth to give him the win. He half-sulked, half-laughed at himself while we ate lunch between games.

"I didn't deserve it," he said. "But I'll take it."

"You find out how to pitch Torre?" I asked.

60

"Keep the ball in the park, you got a chance."

Maloney shook Jay's hand and said, "I still got the long-ball record for one home run but you got the most tape-measure jobs in one game." The Braves had hit three homers off Jay, all of them well over four hundred feet.

The Milwaukee barrage had shaken the clouds that hovered over the field in the ninth. Rain drenched the bleacher fans who had survived the falling home run balls. A fifty-minute shower cooled everything off, including the Brave bats.

Maloney, unfortunately for the Reds, gave up just enough runs to lose the second game to Carl Willey. Maloney, fortunately for me, failed to finish the game. Nunn pitched the last two innings after the seventh-inning rally when Maloney was lifted for a pinch-hitter.

By eight o'clock the field had been finally cleared of ball-players—and drunks. One fan, angered beyond inebriation when he learned that the concession stands had no beer left, ran across the field, faked a slide into second, and stumbled into a park policeman's arms, laughing.

"They ran out of paper towels and toilet paper in the rest rooms, too," my wife told me as we rode back to the hotel.

Don't see how these fans will make it through the season.

The following day we faced L.A. for the first time in Cincinnati. The Dodgers had caught up with San Francisco and were tied for the league lead, three games ahead of us.

"How many left-handed hitters they got playin'?" Nunn asked as the Dodger lineup was announced just before the game.

"Eight, I guess," I said. "L.A.'s got two major league clubs; one hits right-, one hits left-handed. They're tryin' to beat the percentages."

"Hutch oughta tell 'em he's starting a right-hander, then warm up a lefty under the stands and bring him in after they announce their lineup," Bevan suggested.

"Purkey does all right against left-handers," said Zimmerman. "That percentage stuff is overrated."

"Don't knock it," I said. "If it weren't for that Henry and

61

I would probably be out of work."

The percentage theory that claims that right-handed pitchers get right-handed hitters out more easily than they do left-handers is just partly true, and depends on who's pitching. My slider is more effective against left-handers than right-handers usually, because it breaks into them as they swing. I'd just as soon pitch to Snider as Tommy Davis (unless Henry is hot and ready to strike Snider out).

"You can work tonight, Gab," I said. "I'll save myself for the Giants. They're all right-handed, practically."

Purkey pitched as if he didn't want any help, holding L.A. scoreless after the first inning. Unfortunately we could manage just two more hits after Blasingame doubled and Kasko singled for the tying run to open the last half of the first.

The crowd couldn't have numbered 4,500 and they were as quiet as our bats. The lack of enthusiasm threatened to put us to sleep in the bullpen so Nunn suggested we play a word game.

"I name a ballplayer, anybody who ever played in the minors or majors. Then the next guy has to name another one who begins with the last letter of the player I named. Okay?"

There are not many players whose names begin with "I."

In the tenth inning, L.A. tried hard not to score the tie-breaking run. Wills walked, was bunted to second, stopped at third on a single by Willie Davis, then was thrown out at the plate trying to score after Moon grounded to second. It looked as if Purkey might work his way out of the inning and we'd have to think up another word game to play all night.

But Tommy Davis singled, to score Willie Davis with the winning run. Henry relieved Purkey and fanned the last Dodger batter, but he couldn't get any of our hitters excited enough even to tie the score in the last of the tenth.

One word described our offense. It was unprintable.

The next day Zimmerman and Henry spent ten minutes of batting practice tearing a baseball apart. One of Robinson's line drives off the center field fence had split two seams on the ball. The unraveling process fascinated Elio Chacon, who gathered up the strung-out yarn as it was pulled from the diminishing core.

"You save string, Chalky?" Purkey asked him.

"Ah, yes . . . no," Chacon said. Elio pretends to know just enough English to help him feign ignorance when he can't think of a smart answer.

"We're tryin' to find out what makes this dolly jump, Broz," said Zimmerman.

"Why don't you send it to Hook? He can analyze it scientifically while he's in bed. Understand he's really hurtin'," I said.

"Yeah. Those damn mumps went down on him," Zimmerman said. "He has to have ice packs and all that."

I shuddered at the thought. "Hell, he won't be able to pitch for a month," I said. "Wonder why they don't bring somebody up? Why, we might lose the pennant because of a case of mumps!"

"How can we win the pennant?" said Purkey. "They already gave it to the Dodgers in spring training!"

In Vero Beach, Florida, visitors to the Los Angeles training camp had been duly impressed by the thirty-five major league players running around the field. Most clubs have barely twenty major-leaguers at one time and have to fill out their roster with "prospects and suspects." (Some of the writers who visited the Cincinnati camp in Tampa after seeing the Dodgers described the Reds' club as mostly "prospects and suspects.")

The Dodgers obviously had power, speed, and pitching.

"Sure, they got guys who have hit home runs in the past, so they *might* beat you with the long ball. And everybody on the club can run so they *might* steal the pennant. And their pitchers will lead the league in strike-outs, but you know damn well they can't strike everybody out."

"What's more," I added, "they're not doing anything very well so far this year."

"They beat us every time we played 'em," said Henry.

"Don't be such a grouch, Gabby," said Zimmerman. "Let's see if you can fungo this thing outa here." He held up the

63

rubber core of the broken-down baseball. "Looks like a juiced-up golf ball."

"I'd love to throw *this* in a game," said Maloney as he stuffed wads of gray and white yarn into the torn cover of the ball. "Let' em try and hit this outa here!"

"Lemme see that, Tits," Bridges asked Maloney.

"Where you been, Fox?" I asked. "Turner missed you."

"How c'n he, with this sun tan o' mahn?" Bridges said.

"You're somethin' else, Bridges," said Nunn, smiling despite himself. He and Bridges had a phony mutual hate going on between them.

"You wanna use some o' mah sun-tan lotion, Nunn?" asked Bridges, rubbing his hand over Nunn's arm. "Man, you need sumpin'! Yo' head already done worn out five bodies!"

"Don't rub that black stuff on me. It's catchin'. How could I ever go home to Winston-Salem this winter?" Nunn said.

From his position behind the pitcher's mound Pitching Coach Jim Turner yelled to us to "Get the balls in" so he could finish the batting practice; and "Get your runnin' in, you pitchers," so he could record our daily exercise in his little black book.

"The Colonel keeps an eye on you guys all right, doesn't he?" said Bevan, laughing. "Run, you silly bastards. Work, Fox!"

Dodger scouts had obviously informed L.A. on Hunt's inability to prevent stolen bases, but the Dodgers didn't get enough men on base to take advantage of that knowledge and their speed. In one case Maury Wills broke for second, had the base stolen by ten feet, then had to pick himself up and scoot back to first when Willie Davis looped a fly ball into center. Pinson got a glove on the ball, dropped it and threw to second too late to get Davis, who made a beautiful hook slide away from the tag. Unfortunately Davis was out for passing Wills, who had slid safely back into first anticipating a throw from center after the catch that wasn't made.

All of which amused Jocko Conlan, the umpire stationed down the left field line. Conlan ran out to our bullpen to get a drink of water and exchange insults with the ballplayers.

" 'Splain that play to us, Jock," I said.

"Didn't fool me a bit," he admitted. "Those guys can really run, can't they? Ha! That Davis is so fast his head's three feet behind the rest of him. So how'd he make out?"

"Nice call, Jock. You take a rest. We'll take turns standin' on the line for you."

"Just get this thing over with, that's all," he yelled as we took our turn at bat.

Henry relieved Hunt and dazzled the Dodgers in the ninth to save Hunt's win and help us split the series with L.A., and win our first game against them.

"What you do with the center of that ball?" I asked Henry after the game.

"Gonna keep it in my pocket," he said. "May be good luck."

Maybe that's all it takes to beat them.

"Summer's here," I said to myself as I got off the bus and walked down the hill to the ball park. "Look at that flag blow out!"

Talking to myself is symptomatic of summer madness in baseball. Southwesterly winds blowing from home plate toward the center field fence can make any pitcher tend to self-pity. Having cored a 1961 baseball and found it infused with nervous mesons and other sources of atomic energy I could see no excuse for Nature, too, to help make my life miserable.

Surveying the distance to the outfield fences from my infield practice position backing up Henry's fungo bat, I was nearly struck down by a feeling of claustrophobia. Also by a thrown ball that bounced off my leg and was retrieved by Ed Bailey, making his first appearance in Cincinnati wearing a Giant uniform.

"Still getting crossed up, eh, Gar?" I asked him.

"Whaddya say, 'Fess!" Bailey said. "Break anything, I hope?"

I rubbed my right shin with my left foot, unwilling to stoop to being injured. "Forget it. You sure are packin' 'em in here

65

tonight. These fans really miss you, y'know. But then I guess *somebody* ought too, don't you think?"

"Yeah," he said. "Guess I'll have to jerk one outa here tonight for old times' sake."

"Wind's blowin' out," I said. "First time all season. Just for you, I guess. Don't dig in. Tootie's liable to remember all the bad pitches you called for him last year."

"I didn't throw 'em," Bailey retorted.

Indeed, O'Toole did blow his stack during the game. Gordon Coleman made what seemed to be an unnecessarily clumsy maneuver on a ground ball to first. Coleman's awkwardness was often as good for laughs as for indignation, but in his embarrassed haste to retrieve the booted ball he flailed away like a whale out of water.

"Dat Bubbles gonna get killed someday," Bridges said as we watched the Giants take advantage of the error.

"Tootie's gonna kill him first," Maloney said. "Man, he's really pissed off."

On his next pitch O'Toole frantically slapped at Kuenn's line drive, knocking it down but too far away for him to make a play. O'Toole threw his hands over his head in disgust, and soon was on his way to the shower.

"Tough luck he's had," I thought. "Can't get him any runs and can't pick up a ground ball when he needs it."

"Tootie ever learns to control his temper when things go bad for him, he'll be a better pitcher," I said aloud. "Christ, you get as many good breaks in this game as bad ones."

The phone rang, Turner asking Henry to warm up. "Get naked, hoss," I said.

"What's Hutch savin' you for, Brosnan, the senior prom?"

"Go get 'em out. They might boot three or four and we'll tie it up."

The Giants did their best to help us out and, with the tying run on base in the ninth, Jerry Lynch pinch-hit, a managerial move that was loudly endorsed by the remaining fans. Hutchinson insisted, every time anybody asked him, "Lynch is the best pinch-hitter in baseball today." Once in a while he said, "Lynch is the best pinch-hitter I ever saw!"

66

Lynch had already hit three pinch-hit home runs. With the wind blowing out and a fast ball pitcher throwing he was a good bet to make another headline. (Any hitter who can go to the plate, cold, and take one perfect cut at just the right pitch deserves a headline.)

"Get one up in that wind, Jerry," Hutch muttered half to himself on the bench.

Lynch waited for Bailey to call for his pitch, swung his bat in his short, quick, beautifully controlled stroke, and hit the ball hard on a line to right.

"Get up! Get up!" Hutch and everyone else on the bench yelled.

The ball shot swiftly toward the bleachers, no higher than ten feet off the ground; but the exultant cheer of the crowd lasted just a split second as the ball sank suddenly into the right fielder's glove.

"I never hit a sinker in my life!" Lynch said, storming back and forth in the clubhouse.

"You had your pitch," Kasko said, consolingly. "Just missed it."

"I *knew* I'd get a fast ball," Lynch's moaning continued. "But, you know, I never hit a sinker in my life!"

There's a wrong time for everything in this game.

A scheduled day off, followed by a Friday full of rain, disrupted Turner's little black coaching book.

"Colonel's probly gonna run us with a fungo tonight, huh, 'Fess?" asked Bridges. We stood at the batting cage waiting for the batting practice pitcher to warm up so we could take our cuts. Bridges mooched a chew of tobacco from me, and as he stuffed it into his mouth I saw he was wearing glasses.

"Welcome to the club, Fox!" I said. "When did you decide you needed the specs?"

"Mah pitches comin' back at me faster'n ah'm throwin' 'em, 'Fess. Got to do sumpin'."

"You haven't been buggy-whippin' that ball lately either, Bridges," added Nunn.

Purkey pointed at us from the starting pitcher's side of the batting cage. "Look at 'em. That's our bullpen. There aren't two good eyes in the whole bunch!"

Nunn, Bridges, and I wore shatterproof lenses with steel frames; Maloney had on a pair of tinted contact lenses; Hook also wore contacts. Henry, who could see the slightest opening from two hundred yards, laughed smugly at the nearsighted group of us.

"Don't smile, Gabby. At your age your eyes are ready to fail you, too," I said.

"Forget it. That's what booze and tobacco'll do for you," Henry said. Henry, a nonsmoking teetotaler, looked ten years younger than forty-three (and even claimed he was *not* even thirty-four!).

"Listen, you old grouch," said Nunn. "When we win the pennant you are gonna drink a glass of champagne if we gotta force it down your throat!"

"Don't worry about it," Henry said.

Joey Jay was scheduled to start for the third time against Philadelphia. He'd handled them easily in the other two games and they hadn't changed their lineup. Jay proposed to experiment on the mound.

"I'm going to use my 'slop slider' tonight. Just flip the ball over the plate when I want a fast strike. They can't hit any off-speed pitching. If I get in trouble I can go back to hard stuff."

Jay *was* in trouble throughout the game; but he survived only because of three sensational plays in the outfield. The Phillies seemingly weren't strong enough to hit the ball out of the park, and neither Robinson nor Pinson let anything fall safely. Pinson caught one fly ball just as it was dropping over the bleacher screen at the 390-foot mark. That ball *did* get out of the park but it was inside Vada's glove which was still on Pinson's right hand. Herrerra, the Cuban first baseman who'd hit the ball, yelled "*Merde!*," or "I was robbed," when he saw Pinson trot back in with the ball.

Bill Henry eventually relieved Jay when the Phillies came to bat in the ninth inning. Bill had a save in his pocket when, with two out, the Phillies sent up four right-handed pinch-hitters. The first three hit safely and Hutch told me to get the last one out. I did and stole the save for myself. Henry treated the whole thing as a loss, dressed, and left the clubhouse in a hurry.

Gene Mauch, the Phils' manager, enraged because the Phils had thrown the ball all over the ball park to give us the win, threw chairs and towels all over their clubhouse. He could concede us the possibility of winning seven straight from him, but he hated giving anything away.

A Philadelphia writer came to our clubhouse and asked, "You guys would like to play us seventy-five games a season, I guess, huh?"

"Why not? Victory tastes the same no matter how you suck it up," I thought, weighing myself in the trainer's room.

"Broz," said Maloney, "I'm getting married after the season and I read that frequent indulgence in sexual intercourse keeps your weight down. That right?"

I was ten pounds overweight, the scale said.

Sunday's game was closing out our home stand so I put my wife on the eight-thirty train back to Chicago and walked from the Union Terminal to Crosley Field. Her farewell could be described as full of eternal regret. She traveled by train because she's convinced that anyone who deliberately flies from place to place is courting death. (She frowns on such adulterous, morbid romance and is sure I'm going down someday.)

We were scheduled to fly to the Coast immediately after the game so I'd checked out of the hotel in the morning. My bill for the twelve-day home stand provided me with a shocking, sad omen for the days ahead. That room service check, so easy to sign at the time, is practically indigestible when presented for payment several days later. "Bottle of Bourbon—$10.95"! Ridiculous, even if it had been bootlegged on Sunday, a blue-law day in Cincinnati.

Zimmerman's face did nothing to dispel the gloom when he arrived at the clubhouse. His roomie, Hal Bevan, had been sent to the minors when Hutch signed Pete Whisenant.

"Bev gone yet?" I asked.

"No," he said, curtly.

"He gonna report?"

"Would you?" he retorted. "You know what it's like at Jersey City. They don't have anything but Cubans down there."

"And Bevan doesn't even speak Spanish," I remembered. "Wonder why they didn't send him to Indianapolis."

"—— 'em!" said Zimmerman.

A natural reaction. I wondered also why they'd replaced Bevan with Whisenant. Hal was a better hitter, even if he hadn't done much so far for us. Whisenant had a hell of a lot of other things going for him, of course. He had major league experience and could play anywhere in the outfield. Or even catch in an earnest, clumsy manner. Peter also considered himself a sort of inspiring type, who demanded as much from every player as Pete thought that player had in him.

"Someday I'm gonna be a manager," he'd once said. "And a damn good one, too."

Well, we already had a manager, but we could use a change of faces in the bullpen even if Bevan had been a hell of a good agitator and a jolly guy to have around. Best time to make a change is when you're going good.

The Phillies continued to make life pleasant for us, playing well enough to make the game interesting but not too well. Pinson took advantage of two high curves and a sharp breeze to right, and belted two home runs into the bleachers. Purkey breezed right along with him and congratulated Vada in the clubhouse twice, once for each homer.

Two customers in the bleachers paid scant attention to the Pinson-Purkey heroics. They obviously had eyes for another ball, and necked continuously from the sixth inning on.

"Things got so interesting out there," said Avery Robbins, the traveling secretary, "that Lew Crosley thought seriously of putting up a cabaña. You know? Provide a towel, a basin, and a bidet!"

"Why not?" I said. "You could raise the price of admission then for the bleachers."

Sex might even replace baseball as the National Pastime.

San Francisco — May 29

WE left by plane the next morning for a quick, four-day trip to the West Coast. In third place, we trailed the league-leading Giants by three games.

The principal diversion on the jet flight to San Francisco was a game of bridge. The permanent batting practice pitcher, Ray Shore, who made road trips with us, had asked to join our more-or-less continuing game. Shore is a huge man, an ex-minor league relief pitcher who used to warm up by throwing from thirty feet behind the regular bullpen mound.

"I'm kind of a butcher at times," he explained, "but I like to play."

"Where's your apron?" Lynch asked.

The stewardess brought two decks of cards and we played for three and a half hours. At a penny a hundred, the stakes required more levity than concentration to provide entertainment. Shore proved to be quite capable, and suggested that the symbolic apron be passed around after each sloppy hand. The blood flowed freely, almost amusing the kibitzers, those deadly serious nonplayers.

"Let's play tomorrow night after the game," Lynch suggested. "We got a double-header the next day."

"Nobody plays bridge on a night off in Frisco," I insisted, vivid reminiscence splitting my countenance in a grin.

Ken Hunt made the day worth celebrating, pitching his first complete game in the majors despite the umpiring of Frank Dascoli. Frank, ordinarily the best ball-and-strike man in the league, had apparently lost his power of concentration. His feud with Warren Giles, president of the league, had made sports page news during the week. His calling of low pitches had all the earmarks of bad guesses. He played no favorites, blowing pitches for both sides.

"At least you're consistent, anyway!" Hutchinson yelled

after Dascoli called Bailey out on a low curve.

Bailey had smiled broadly at our bench after the first couple of pitches had gone against us. His smile looked a bit forced after the left-handed Pinson hit southpaw Mike McCormick's curve ball out of the park for Vada's fifth straight hit off Mike. Bailey, who couldn't hit a left-hander's curve, didn't think any left-hander should hit a curve. He couldn't convince Pinson even if he'd apparently assured McCormick.

"When's he gonna learn?" Jay asked.

"Who?" Whisenant asked. "Mike or Bailey?"

The San Francisco writers, a pack of unsophisticated news-scoops, crowded into our clubhouse after the game asking inane questions. Like: "How do you guys keep doing it? You're not supposed to be beating us like you are, are you? Are you really that good?"

The Roman philosopher, Seneca, once said: "You can tell the character of a man by the way in which he receives a compliment."

Hutch parried the left-handed compliments diplomatically but his face wore a slight, properly perplexed smile of pride.

Pinson insisted he was just doing his job. Robinson sniffed at the suggestion we might be inferior rather than properly placed near the top of the league. Hunt just grinned happily.

What the hell! If somebody says you're good, accept it as the truth! When he says you're lousy he means it, undoubtedly. Plenty of time to knock yourself when you're going bad. Enjoying success modestly doesn't allow you the right to cry wholeheartedly when the beer tastes foul.

San Francisco being a Night Town, à la Joyce, the scheduling of a morning game the next day as part of the Memorial Day double-header might have been intended to catch late partygoers on their way home. The prospects of a big crowd seemed dim although the Giants' front office predicted a sell-out.

The ten-thirty starting time was more likely a preventive measure occasioned by the climatic conditions at Candlestick

Park. Afternoon "breezes" are so brisk on the Point that Candlestick is the only park in baseball where a second baseman is not allowed to chew tobacco. Should he turn his head to spit, his juice would strike the right fielder in the eye.

Everyone on our club made the eight-thirty bus. Everyone on the bus was as grumpy as Henry.

"What a hell of time to play a ball game! We gonna hit, Hutch?"

"No," he said, grumpily. "We'll dress, warm up, and beat hell out of 'em. Won't even take infield."

Hutchinson stared at the sports page subheadline: "Are The Reds For Real?"

"See where Sam Jones is starting one of the games," he said, smiling. "Hope we get him in the first game. He won't even be awake!"

The street exiting from the Bayshore Freeway was choked with traffic.

"Either there's a hell of a fire up ahead, or we're a hell of a lot bigger attraction than I thought," said Avery Robbins, rubbing his hands together as he contemplated the check he'd take from a sold-out park.

The entrance gate at the parking lot was blocked. A cop waved us around, stubbornly refusing to believe we deserved to get by as celebrities. Probably thought the Giants were the occasion for the crowd.

A gatekeeper recognized us, finally, but could find no way to usher us to the clubhouse entrance. Hutch climbed down from the bus and led us through the crowd, which parted before us grudgingly, no doubt thinking we were trying to beat them to the ticket window.

Nearing the clubhouse we could see and pity one ticket seller screaming that he had no more seats to sell. A disappointed but unnecessarily violent lady fan cursed him, inciting a mob to storm his position and smash his window. Police ran to his rescue as we made it to the clubhouse door.

"Where was it those two teen-age broads had the fist fight in the stands?" I asked Nunn.

"Milwaukee, wasn't it?" he said.

"Baseball makes broads aggressive, doesn't it?"

Jim Maloney started for us against Jones, who departed at 11:15 A.M., rubbing his eyes. Maloney, proud to see so many fans out to watch a native Californian, had stroked a 375-foot home run off Jones. Willie McCovey, the Giant first baseman, had rushed in toward the plate, expecting Maloney to bunt with a man on first.

"Man, McCovey damned near turned white!" said Schmidt. "Malone pulls that ball on a line and Willie is a dead mother!"

We had four runs in the fourth inning so the bullpen went back into the runway to listen to the auto race from Indianapolis. In the sixth, suddenly, Maloney lost his control, and by the time Hutch got me heated up the bases were loaded, nobody out. I wormed my way out of that jam and had retired nine men in a row going into the ninth. We led 7-2, as the wind picked up unexpectedly strong, as if it were already three in the afternoon.

Davenport sliced a low outside slider down the right field line, the ball eluding Elio Chacon, who thought he had it easily, had to chase it, then dove desperately as it blew away from him for a triple. He said that he was ashamed of himself, but he was less embarrassed than I was when a gust of wind blew me off the mound as I made my next pitch. First balk of my career.

To make the day more memorable, I gave up home runs to Landrith and Hiller, two little guys who just shouldn't do things like that. Henry came in to save the game, and did so after Mays hit the third homer of the inning.

The excitement was so invigorating that the winner of the auto-race pool had to ask twice before he could collect his money. Henry insisted that he hadn't let Mays hit a home run just to bring the tying run to bat and give him a chance for an easy save.

"Wasn't nothing easy about it," he insisted.

"Don't I know it," I said.

In the ninth inning of the second game Hutch ignored both of us, bringing Purkey in to get the last three outs. The wind

74

blew just as hard, maybe harder, but Purkey threw nothing but sinkers and even at Candlestick a ground ball can seldom make the bleachers.

At dusk, glowing with triumph, a momentary grip on first place, and a few Beefeater martinis, we resumed the bridge game on the plane to L.A.

Los Angeles — May 31

IN a theory-fumbling effort to prove his point one Dodger sportswriter cited the Los Angeles casualty list as reason why the Dodgers were not leading the league. His injury roster listed everything from a "broken elbow" to "general aches and pains" and took up so much room in his column he had room for just one unoriginal opinion: "Are the Reds for real?"

Our writers, were they willing and able, could have made a hospital case for us, in like manner. We could match Chacon's spiked knee to Snider's elbow. And Robinson's swollen arm (target for several knockdown pitches in the last Red-Dodger series) had as many negative connotations as Larry Sherry's sprained ankle. For good measure we had Jay Hook's mumps to compare with Charlie Neal's chicken pox. All in all it looked like we deserved at least a tie with L.A.

The Dodgers had won three in a row despite their physical disabilities. Joey Jay, after a sixth win that would tie him with L.A.'s Koufax as league leader, spent most of his batting practice time trying to loft a ball over the left field screen. His frustration did not escape my notice since I had plenty of time to watch and run. Turner had said, "Take some extra laps tonight, Captain. We won't use you in this game probably. Pitching in that wind up there tends to stiffen you next day, doesn't it?"

Mute and grateful, I agreed with him. Any reason for not having to pitch in the Coliseum is a good one. When I wasn't watching Jay swing I admired the lovely young things who paraded through the stands and sat behind the Dodger bullpen.

Even on this cool night they revealed the best in female fan form.

"Why don't we get some of that stuff behind *our* bullpen?" asked Nunn.

For seven innings our bullpen was too busy to check anything but the progress of Dodger runners trying to tie the score. Jay allowed them to catch up at 2-2, 3-3, and 5-5; but each time Drysdale and Farrell, the Dodger pitchers, gave back the lead. Gene Freese's second home run of the game put us ahead for good in the eighth. Jay retired two men in the L.A. eighth, threw a long ball to Roseboro, and handed the ball over to Henry, who fanned Howard for the third out.

Bill loaded the bases in the ninth to give me a chance to get heated up in the bullpen. When I got out to the mound Hutch turned to me with more of a resigned than confident look on his face.

"Nobody out," he said. "See what you can do."

Well, either you do or you don't. A tired arm that isn't sore often will operate just as you expect it to, and not give you too much when you want just enough spin or power on your pitch.

With Tommy Davis hitting I had no problems. Or rather just one solution. Make him hit a slider on the ground. He pulls, usually. If he hits the pitch as he should the percentage says the left side of the infield has a chance at a double play. Davis took two sliders low and away for called balls, and the noisy crowd almost penetrated my simple-minded concentration.

Zimmerman called for another slider, and Davis hit it to Kasko for a double play, as predicted. One run scored, but we still had the lead and only one more man to get. Fairly hit the first pitch on the handle of his bat. Coleman jumped for it, spread-eagled his legs, hung in the air just long enough, caught the ball, and yelped happily.

Jay, who had given up hope for his win, echoed Coleman gleefully in the clubhouse. "That's the way to win 'em!"

He had to be kidding.

Cincinnati — June 2

Lou Smith, sports editor of the Cincinnati *Enquirer*, applauded the Reds' feat of winning four games on the Coast by writing a column which might well have deserved a copyright for wishful thinking. Strongly implying that the smart fan would order World Series tickets for October seats at Crosley Field, Smith served notice on the other National League clubs that Cincinnati was the team to beat. His desire to be first to jump on a bandwagon that was at least two months away encouraged more anti-press snickering in the Red clubhouse.

"Lou's just getting in position to jump all over us when we don't win it," said Lynch.

Hutchinson congratulated the team for its California harvest. "You did a hell of a job, and I'm proud of you," he said. He picked up the score card listing the Cubs' lineup, pursed his lips, and continued. "But that's all done now, and we got a lot more games to play. These guys have been hitting lately and they have some guys that can hurt you. Don't hold 'em cheap. Purk, you want to go over their hitters?"

Purkey described, succinctly and with professional aplomb, just how he intended to pitch each Cub batter. His intentions, well meant and impossible to fault, did not impress the Cubs, who chased him after five innings.

The Cubs had come into the park with as many nominal "managers" as they had players on the field during the last half of the first. They had devised an experimental coaching system in which any of nine different men might at some time during the season be named "head coach." (If the players chose to think of him as manager he'd acknowledge the title, no doubt.)

The Cubs introduced a further innovation; they required their pitcher to wait his turn at bat in the batting circle. Treating him as if he were just as good a hitter as any other man in the lineup, I suppose.

The psychological aspects of Chicago-style management were admirable. For instance, any player who did not like his manager at the start of the year could absorb, patiently, all real and imaginary abuse, aware that a change, maybe for the better, was just around the next losing streak. Smugly unaware of their relatively uncomfortable position at the bottom of the league, the Cubs and their nine-headed manager brought along a rackful of hot bats with which to play the Reds.

In the ninth inning the Cubs took their last turn at bat, holding a 6-1 lead behind the pitching of Jackie Curtis, a little southpaw who looked like he had a sore arm and was saving himself from any untoward strain while pitching. His pitches had to be called "off-speed" because they certainly were neither coming to the plate fast nor moving away from it any faster. Jimmy O'Toole, another little left-hander who throws pretty hard, shook his head, feigning amazement. "You wouldn't believe it if you didn't see it!"

Hutchinson bristled indignantly on the bench. "We're dead-ass, that's all. Swing the damn bats!" He shoved Pete Whisenant behind the plate in the ninth to see if Whiz could actually catch. He had said he could, and Bob Schmidt's sore knee prevented him from replacing Zimmerman after Jerry had gone out for a pinch-runner.

Whisenant, on a 3-2 pitch, tried to catch the runner on first as he headed for second on the hit-and-run. Neither the shortstop nor second baseman covered second since the pitch had been low, the batter had drawn a walk, and the base runner was entitled to second base. Whisenant's throw went into center field, the base runner went to third, and Banks scored him with a fly ball. For the moment it was simply embarrassing.

Curtis could retire just two men in the last of the ninth, and left the game with the bases loaded and two runs in. Elston relieved, tried to throw a fast ball by Lynch and Jerry tripled to left center to make the score 7-6.

"That Lynch is somethin' else, ain't he!" said O'Toole. "We oughta be tied up."

That was something else, however.

Two hours before the next day's game started I walked over to the left field foul line intending to take a few extra laps to shake the Scotch out of my head. Jerry Kindall, the

Cubs' shortstop, came down the ramp yelling to me to wait for him. Kindall, an earnest, religious young man, was a former roommate of mine when I played at Chicago, and we'd had many nighttime squabbles over religious faiths and related superstitions. He didn't want to run, just to visit, so we went into the dugout where the sun and Turner couldn't see us fraternizing.

Kindall described his trip to Berlin during the winter on behalf of the Lutheran Church; and I reminisced about my trip to Munich and Wiesbaden on behalf of pleasure. Kindall suggested we have dinner after the game and I agreed, halfheartedly. I could think of better things to do with my Saturday night.

"Meet you at the hotel then," Kindall said.

We met earlier—in the seventh inning of the game. I should have left for the hotel in the fifth.

Ken Hunt started for us, nervously watched by Schmidt and Whisenant, who'd taken turns warming him up.

"He's got great stuff today," said Schmidt. "Monday he was lousy warming up and got better every inning."

Hunt couldn't have been better than he was for the first five innings. He had a perfect game going, a fact which I noted, aloud, just before the Cubs got their first hit.

"You had to open your big mouth, Broz!" said Schmidt.

"That's all right, Bross," said Whisenant. "O'Toole said it, too."

This doubly jeopardized Hunt, of course. No one is supposed to mention a pitcher's no-hitter till it's finished. Hunt lost his control after the first Cub hit, getting progressively wilder with each pitch.

"What happens to a pitcher when his control goes, Bross?" Whisenant asked me.

"Watch his legs, Pete. His rhythm is all shot to hell. You lose your coordination and you don't know where the ball's going."

Hutchinson lifted Hunt in the seventh with two Cub runs in and two men on. Kindall was the first hitter I faced and I knew I'd get out of the inning easily with a slider. Low and away—*not* low and inside. Kindall hit *that* slider over the center field fence.

Hutch bearded me in the dugout after the inning. "What the hell's goin' on?" he said. "You get the good hitters out and that guy hits you like he owns you!"

So did two other Cubs, in the eighth. Hutch came out to get me, mollified by circumstances that were clearly out of my control.

"Guess they just got hot bats, that's all," he said.

Howie Nunn, my current roommate, relieved me and threw a *high*, inside slider to Kindall. He hit it off the top of the scoreboard to drive in the runs that made me a forlorn sight walking all the way back to the hotel, a losing pitcher.

The doorman did not notice me slinking into the foyer. He was working a patron who'd checked out of the hotel, and said, "The Reds really choked again today. That puts the Dodgers in first. They'll never win the pennant."

I didn't even eat dinner that night.

A Sunday double-header, the next day, concluded our series with Chicago.

"The jinx of Time, Inc., still works, eh?" asked Tex Maule when I walked onto the field just before batting practice. Maule, writer for *Sports Illustrated*, had been assigned to find out if the Reds really, really were for real. An accompanying photographer, Art Shay, bugged me gently for a few poses. Shay and I had played handball together during the winter and he assured me that any close-ups of my red-white-and-blue eyes would not be used in the magazine.

"You doin' a story on our pitching?" I asked Maule.

"Pitching *is* the story, isn't it?" he countered.

"Since you and Shay showed up it's been a farce, I'd say," I said.

The Cincinnati sportswriters jumped off their bandwagon onto the Red pitchers' backs. Not only were we all suddenly lousy but some of us were in danger of being shipped out. Nunn and Bridges, particularly, were warned not to send out any laundry; it might have to be delivered to Jersey City.

"——— ——— ———!" said Nunn. And Bridges. And Maloney. (And I took notes to remind them of what they said.)

Bridges and Nunn were so incensed that they grabbed their rifles and went to the right field corner to practice shooting.

One of the late Powell Crosley's last decisions as owner of the Reds was to set up a course in "instinct shooting." Using air rifles each player shot BB's at small targets tossed into the air by the shooting instructor. Purpose of the course: to improve concentration of mind and body on a single, isolated object. The targets selected became progressively smaller until the instructor asked each man to "look at the shiny spot on the BB" as he tossed one into the air.

"I didn't hit any BB's," said Nunn as we prepared to do our running. "But those ——— writers better watch their step!"

"Howard, next time you pitch well and they want to know how you did it, what you gonna say?"

"I don't know 'em!" Nunn said.

An old biddy wearing a Reds baseball cap over her angry brow yelled, "What's wrong with you bums?" as we neared the foul line box seats.

"Lady's talkin' to you, Broz," said Nunn.

"I don't know her, Howie."

Even Hutchinson took a critical attitude toward the play of our last two games. To his collective ass-chewing he added the typical fanlike exhortation: "It's now you gotta bear down, make your move. Stop this carelessness, bad base-running, wild swinging. And you pitchers—my God, have an idea of what you're trying to do out there!"

Jim Maloney, one day older than twenty-one, was the man chosen to lead us back to the path of righteous, winning baseball. He was most careful for eight innings, and even scored the first run of the game in the third.

"Tits don't care about those hot bats, I guess," said Schmidt.

"Tits don't care about nothin'," said Nunn.

"Hutch says Maloney's gonna be a great pitcher someday," I recalled.

He was good enough to go nine, giving up just one run on a long homer by Altman, the Cubs' hottest bat. We ate lunch between games, quickly, before the writers could get from the press box to our lunch table.

"They cut you up at breakfast, then eat your food at noon," said Maloney. "Let's go get 'em again, gang. Ain't done a thing yet." Then he showered, finished for the day.

The Cubs, acting as if they'd been denied lunch, feasted on Jim O'Toole's first-inning pitches in the second game. Back-to-back homers by Santo and Banks put them too far ahead to catch.

In the sixth inning, Henry, still hungry apparently, suggested that we order some popcorn and peanuts. "Might as well enjoy the game. Hutch don't trust us, Broz, after yesterday."

We ate several bags of goodies, and washed them down the drain while Nunn and Bridges mopped up the game.

"Everything shipshape, Captain?" Schmidt asked, hanging the wet broom from the bullpen railing.

"Okay, Sergeant," I said. "Change the order of those flags on the roof. The Giants won. We're half a game out now."

"Latest odds from Vegas says the Yankees and Dodgers are in," I read from the paper. "L.A. is two to one to win the pennant."

"So what?" said Nunn. "Tell me something interesting. What's the odds a man will break a tooth off eating ice cream?"

"Why?"

"I just did it. Look."

"You look just gummy, Roomie!" I said. "Tell the writers you were defending their honor in Newport last night."

In the clubhouse meeting to go over the Braves Hutch insisted that there was no panic in the front office, despite the generally derogatory public explanations of our slump. We'd made headlines on the road, however, and the fans wanted to see some *reason* why we weren't in sixth place where we belonged. Twenty thousand of them showed up (on a Monday night!) to sit and stare.

The queasy air of concern led to a minor shifting of scene

and attitude in the dugout. Jim Turner, taking sudden interest in what went on in the bullpen, asked Henry and me to sit on the bench for half the game.

I reacted negatively to Zimmerman's hint that the hitters might be looking for my slider and asked Maloney, defensively, "Tits, let me use your hummer. I need another pitch."

Don Blasingame, father of a new-born baby, rejected Dr. Rohde's outstretched hand. Don rubbed the sleep from his eyes and said, "Forget those pep pills, Doc. I got jammed three times yesterday!"

The Braves paraded past our dugout from their clubhouse, flinching from an expected barrage of bench jockeying. Charlie Dressen had just publicly criticized his entire club for: (1) starting a small brush fire in the rear of their bus after they'd lost a game to Philadelphia; (2) breaking the midnight curfew in several places; and (3) making him, Charlie Dressen, look bad.

He concluded his depressing sermon with threats that he'd make a few personnel changes. "You don't think I'm daffy enough to go with what we have, do *you?*" he said. In a way he may have destroyed faith in the confident Dressen demeanor that always forged ahead dragging his team with him.

"Check your matches here, men!" Pete Whisenant yelled, as the Braves' bullpen crew filed by. "Don't let little Napoleon get you down, boys!"

The Braves were up and after Joey Jay in the first inning, scoring all their runs on homers by Mathews and Adcock. But Jay settled down and held on till the seventh. After Bell hit for him, I relieved him on the mound. Having retired the side in order I watched joyfully as Robinson hit Burdette's slider over the scoreboard with one on. Dressen walked out to relieve Burdette with the Dominican, Federico Olivo. Olivo was making his major league debut and had to make his first pitch to Jerry Lynch. That's a tough way to break in. Lynch also homered.

In the ninth inning I convinced Zimmerman—and Hutchinson—that, yes, they might very well be looking for my slider. Anyway they hit it, and had the tying run on base when Lee

Maye, a left-handed hitter came to the plate. That brought Hutch out from the bench, and Henry in from the bullpen.

And that's all she wrote.

"Gabby, you get the easiest saves I ever saw!" I said, shaking his hand in the clubhouse. "All you ever have to do is get one man out!"

"You suck up easy wins; I'll save 'em for you," he said.

How can you knock that combination, Vegas?

"Blazer, did I see you drinking a beer after last night's game?" I asked. Blasingame shuffled his shower shoes on the locker room floor and half-grinned.

"Yeah. I'm tryin' to keep my weight up. This night life's killin' me."

"Your baby got colic?"

"No. But she doesn't sleep much. And you just doze all night waitin' for her to cry!"

Henry laughed, having survived and forgotten *his* early parenthood. "Listen, Blaze," he said, "you better send that baby back to the hospital. We gotta win a pennant."

Whisenant insisted that I stay on the bench again for six innings. We'd won a game with that format the night before, so why not stay with it?

"Besides, we need you to help Otis yell," Pete added, facetiously. About the only time I ever open my mouth on the bench is to stick a needle in somebody's psyche or a chew in my jaw.

"Otis makes so much noise it's distracting, Whiz," I said. But I went along with the superstition.

"Otis gets on Dressen's nerves, too," said Whisenant. "Look at Spahnie."

Spahn stood at the edge of our dugout, mouth wide-open, neck muscles straining, in a silent burlesque of Otis Douglas cheerleading a rally. Hutchinson laughed loudly at Spahn, but Douglas sat back on the bench, primly ignoring Spahn's satire.

"What the hell's going on, Hutch?" Spahn yelled aloud. "That guy is drivin' Charlie nuts!"

"Atta boy, Otis!"

Carl Willey's pitching for the Braves presented a case study of premeditatedly difficult technique. Behind on every hitter, 3-2 on many, Willey *labored* throughout the first four innings. His professional knowledge and equipment were enough to warrant professional respect, but:

"He sure makes it tough on himself," said Whisenant.

"He doesn't dare anybody, does he?" asked O'Toole.

"He's a good pitcher," said Jay, who once roomed with Willey.

"He'd be a better pitcher if he forced hitters to come to him instead of going to them all the time," I said.

"They're waitin' to get beat, boys," Douglas yelled. Full of impregnable optimism.

Purkey dangled runs in front of the Braves for three hours, the time it took to play eight innings. He gave them thirteen hits and a base on balls, which, to the amateur or uncool spectator, might seem to be inviting all sorts of trouble.

Purkey, though he permits hits, shuns runs; and he still had a one-run lead when he came to bat with men on second and third in the eighth. Purkey, though he swings hard, doesn't hit well, so Hutch sent Bell to pick up the runs offered by the Braves.

Olivo, making his second major league appearance for the Braves, walked Bell, then Kasko, then Blasingame, forcing in two runs, and providing us with a comfortable lead for me to hold in the ninth.

Bolling hit my second pitch, Mathews the third, Aaron the fourth. None of them went out of the infield, so we all went home.

"Don't tell me about easy saves!" said Henry.

"Purkey had 'em tired out," I admitted.

Otis Douglas lost his voice in the eighth.

"Broz, is that a spitter you been workin' on?" Whisenant asked me.

"No, Peter, the spitball is illegal."

"Well, it *looks* like a spitter," he insisted.

"It's a fork ball. I figure I'm going to need another pitch to stay in business two more years, so I'm working on that. You like it?"

"It's a good one! You oughta use it in the game."

"No. It's not ready yet. Takes at least a year to get a new pitch down to the point where you can control it well enough to take a chance in a game."

"You may be right. Whenever you or Gabby go in you got to throw your best stuff and make 'em hit it. You oughta hurry that fork ball up, though. Any pitch that looks as much like a spitball as that has got to have a future."

The spitball was banned by the rules-makers at a time when pitchers carried sandpaper, slippery elm, files, razor blades, and pine tar with them to the mound. Any of these artificial stimulants when applied to the ball gave a man a new pitch. After the batters usurped control of baseball all foreign aids to pitchers were declared illegal. They now must battle bare-handed in the arena, and working on a new pitch takes research and patience.

When a pitcher turns thirty he will often work, during the season, on a new and difficult pitch or delivery, mastering it on the sidelines to use in his declining years when he passes thirty-three. It is his Social Security Pitch, with which he hopes to sustain himself just a little while longer.

Coaching, the teaching of fundamentals, usually recurs during the second month of the season. As if we'd never done it before, never spent days in the spring training batting cage practicing, we were now forced to give up half our batting practice to study *bunting*. Just the pitchers.

"Ain't no*body* gettin' any runners over on this club," Bridges grumbled. "Why's we got to practice buntin', 'Fess, the way I buggy-whips dat ball?"

"Fox, this is something every batting coach has to do, pretend he's teaching pitchers how to bunt. That's how he gets paid."

"What we oughta do is practice fake bunts," said Jay. "The way every infielder charges in on a bunt, there's no way in the world to get a guy over!"

Frank Thomas, the Braves' left-fielder, stuck his head in the

86

Cincinnati dugout just before we took infield practice. Tapping sportswriter Earl Lawson on the shoulder, he said, "How come you don't talk to me any more, Earl? When I was goin' bad you were always hangin' around."

Lawson smiled, sheepishly, and Thomas, sticking his nose back up in the air, walked away.

"He must be going good, I guess," said Lawson. "That trade the Cubs made has to be the worst of the year. Thomas for Roach!"

"Frank's all right," said Hutch. "But what a disposition! Say good morning to him and he wants to know what you mean by it!"

During the game Thomas made a one-handed catch of a line drive to help Nottebart out of the only trouble he had all night. Nottebart retired Robinson four times in a row, twice with men in scoring position.

"Robby hits either time and we're still in the game," said Whisenant.

"If Robby doesn't hit we don't win. That's the way it's been going lately," said Hutch to Lawson. "That kid pitched a hell of a game for them.

"Well, Robby'll get 'em tomorrow."

Thunderclouds blown by a twenty-mile-per-hour wind added a black discontent to the day-game-after-a-night-game blues. Bob Schmidt, warming up Maloney, said, "I'd rather catch a double-header than this kind a game."

I stood at the bullpen plate, pretending I was a hitter to give Maloney a target off which to gauge his pitches. "Yeah, man. We need a laugher today. Hope we can get a couple up into that wind. Juice two or three off Spahn quick."

"He's only had three days' rest," said Schmidt. "Maybe he's getting too old for that much work, huh!"

"Don't bet on it."

Humidity and exercise drenched Maloney's shirt even before the game began. He dipped a sponge in the bucket of ammonia and water, ran it over his brow and neck.

"Hope he has a couple of easy innings," said Turner. "Sit

down and cool off, young man!" he said to Maloney. "Don't drink too much water today. Use that sponge."

"Stick your head in the bucket, Malone!" O'Toole suggested.

"Let it all hang out now, Tits," said Whisenant. "Don't hold back out there."

Maloney took a deep breath, picked up his glove, and started out to the mound.

"That kid ain't impressed with anybody," Whisenant said. "He needs a kick in the ass sometimes, though. Cocky. Just like Tootie was a couple years ago. Right, Tootie?"

"Sure, Pete," said O'Toole. "Anything you say."

"You bonus kids are all alike. Somebody once asked Frank Baumann whether he'd sign today for eighty G's and sit on the bench, or forget the bonus and get some experience in the minors. He said, 'I'd still take the money and put it in the bank.'"

"That's right," said O'Toole, who had banked fifty grand when he'd signed. "Where can you put experience?"

"In your head, you dumb Irishman! That's what you make your living with!"

Spahn lasted just five innings, and when Freese hit a three-run home run off his reliever, Drabowsky, Maloney had a 10-2 lead, the first time all year we'd scored ten runs in a game.

"Atta boy, Augie!" Whisenant said, shaking Freese's hand. "I think we got a laugher goin'. You can quiet down, now, Otis!"

Maloney walked Bolling to start the seventh and Hutchinson slapped his own forehead in disgust. "How can you walk anybody with an eight-run lead? Let 'em hit the damn ball!"

Mathews and Aaron then hit successive home runs and Hutch called Bridges in to relieve. Adcock and Thomas greeted the Fox with two more homers in a row, a new major league record. Both drives cleared the scoreboard, landing near a group of workmen razing the building across the street from the park.

Wally Post said after the game, "I tied myself down out

there when that wrecking crew quit working! Nice goin',
Bridges!"

"Well, mah arm's tired, man! Ain't no coach in the bullpen.
Dey don't know when you's tired!"

Bill Henry started the eighth inning in place of Bridges.
Nobody laughed in our dugout. Everyone hoped that Gabby
could just get six more outs before they hit some more long
balls.

Henry got two men out, but when Mathews homered and
Aaron lined a double high off the scoreboard, Hutch waved
me in to fan Adcock.

Don't let 'em hit the ball, that's the plan.

In the ninth, with one out, Torre singled through my legs
and Roy McMillan, an ex-roommate of mine, came to the
plate. He chopped at a low slider and bounced it to Freese
who started a double play. Blasingame's pivot was slow and I
thought McMillan might have a chance to beat the relay. But
I could have relaxed. Jocko Conlan had his right arm in the
air even before Coleman gloved the ball.

"Nice call, Jock," I said, following him as he ran up the
ramp to the umpire's dressing room. Three hours and fifteen
minutes had elapsed, sweatily. McMillan really had had no
chance.

St. Louis — June 9

THERE seems to be no way to travel to St. Louis comfortably
during the summer. During one plane trip from Cincinnati,
the Reds had to fly south to Memphis to avoid a squall line
which refused to get out of the way. Eventually we flew
through the storm, and were tossed about like a spawning
salmon heading upstream. After a three-hour flight (scheduled
for one hour, twenty minutes) we landed with a foot-wide
strip of stabilizer sheared off by lightning. Don Newcombe
turned white and three other pitchers lost forty-eight hours'
worth of meals.

To avoid a similar traumatic situation we took the over-
night train after the Milwaukee game. It's possible that we
went through Memphis again, to avoid the railroad tracks.

The night-long jostling caused no vomiting, but it prevented sleep. Hutchinson, cross as a bear as we filed aboard the bus to the hotel in St. Louis, reprimanded the traveling secretary for the rough trip.

"We won't be taking any more trains," he insisted, and his decision was seconded by everyone who could open his eyes or mouth.

The Cardinals welcomed us to Busch Stadium like ex-teammates. On our roster were eight players who once played for St. Louis, plus a manager and a coach who once worked there, too. For thirty minutes photographers herded various groups of Cards and ex-Cards together for captionable pictures. Kasko and Blasingame, ex-roommates of Joe Cunningham, insisted that Joe take off his cap for an informal, hair-raising shot. Cunningham, who has more hair on the barrel of his bat than he does on his head, refused to doff his cap.

"Guess Flakey is getting sensitive in his old age," said Kasko.

"He's married, now, too," explained Blasingame.

"Why'd they want a shot of me and you?" Henry asked. "I never played here."

"Broeg probably asked for it," I thought. Bob Broeg, sports editor of the St. Louis *Post-Dispatch*, had been needling Hemus, the Cardinal manager, for his bullpen problems. At one time, Hemus had had three-fourths of the Cincinnati bullpen on his roster.

"If Hemus had our bullpen he wouldn't be worryin' about his job."

"Think they'll let him go?"

"I couldn't care less," I said.

Broeg walked up to us and said, "You and Gabby are doin' a hell of a job, aren't you? Wish we had you over here."

"What have you got in the jug?" I asked, pointing at his thermos bottle.

"Milk. I got an ulcer."

I always said sportswriters take this game too seriously.

Jim O'Toole, his pride warped by three straight poor performances, started warming up twenty minutes before game time. His reasoning was sound. Any pitcher who depends on his control for effectiveness must practice by throwing over and over again to spots in the strike zone.

"Jesus," said Nunn. "O'Toole's gonna pitch a whole game before we ever start!"

"Bet he's thrown 150 pitches already," I said. "Pretty hot tonight, too."

O'Toole's intentions were better than either his control or his stuff, and he was gone in the fourth inning. St. Louis had six runs, a three-run lead, and the same offensive power that had produced forty hits in their last four games.

"They're hot," said Jay on the bench.

"We don't have any more life than Hogan's goat!" Turner complained.

"We're deader than Kelcy's nuts!" said Sisler.

"Yeah, dead," Bell echoed.

Hutch asked Bell to hit for Hook, who had made his first appearance since the mumps left him. Bell lined a single to right but inspired no resurrection of hitting spirit; and Nunn gave up two more Cardinal runs in the seventh to ice the body.

"You got a little sunburn this afternoon," Doc Rohde said in the trainer's room after the game.

"Yeah, Doc," I said. "We played bridge by the pool at the hotel. Lost that game, too."

"Can't win 'em all," he philosophized.

It usually takes a succession of pleas, warnings, and threats to clear the clubhouse of ballplayers before a game starts. The last-to-leave coach yells, "Ten minutes!" and rouses the regulars; word that "The umpires are out!" starts a more general exodus; and "You can't see the whole game if you don't see the first pitch" reminds anyone left that "The Star-Spangled Banner" has been announced on the field.

The Cardinal management, anxious to get Saturday's players started on time, scheduled a pregame fashion show. The prospect of seeing a couple of bathing-suited broads precipitated a rush to their respective dugouts by both clubs. Convertible cars, each bearing a broad sitting on the back of the car's front seat, circled the park in a pleasing halo. Missouri's heat and humidity brought out the best in most of the pretty pink complexions shown. Each car had a red-faced Cardinal player as escort. Bob Miller, young bachelor right-hander, opened the door of the car that unloaded before our dugout.

"Hey, Bobby!" Blasingame yelled. "Get any phone numbers?"

Miller played it properly coy, and Blasingame mused, "I used to get that job all the time."

Blasingame had remained single for five years as the Cardinal's star second baseman. His return trips to Busch Stadium often inspired him to reach premarital heights. On the field.

Today was no exception. He had four hits, off Curt Simmons, all of them bleeders that barely reached the outfield. As "Star of the Game" he was asked to appear on a postgame radio show.

"Hope they don't describe those hits," he said.

"In tomorrow's box score they'll look like line drives, Blaze," said Freese.

One of Blasingame's bloops had driven in the first two runs in the fifth to give Joey Jay the lead as he went to the mound.

"Now's when you pitchers got to bear down," Whisenant said. "Make yourself think it's 0-0 instead of 2-0. Bear down out there."

"Get off the pitchers, Whisenant!" O'Toole said. "You sound more like a coach every day!"

In the seventh inning Stan Musial pinch-hit for Lillis. Musial's appearance always excited the crowd as much as it concerned the opposing pitcher. Jay retired him with one pitch, however, exciting a natural question of Catcher Jerry Zimmerman.

"What did you throw Stan?"

"I went out and asked Joe how he was gonna pitch him. He said he was going to throw sinkers and curves. And I said, 'Nah, Broz says he don't like sliders.' So we threw him one and he hit it on his fists."

Musial once confessed to me that the slider gave him more trouble than any other type of pitch. So, instead of hitting .350 he hit only .310 against slider-ballers. An almost insignificant advantage for pitchers.

Bill Henry, unreasonably self-conscious about the home run Mathews had hit off him the day before, said, "I guess I'll work on another pitch, too. Broz, how do you hold your slider?"

"Forget it, Gab," I said. "For Christ's sake, don't start foolin' around with that thing. Hum that seed! That's all you gotta do."

In the ninth, Henry did just that to save Jay's win. His eighth save and my eight gave us a right to order extra prints of the "REDS' HOT FIREMEN" picture from the paper.

"We'll hang it in our lockers. You have a good day, you get it. And vice versa."

It's a good idea to remind yourself that you can do a good job. Seeing is believing, as they say in Missouri.

Sunday double-headers, before a packed house, can be a monumental drag if you lose both games, a frustrating exercise if you split the two games, and a fun day if you take everything.

Scoring four runs in the first inning of the first game and four runs in the ninth inning of the second game helped us while away the sunny Sunday hours. The bus broke down on the expressway to the airport, the plane was an hour late taking off, and Pittsburgh was closed up by the blue laws, but we'd regained first place from the Dodgers and obviously it was one of the Reds' better days.

At noon our prospects had failed to stir the sleepy sportswriter from Dayton, Ohio, who sat on the dugout bench thinking up reasons why the Reds were winning. His questions reflected his pessimism, an attitude to be avoided until you're five runs down in the last inning. I picked up the new, steel-colored, heavy bat that hitters swing in the on-deck circle to make themselves feel strong.

"What is that?" asked the writer.

"That, Froggie, is an extruded aluminum football. What the hell did you think it was!"

He laughed heartily enough to set his stomach in motion,

a fascinating sight. If he'd only change his philosophy he could play "The Night Before Christmas" without props.

Don Blasingame led off against Ray Sadecki, the Cards' young left-hander who'd beaten Cincinnati four straight times. (And was not yet twenty-one!) As Blasingame swung hard at Sadecki's first pitch and missed, Whisenant said, "If I were manager and Blasingame ever hit a fly ball I'd fine him. He oughta hit nothing but line drives."

Blasingame hit the next pitch onto the right field pavilion for a home run.

"That's another reason you're not a manager, Pete," said O'Toole.

"He should still try to hit line drives all the time, a little guy like that. Let the big boys hit the long ball."

Freese, a bigger boy than Blasingame, hit a three-run homer later in the inning to give Sadecki a taste of adult living. He stayed in for four more innings but the Cardinals couldn't do anything with Hunt's hanging curve but hit line drives at somebody.

Hunt, slightly embarrassed at his good luck, said, "All I'm tryin' to do is throw strikes!"

"Well, throw 'em. Don't worry about it," Whisenant advised him. "Ain't nobody been killed yet!"

Hutchinson sent Marshall Bridges to the bullpen "just in case." The Fox half-smiled as we started to throw. "Guess ah ain't on the block yet, 'Fess. Didn't think he'd evah trust me no more."

Hunt needed no help, however, and looked particularly strong in the clubhouse eating a sandwich between games. Whisenant pounded him on the back and shook hands with every man on the club.

"Got to push in this second game now, boys. Gotta jack ourselves up. Ain't done a thing yet today."

"Maybe L.A. will lose, Pete," I said.

"To hell with them. Can't depend on anybody to help us out. You gotta win it yourselves."

Purkey battled the Cardinals for seven innings in the second game despite a sore elbow. Between innings Doc Rohde slathered the elbow with Capsolin, an ointment that relieves pain *in* the elbow by blistering the skin covering it. With Purkey scheduled to hit in the eighth, down by one run, Hutch told him he'd done well enough. "I'll use a hitter if we get that far. Broz, go heat up."

Blasingame, second man in the lineup, led off and it seemed unlikely that we'd get "that far." But by the time the Cardinal bullpen was through making mistakes eight men had hit and we had a two-run lead.

I walked Cunningham to start the Cardinal eighth, bringing up the tying run and setting up my ninth save when the next six hitters failed to reach base. Our four-run ninth made the job easier, and prompted Purkey's congratulatory remarks. "Nice goin'. I can see why you walked Cunningham. You must have known something."

Freese, having batted in seven runs during the day, wasn't a bit depressed when the bus broke down. He joined a family picnic in a backyard adjoining the roadside.

"Bunch of Polacks," he said when he returned to the bus with a bagful of beer bottles. "Couldn't play horseshoes but they had plenty of beer."

"They'll call you for passes next trip in, y'know."

"It's worth it," said Freese.

Pittsburgh — June 13

FOR every ballplayer, on every ball club, there is one ball park for which he has few good memories, and in which he feels uncomfortable. For two years, Forbes Field in Pittsburgh had been a bad-news scene for most of the Cincinnati Reds.

"Remember that game last year we had a five-run lead in the ninth? Hutch sticks Henry in because Gabby needed the work. The Pirates knock him out and then Skinner hits a two-run shot into the stands and we lose, 6-5. Remember that, Gab?"

"Forget it!"

"Remember, Broz," said Nunn, "when Stuart hit that ball

over the light tower? Longest ball I ever saw thrown. You musta been strong that night."

"Forget it."

"Remember when Hutch threw the chair across the clubhouse here? Nearly killed the clubhouse boy. Think we gave 'em a double-header that day," I recalled.

Apparently no one could think of anything pleasant to remember as we started the game. A smoggy haze added to the generally dim view of our prospects.

"This *oughta* be a good park to pitch in," I noted. "Especially at night. Look at that light pole. Must be seven bulbs out."

"Gibbon oughta be rough here," said Schmidt, "the way he can hum."

"He hasn't finished a game all year, the paper said," I said.

In trouble in the first inning, Gibbon fanned Wally Post to retire the side. He had no more troublesome innings until the ninth, and he fanned Post twice more during the game.

"Wally hasn't had a loud foul off Gibbon in two games," Nunn said. "Last time we faced him he struck Post out three times."

"Some guys just can't hit certain pitchers," I said. "Wish I had some cousins like that."

Maloney walked Mazeroski with the bases loaded in the sixth to force in the second run of the inning and the winning run of the game.

"Tits is high with everything tonight," Schmidt said. "If he'd just concentrate on keeping the ball down when he warms up he'd be better off."

"Turner wants him to practice his slow curve," Hook said.

"Turner wants everybody to practice his slow curve," I said. "The way he talks you'd think the slow curve is the best pitch in baseball."

"Ever listen to him when we go over hitters?" asked Nunn. "Nobody in the league can hit a slow curve. Unless he's been around for ten years."

"It's a good pitch to have," said Hook.

"Yeah," I said. "But Maloney doesn't have it. At least he

96

can't control it. He's already walked six men foolin' around."

"Maybe he took two Benzedrine pills 'stead of one!" said Schmidt.

"That *would* tend to make you high," I guessed.

"There's one good thing about this park," said Whisenant the next night. "They play the best music before the game."

With Erroll Garner swinging through the P.A. system we took a forty-minute batting practice and watched to see the Milwaukee–San Francisco score posted on the board.

"Giants are hot again," I said. "Only a game behind us now."

"Only half a game, Broz," said Jay. "They won, 11-2. Bombed Spahn. I heard it on the way to the park."

"Looks like he's had it, finally," I said. "Doesn't look like he'll win twenty this year."

"Whitey Ford oughta win thirty the way he's going," said Purkey. "He's got ten already, hasn't he?"

"I don't know," I said. "But he's the best left-hander in the game. Wonder if Bevan agrees with me now."

"How's he doin' at Jersey City?" asked Purkey.

"Hasn't been hitting much, I guess. It's a bad year for catchers."

One of the reasons given by Pittsburgh writers and fans for the Pirates' slow start was the slump of Hal Smith, the No. 2 catcher. In 1960 he'd helped win the pennant, swinging a big bat against left-handed pitching. When he faced O'Toole in the second inning of the game, he was hitting under .200. So Tootie walked him.

"Why didn't he walk Stuart?" Henry asked.

Big Stu, booed by the fans when he came to bat, had hit a two-run home run to give Pittsburgh the lead.

"Hutch says there's a campaign on to run Stuart outa town," I said. "Wish they would before he kills us again."

"They're all a bunch of front-runners," said Schmidt. "If Pittsburgh doesn't win again this year they'll run 'em all outa town!"

"Wonder if they'll make a trade tonight?" Hook asked.

At midnight the trading deadline was due. After twelve

P.M. Pacific Coast time, no interclub trades could be made, under the rules. (Under-the-table trades, involving waivers and gentlemen's agreements, were not only possible but likely.)

O'Toole threw 118 pitches in eight innings. Eighty of them were strikes and he had a 4-3 lead going into the last of the ninth.

"Tootie oughta waste a pitch once in a while when he's got two strikes on a hitter," said Whisenant. "They already got three hits on 2-0 pitches."

"So what!" I said. "What difference does it make *when* the guy gets a hit?"

"It's not good pitching, Broz. You know it. Besides, Hutch doesn't like it."

When Groat singled on a 2-0 pitch with one out in the ninth, Hutch jerked O'Toole and brought me in. With five right-handed batters coming up in order, the perc·ntage indicated the change.

Clemente swung at, and missed, two low sliders, then took a third one just off the plate.

"I'll give him a low fast ball away and then come back with the slider," I decided. But Clemente topped the fast ball and it rolled ten feet out toward the mound. I let it roll, thinking Zimmerman might get to it before I could. It came further than I'd judged, and Jerry couldn't make a play.

"My ball," I said to him. "Couldn't get off the mound, that's all."

"Forget it," he said. "Make this guy hit your pitch now."

Stuart had beaten me twice before with home runs over the left field scoreboard.

"If he pulls me tonight, he's gonna have to step across the plate," I muttered to myself. "Everything away from him," I told my arm.

Stuart took a low slider for a ball, then hit a belt-high slider just off the outside corner. It was hit well, but to right center, and Bell ran back toward the fence, drifted with the ball toward the screen, and jumped up against the low wall in front of the stands. The ball caromed off the screen just over his head, bounced away from him, and by the time Pinson recovered it Clemente and Groat had both scored, and we'd blown another one.

The clubhouse gloom was opaque. Hutch stared at me, accusingly. O'Toole, who needed the win, wouldn't look at me. Even the beer tasted lousy.

"Let's go get loaded, Roomie," I said to Nunn.

"Better not, Rooms," he said. "Hutch might check tonight."

The two o'clock curfew check is a disciplinary threat seldom invoked by Hutchinson. He'd used it once, in L.A.

But what the hell. It was only a hundred bucks.

"What kind of mood is No. 1 in?" I asked a Pittsburgh sportswriter standing behind the batting cage.

"Hutch?" he replied, looking down at his note pad. "Still hates this ball park. Says if a man fields a ball on this infield he should be awarded a Distinguished Service Medal. It's not that bad, is it?"

"Well, yes, it is," I said. "I need a favor from Hutch. Did he talk about last night's game?"

"He asked me if I'd ever seen Stuart hit a ball to right field like that and I couldn't remember any."

"It's buggin' him then, I guess."

Twenty hours had passed since Stuart's double had beaten me and snatched a win from Hutchinson. I could only hope he'd forgiven if not forgotten my pitch. I'd done penance all night and looked like it, but I had to ask him for a favor.

What I needed was a week off, really. We'd played sixty games, nearly half a season, with very few days off. It never seemed to rain any more. All I was asking for was permission to fly to Chicago from Philadelphia and spend the off-day Monday with my family.

"What do you think?" I asked him.

"Well," he said grumpily, "it's not so much what I think as it is what everybody else will think. You know you're not covered by insurance with the club in a case like that. The front office wouldn't like it. And it's the kind of exception I'd have to make for everybody if I made it for one. Why do you have to go?"

"Hutch, I haven't seen my family since the season started, except for two days."

"So what? I haven't seen mine either. And I won't see them all together until October." He stared out over the center field fence, looking at the same prospect I saw, I suppose. "Look, Jim, you knew what you were getting into when you signed a contract."

His refusal I could have expected; his reasoning hurt. When I signed my first pro contract I was seventeen and glad to get away from home for six months.

"How does your arm feel?" Hutch asked as I started up the dugout steps. "You've been throwing a lot lately."

"I'm all right. Christ, I made a bad pitch to Stuart. Forget it."

In the clubhouse meeting Joey Jay, the starting pitcher, went over the hitters. Holding a score card in one hand, a cigar in the other, he exuded all the confidence that seven straight wins could give a pitcher. Jay had never won a game at Forbes Field so he was due; the Reds had won just five in two years so they were due; and Mizell, the Pirates' starter, was off to a bad year. (For some unaccountable reason—at least the Pirates couldn't account for it—we were in first place, four games ahead of Pittsburgh.)

Hutchinson held the meeting over for a few remarks.

"We just lost two tough games. But let's not panic. Get out there and swing those bats. Let's score five in the first and go from there."

Mizell retired just one batter in the first inning, and we scored four runs, which satisfied Jay, who made no mistakes for six innings.

"Looks like a good day for a laugher, Broz," said Nunn. He scanned the bleachers behind the bullpen, admiring the view. It was Ladies' Day and the stands were full of la belle broads from Pittsburgh.

"See anything you like, Roomie?" I asked him.

"This is a *good* town!" he said.

"Are all those broads your passes?"

"Hell, no!" he said. "My passes go first-class. You know that."

"That redhead looks interested. Let's ask Murph to sound her out."

One of the unusual features of the Forbes Field bullpen is the service provided by a character called Murphy the Gimp. A bedraggled exile from Boozeville, he uses Irish brashness and a kind of idiotic charm as a liaison between such broads and ballplayers as may want to make a connection. Later.

Murph reported that it wasn't the redhead but her friend, the fat blonde, who had eyes.

"That figures," said Nunn. "Tell her we're leavin' town tonight."

On the bus to the airport Jay sat next to me, puffing contentedly on a pipe.

"You always smoke a pipe when you win?" I asked him. "Usually you got a cigar in your mouth."

"Pipe relaxes me," he said. "You should try one."

"Gives me heartburn."

"Why do you chew tobacco then?"

"Relaxes me," I said. "It's a nasty habit, though. I'm going to give it up when I quit playing ball."

"Me, too," he said, smiling at the many good chewing years he had before him.

Philadelphia — June 16

"WOULD you like to pitch in the American League?" Larry Merchant, the bearded sportswriter, asked me before the game.

"Look, Merchant, I made one bad pitch the other night but I'm not ready to quit this league yet!"

"No offense, man. That's not why I asked. I talked to Frank Sullivan about the difference in pitching in each league. He said those big American League parks are just made for pitchers like you that throw nothing but sliders."

"It's an inferior league, too. Print that. Came from the horse's mouth."

"Which horse?" Merchant asked.

"Pete Whisenant, of course. He's managerial material, you know."

"For night games, I suppose."

"No, listen. Pete's settled down. He's serious when he talks baseball."

"Sullivan was serious, too, for a change," said Merchant. "Usually you can't tell whether he's putting you on or not. While I'm talking with him he points at one of those mass pepper games they have and says, 'We got a guy on our club who has such bad hands his glove is embarrassed!'"

"Who's that?"

"Never mind. You guys have a big enough advantage already when you play the Phillies."

Having won eight straight from Philadelphia we might have feared the law of percentages. But we hadn't really whomped them yet, winning low-score games most of the time. Every other team in the league had been bombing Philly pitchers, so:

"Time to let out a little shaft, boys!" said Jerry Lynch. "Let's open a little gap."

With L.A. playing the Braves we had a good chance to pick up a couple games on the Dodgers, with whom we were in a virtual tie for first place.

The P.A. announcer changed the pronunciation of John Buzhardt's name, while listing the opening lineup. Probably trying to change John's luck. Instead of accenting "*Buz*" he emphasized the "*hardt*," but it put no life into the Phils' attack. Demeter did hit a home run to give John a 1-0 lead in the seventh, but that was the only runner to get past second base.

In the eighth three Cincinnati singles tied the score and when Jerry Lynch batted for Zimmerman, Phil Manager Mauch pulled Buzhardt for a left-handed reliever. Lynch snorted at this percentage strategy and lined a double down the left field line, the ball skidding beneath my legs as I took my warm-up pitches. Although we now had a 2-1 lead, Hutch pinch-hit for Hunt and we soon had two more runs, gifts of Demeter, who caught a long, foul fly ball and threw too late to get the runner tagging up at third after the catch. Demeter's throw bounced off Pete Whisenant as he slid into the catcher and Elio Chacon, running for Lynch, scored a fourth run.

The Phillies were depressed by their own faulty generosity and waved halfheartedly at my relief pitching. Three up, three down.

"I hung five sliders in a row to Amaro!" I said on the bench. "I ain't got a thing!"

"So what!" said Hutchinson. "You're getting them out, aren't you?"

Elated at such confident analysis, I tried it again in the ninth. Three up, three down.

Hutch must have known something.

Halfway to the ball park on the short-cut bus route through Philadelphia's Little Harlem there is a sign that reads: "Have You Been Born Again?"

Seen on Saturday morning through sleepy eyes it never fails to shock me into a yawning semblance of life. To a ballplayer, traditionally forced to be as superstitious as a Congolese tribal priest, such psyche-stirring posters *should* start the brain moving.

On the Philly roster there were two ballplayers who took religion seriously. They belonged to the peculiar sects that equate athletic prowess with purity of heart and morals. Perhaps the competitive nature of major league baseball fires the preachings of such religious buffs. It doesn't improve their hitting.

At that, the Phillies seemed to be doing their best to make believers out of the Reds, especially inspiring us with the tenet: "Philadelphia can't beat Cincinnati." A fevered rush for the baptismal font could have been expected from the Reds. Any old preacher would do. Give him the ball and let's get on with the ceremony.

Twenty-three thousand kids helped five thousand paying customers fill the stands thirty minutes before the game. For eight and one half minutes the kids, all of them at that age which Ilg and Gesell admit is obnoxious, were relatively quiet.

"By the fourth inning, the bullpen will sound just like

home," said Zimmerman.

"You've only got four kids, right, Jerry?" I asked.

"Yeah, but it's a small apartment and they're always in the same room I'm in, and they're noisier."

The gradual swelling of juvenile tempers reached the plateau which only experienced parents can tolerate.

"Oh, my God!" said Nunn. "I can't stand it. Remind me never to have any kids. In fact, I don't think I'll get married."

"That a boy, Rooms. Don't take any chances."

Robin Roberts started for the Phillies. Once upon a time that prospect was enough to send hitters into hiding. Fortunately for them Robert's mind had not matured as fast as his arm. Instead of learning a new pitch or changing his style of pitching, Roberts pretended he was young Robby, the fireballer. And didn't fool enough people often enough to retire enough of them before they retired him. To the showers.

There is a reasonable axiom in pitching that says: "Don't walk anybody and everything will be all right." Nothing, of course, is always all right. Roberts would admit that privately, maturely. But then he'd throw nothing balls in the game just to get the pitch over the plate and prevent a base on balls. The results were frequently similar to the sight of Gordy Coleman's second- and fourth-inning home runs. Really long balls!

When Roberts agreed with Mauch that he'd had enough in the fifth inning, Al Barlick, the extra umpire working the left field foul line, came to our bullpen for a drink of water.

"Look at 'em! Look at 'em!" he said, having quenched his thirst. "Look at all of 'em on the mound. This Philly club has more huddles than a football team."

"They kick as many balls, too, Al," I said.

"Yeah. Ha, ha!" he said. "That's pretty good, Brosnan. You guys are really goin' good, y'know."

"We're gettin' the breaks," I said.

"Nuts. You're makin' your own breaks!"

"Okay, Al."

"Listen," he went on, "tell that Hunt he should throw his curve side-arm more. He hangs his other one too much."

"They're waitin' for you, Al," said Jay.

Barlick ran down the line to resume his nap.

"Even the umpires are with us," said Jay. "They're real friendly all of a sudden."

"Front runners!" said Zimmerman.

"Ah've seen everythin' now," said Bridges. " 'Magine umpires teachin' us how to pitch!"

"Shut up, Charcoal!" said Nunn, resuming his fake feud with Bridges.

"Charcoal! Why, you puny, snaggle-toothed—!"

After a while such noises blend with the roar of the kids. In the seventh Mauch let Baldschun absorb a six-run blast because he wanted to use a pinch-hitter in the Philly half of the inning.

That made it a laugher.

Sunday was an open date for the Yankees. New York is just one hundred miles from Philadelphia. Cincinnati led the National League. And every sophisticated New York sports editor had to find out why.

So there was a crowd of New York writers and baseball commentators in our dugout before the double-header. Their question: "How can you guys keep goin'?" was unanswerable. (Some answers were unprintable, the question being an insult at least.)

Frankie Frisch, an old-time ballplayer, interrupted my pepper game, introduced himself, and said to me, "What have you got against us old-timers?"

I pleaded peace, but he insisted. "You really knocked us in your book. Why? I don't have anything against ballplayers of today. They don't play the game like we used to, though." He said it proudly, as if the game had been better then.

"You don't knock me, I won't knock you, sir," I said. I truly had nothing against him, Frankie Frisch. As a commercially sponsored sports commentator he paid good money for interviews. And if he just asked me, I'd be all for him.

He didn't so I went to the bullpen.

Bob Schmidt came hobbling from the bench in the first

inning, groaning, "My God, I'd rather warm up anybody in the world but Maloney. He musta bounced sixteen curve balls off my knees!"

Maloney played no favorites. Before he was relieved by Howie Nunn in the second inning he'd bounced several more curves off Zimmerman's body, and had walked in two runs. Nunn threw a double-play ball to Del Greco to get out of the inning, and then shut out the Phillies the rest of the game as Bridges shouted encouragement.

"Looka theah! Look at mah buddy! Watch him wehrk! Wehrk, Nunn, wehrk!"

"Thought you and Nunn weren't speakin'," I said.

"But he's mah buddy, 'Fess! Look at 'im go!"

Wally Post hit a three-run homer in the fourth to put us ahead. (Post had hit ten balls out in batting practice, impressing the crowd but distressing Coach Reggie Otero, who was in charge of the baseballs. "We don' have any more balls, you dumb Indian!" he yelled at Post. "Go up to the clubhouse!")

Post's homer was enough, but Freese also hit one, and even Nunn got a base hit, transfixing Bridges. He shook Nunn's hand four times in the clubhouse, whispering, "What you gonna say to dem writers?"

"Yeah, Rooms," I said. "They wanted to ship you out, y'know. What are you gonna say when they ask you how you did it?"

"—— them!" said Nunn, laughing.

Post hit another homer in the second game and Freese had four hits. All in all it was Laughsville. Three boys jumped from the stands during successive innings, ran around the bases and slid into home. The second runner missed third, so Freese made sure the next one touched the bag. All three were ejected from the park and missed the rest of the game.

Probably figured they missed nothing.

Cincinnati — June 20

MOST major league clubs today have two or three pitching jobs that offer the most pleasant chores in the field. The hours of batting practice demanded by the hitters require the hiring of batting practice pitchers. These strong-armed, usually overweight throwers are required to do no more than get the ball over the plate for fifteen minutes a day. And they get paid for it.

My brother, Pat, a right-handed ex-professional pitcher, performs this pleasant duty when the Reds are in Cincinnati. Pat spent four years in the minor leagues learning how to get the ball over the plate; and regretted his mastering of this facility because too many hitters liked what they saw and belted him right out of the game. Absorbing these lumps in batting practice without fear of embarrassment should, I'd think, satisfy him that he's learned a way to play the game. Even if he can't make a living from it.

"There's only one job," he once explained, myopically, "where if you don't do it you're fired—selling!"

"Hold on, man," I said. "How about if you hang a curve ball with the bases loaded and lose the game by one run?"

"There are few quicker ways to lose a job," I went on. "Last year I saw a pitcher do that. The general manager was eight hundred miles away, watching the game on TV. He put down his beer, picked up the phone, and sent that pitcher to the minors!

"We were playing a double-header and that poor pitcher was sitting next to me in the bullpen in the second inning of the second game. He probably was ashamed to sit on the bench. Well, they phoned from the bench, told him to take off for the clubhouse. They practically stripped him of his uniform. And sent him to Havana!

"So don't tell me about tough ways to make a buck, brother."

With the Cardinals and Stan Musial in town, and a first-place club with a five-game winning streak to attract them, 32,000 fans packed Crosley Field. They paid good money, too, pleasing the Red management and exciting each Red player.

"Let's go ask for a raise, Robby," I said. "They sure as hell didn't figure to draw this many this season."

"Line forms at the right," he said.

Robinson's bat had been responsible for more wins than the front office probably would care to admit after the playing season ended and contract season arrived. He had had an especially devastating series against the Cardinals in St. Louis and picked up at the same tempo, driving home the two runs that gave Hook his lead in the seventh.

With two Cardinals on base, Carl Sawatski, who had beaten Hook with a pinch-hit home run the season before, batted for Lillis. Hook, a determined young man, had shut out the Cards for six innings and was anxious to join in the public acclaim being accorded all the other young Red pitchers. Recalling that Sawatski had beaten him on a fast ball before, he threw Carl nothing but curves. But Sawatski proved he could hit them, too, and we trailed 3-2 going into the ninth.

With a man on second and one out Ray Sadecki threw what looked from the bullpen like a perfect pitch, a curve low and away. But Jerry Lynch, living up to Hutch's accolade as the best pinch-hitter in baseball, stroked the curve to right center to tie the score.

Out went Sadecki, bewildered probably. In came Bobby Miller, nervous possibly and wild certainly. In the eleventh inning Miller walked three men, the last being Blasingame, who drew credit for driving in a run, and who couldn't have pleased me more since I drew credit for the win.

"That last pitch was just bad enough," Blazer said to me, exchanging mutual congratulations. "I didn't know about Secory. If the pitch was any closer I'da swung."

"Atta boy, Don. *Your* eyes are better than any umpires!"

Joey Jay pitched and lost the second game, ending two winning streaks, ours at six, his at eight straight. Which fulfilled the law of percentage, and proved the popular maxim: "You can't win 'em all."

Why not?

At a time when we led the league by two games; at a time when I could seem to do nothing wrong most of the time on the mound; at a time when people on Cincinnati streets seemed to admire me just because I played for the Reds; in the middle of a sunny summer afternoon I decided to quit baseball. Speaking aloud to myself, alone in my hotel room, I said, "I've had enough." Then I put down my book, poured myself a Scotch, and walked to the mirror to see if that was really me sounding off. It looked like me.

The grind gets rough whether you're winning or not. Success is as difficult to endure as failure.

I swallowed the drink, gave myself an encouraging wink, sat down again, picked up my book, *Advise and Consent*, and read the answer to my hallucination:

> Men do not often act on such impulses, which are immediately thwarted by reminders that this is a workaday world, after all, and here they are, after all, and such gestures would be completely irrational, after all, and what in hell are they thinking about, after all; and so they don't do them.

And so I reported, a little wobbly, to the ball park on time, feeling fortunate that I'd learned to read at an early age. Blasingame handed me the afternoon paper.

"You see this?" he asked. "Hal Smith has to quit."

Smith, the Cardinal catcher, had suffered a mild heart attack and had been advised never to play ball again. A witty little guy, one of the best receivers in the game, he probably hadn't even thought about quitting. And he must have accepted the news more bitterly than his published quip showed.

"They put me in the hospital just when I had an eight-game hitting streak. Guess they must have suspected something!"

"A damn shame!" I said, a remark echoed by every player in the game who knew Smith.

("At least," I thought, "he's got a good reason!")

Ken Hunt started for us against Ernie Broglio.

"Broglio's been havin' his troubles, Broz," said Whisenant. "What makes a pitcher win twenty one year and flop the next?"

"Ernie probably doesn't know either, Whiz. I sure as hell wouldn't. I never won twenty."

"Well, let's grind it out, boys!" Whisenant yelled. "Day off today. Only one game to play!"

St. Louis gave Broglio a run to work on in the first, but he gave back two before fanning Bell on a good, overhand curve ball. In the third inning, in the same situation, he threw Bell the same curve and Gus hit it out of the park for three runs.

"So whaddya goin' to do!" Broglio's expression said as Hemus came out to talk to him. Broglio turned his back on Hemus, and Solly took him out of the game.

Hunt's fast ball subdued the Cardinal bats for four innings. Then a blister on his pitching hand broke. Wiping the blood on his pants between pitches he switched to slow stuff and carried on. Robinson hit another home run and the bullpen talk turned to pennant prospects.

"We jus' gotta win it, now," said Bridges. "Ah gotta mortgage ah wanna pay off."

"What are you going to do with your share of the Series, Gabby?" I asked.

"Gonna buy me about a hundred acres up in the Big Thicket."

"Where in hell's that?"

"Up near Houston. They had seven inches rain in Houston today. Lots of pasture growin' up there."

"When you going to quit this game, Gab?"

"I don't know. Do you?"

"Sure. Two more years," I said.

"Why?"

"I don't know."

Still don't.

At some time during the season each manager must make changes in his player roster. If he makes the right ones at the right time he may jack his club up right into the pennant race; and he looks so good he receives votes as "Manager of the Year." If he makes the wrong moves the club looks bad.

About halfway through the season at least one manager must make more serious changes in the roster. He can see that there is no pennant for him in the near future. He rationalizes his wholesale changes by saying, "We're building for next year." If he has a bunch of young prospects he can bring up from the minor leagues, he says, "We're building for the future and we'll see what the kids can do."

In 1960 Solly Hemus had gathered together a veteran club that ran the pennant race down to the wire before finishing third. In 1961 the same club did not satisfy him so he went to the kids, of which the Cardinals had many.

St. Louis had put a million dollars a year into kids' pockets, which is as good a reason as any for the increase in population. Some of these bonus babies died in infancy on farm clubs; some had started to mature. Hemus was anxious to make men of them and brought them to the majors. Some of them weren't ready.

In six games, Cardinal Shortstop Julio Gotay had made six errors, all of them costly. Larry Jackson, whose luck seemed to be going from bad to worse all season, could not have been much encouraged to see Gotay, a ballplayer with uncontrolled potential, just over his right shoulder as he prepared to pitch.

Gotay couldn't help much when Robinson hit a Jackson pitch out of the park in the second. But he had two chances in the fourth inning, throwing one ball past first and another by third, giving us two runs and a lead we didn't lose.

Jackson, who had suffered a facial depression when a splintered bat bounced off his jaw in spring training, had a forlorn look of mental depression when he left the game in the seventh. Down by four runs, he had to be resigned to the knowledge that his relief pitchers probably would give up another run or two. They'd done it all season.

Hemus allowed the first reliever to pitch to only three men before he jerked him. Bob Miller, the next relief man, was greeted by a chorus of boos from our bench.

"Good God, we'll be here all night now!" said Robinson.

"Shaky sure likes to take his time," said Blasingame.

"Ever see a guy fidget any more than him?" said Whisenant.

Miller's carefully rehearsed gestures, repeated before each pitch, seemed to include the Sign of the Cross.

"What's he doin', prayin' he won't have to throw the ball?" Robinson said.

Miller's time-consuming stint on the mound apparently undermined Purkey's ambition to go nine, and Hutch pulled me in to protect the lead. As an ex-Cardinal I got the special kicks any pitcher gets out of beating his old club. But time was wasting and I had promised a radio commentator that I wouldn't use any more than twelve pitches an inning if possible, to expedite matters.

I needed just nine to get the four outs necessary for a save. Nunn and I were out of the clubhouse thirty minutes later talking to Broglio at the Cardinal bus. Ernie carried a large paper bag full of toys.

"Where you been, Ern?" I asked.

"They had a fire sale in the toy store."

"You guys headed home from here, I guess. They have any green jelly beans?"

Nunn hailed a cab and we said good-bye to Broglio and Cunningham. Joe had hit one of my sliders on his fists and popped up in the eighth.

"You're not getting around as quick as you did before you got married, Joe," I needled him.

"Yeah, sure. I know," said Cunningham. "And now I'm pregnant, too."

"Congratulations."

Nunn lit a cigar as the cab pulled away from the park. Smoke wreathed his smile as he said, "Rooms, you think Hemus'd like to have us back in his bullpen?"

"We're too old, Howie."

The message chalked on the scoreboard at the clubhouse entrance read: "We Are Sold Out Tonight and Sunday. Passes For Immediate Family Only!"

Ordinarily each player is entitled to two free tickets. Ordinarily, therefore, the club has to provide fifty free seats to friends of the players. Such largesse kindles slow-burning fires of penurious indignation in the front office. When a sell-out is envisioned the front office slams the gate in the faces of cheer-full friends of the players and invites the front-running second-guessers. Players' families are welcome, however, and the Family Pass List carries the names of many fictitious sisters, uncles, and cousins.

"The whole town's talkin' about the Redlegs," sang Avery Robbins, parodying a popular song of romance. The Ballad of the Year was to be played each day of the weekend, and the nickels were piling up.

"This is it," said the sportswriters. "The Big Series. With a capital 'S.' "

"Ninety games to go and you'd think we were playing for the pennant!" said Henry.

"Let 'em talk it up," said Lynch. "We're the hot club right now."

So the Dodgers weren't so hot, then?

Even before the Dodgers came out to take their batting practice the box seats behind the bullpen had started to fill.

"Those the best seats you could buy?" I asked my young cousin.

"They're sold out, they said," he replied.

"I'd have gotten you passes, but you know how it is when they are sold out. Family only gets free tickets."

One never gives passes to *real* cousins. Males, especially.

Hutchinson dispensed with a pep talk, nor did he ascribe any particular importance to the game with L.A.

"Just play the way you have been. Nobody can ask for much more." He paused, rubbing his chin, and continued. "If they want to play rough, that's the way we'll play. If they throw at us we'll throw at them. Tootie, you know these guys. You and Jerry go over them with the pitchers. That's all. Let's get Drysdale early."

The umpires apparently had had orders to keep the game clean. When Drysdale, incensed because Freese had taken a healthy cut at Don's curve ball, decked Gene with a head-high hummer, Augie Donatelli shook his ball-and-strike indicator at him. Naughty Donny.

O'Toole, equally incensed because Tommy Davis had banged Jim's slider for a double in the second, hit Davis with

a pitch in the fourth. Donatelli excused O'Toole, which made
L.A. Manager Alston mad.

On a double-play ground ball, Robinson banged into Wills
at second, knocking him high into the air. The atmosphere
reeked of the pro gridiron, exciting Otis Douglas, who yelled,
"Hit him!" when Coleman had a shot at Wills on another
double-play pivot. Coleman missed Wills, disappointing the
entire Cincinnati bench.

"Otis," I said, "when the fight starts who do you want?
Howard?"

The Dodgers' Frank Howard, standing six feet six inches,
and weighing 250 pounds, presented a different sort of problem
than little Maury Wills, who weighed only 160 in a dirty
uniform.

"I'll butt Howard with my head," said Otis, promptly.
Otis is only five ten, and obviously had figured the play ahead
of time.

O'Toole and Drysdale both departed in the sixth and the
bullpens took over. Howie Nunn stopped the Dodgers for
three innings before his arm stiffened. I pitched the ninth,
using just twelve pitches. Which was just enough.

Perranoski matched us till the last of the ninth, when Freese
doubled to start the inning. Coleman sacrificed him to third
and Lynch pinch-hit. Perranoski walked Jerry on purpose,
and Gernert hit for me. Sherry relieved and walked him.
Kasko then lined a single over Davis's glove and I hurried to
the clubhouse to shake Nunn's hand for setting up my win.

"Let's dig that bash with Buddy Morrow's band tonight,
Rooms. We won't work tomorrow, right?"

We reassured each other with the same line all night.

The only trouble with a musician's party is that it doesn't
start until after work. Therefore, the first glass is poured at
about the same time dairy cows are releasing milk for the
morning delivery. Since the party lasts as long as it should,
the next day often is half-shot before the night ends. It gives
one an entirely new perspective on the game of the day.

I hadn't seen the sun rise in a long time. There may be

aesthetic angles to appreciate, but I couldn't find any. Seen through a glass of Scotch the sun looks like a fertile raw egg. (Perhaps that was the reflection of my eyeball.)

Jim Turner asked me two questions when I walked into the clubhouse: "Why the dark glasses?" and "How's your arm feel?"

I had difficulty raising my arm to remove the glasses so that he could see the answer to the first question. Having worked in three games in four days I could reasonably be excused for the day. So when I said I was a little stiff, Turner told me to rest.

"We won't use you unless we have to," he said. That wasn't completely reassuring, since by definition a relief pitcher's job is determined by necessity. But Hutchinson knew me and my arm. I could figure on not working. The arm, once heated and exercised in a game, needs about twenty-four hours to recuperate fully. The effectiveness of a pitcher who works a day game after a night game is somewhat limited.

While the Dodgers took batting practice I stretched out on the bench in the bullpen and tried to nap. Dick Farrell, the Dodger relief pitcher, caught me sleeping, recognized the problem, and dropped a chair onto the bullpen floor. Just to be friendly.

"No sleeping in the bullpen, Brosnan," he said.

"Thanks, Turk. I'll remember you in my nightmares," I said.

The reverberations of the bouncing chair started a chain reaction in the stands as 28,000 fans clattered noisily to their seats. Since the game was being televised, locally and nationally, the club had scheduled special group rates. Knot-hole Day for the kids, Ladies' Day for the broads, Senior Citizens' Day for old-time ballplayers. The cheering, whistling, and second-guessing were enough to waken the moon. And, sure enough, it soon took its place in the sky next to the sun. A beautiful day for a ball game.

Maloney and Koufax warmed up to start the game. Both are young, hard-throwing, and inclined to be a little wild.

Maloney refused to have anyone stand at the plate as he heated up.

"Afraid I'll hit you," he said.

He didn't have that good a control. In less than five innings he threw 124 pitches, most of them outside the strike zone. Jocko Conlan, umpiring behind the plate, was as hot under the collar from Maloney's wildness as he was from the sun's rays. Sponging himself with ammonia water between innings he said, "That kid is driving me outa my mind. Tell him to get the ball over the plate."

"Just call 'em when they're in there, Jocko," Whisenant advised him.

Koufax had a little better control than Maloney, but not as good stuff, and he was bombed out in the third. Maloney followed him in the fifth, Bridges and Hook pitching parts of the next three innings as the Dodgers hit three home runs and took the lead.

L.A. gave the lead back and Bill Henry started the ninth with a 7-6 lead. Henry got the first two men, but Howard lofted a high fly ball that blew into the left field screen, and after Wills singled, Gilliam lined another home run into the screen to put L.A. ahead again.

Roger Craig, one of L.A.'s starting pitchers, began the ninth. Drysdale and Podres, two other Dodger starters, heated up in the bullpen.

"They're really going all out, aren't they?" I said to Nunn as we both tried to get loose in our bullpen.

"Let's get 'em tomorrow, Rooms," said Nunn. "How about it?"

Saturday just wasn't our day.

Within forty-eight hours I'd proved to my satisfaction that (1) sleep is good therapy for a tired arm; and (2) the Dodgers were no better than the Reds. Splitting the first two games of the Big Series had allowed us to keep a two-game lead. The Dodgers would not leave town on top, a bitter disappointment to the L.A. reporters, who thereby lost a chance to tell the tales of superiority that flavor their writing.

The interview-opening question: "How can you guys keep it up?" had changed to: "Are you getting a bang out of this first-place fight?"

Being recognized as bona fide contenders instead of upstart pretenders was a dignified step forward. If L.A.'s failure to stomp us could be interpreted as the stumbling of a clumsy Goliath, then we could cheerfully play David, take our slingshots, and beat hell out of the ol' monster.

"I'm convinced you love this sense of dramatics," said Sy Burick. "Your indifference is just an act."

I hadn't really been indifferent the day before when Sy had claimed I relished working the bullpen. Chatter made my head ache, that's all.

"Certainly I get my kicks doing my job," I said. "But you're trying to make too big a thing out of it, I think. After all, the pressure's on every hitter, too, that I face in a jam. He feels he *has* to drive in the tying or winning run just as I feel I *have* to get him out. The thing is I *know* what I'm going to do. He doesn't. He *can't* until I make my pitch."

"Nevertheless," he insisted, "you get a big bang out of any type of pitching, even if you don't act like it."

"Okay. Okay. I love my work."

A homer-hitting contest preceded the game. Four men from each team took turns trying to hit five fair fly balls over the fence. With a southwest wind behind them and $225 before them, they picked their pitches and whaled away. (Naturally, no self-respecting pro will hit home runs for nothing.)

The Dodgers hit more than the Reds, too many to watch, really. Hurt's a pitcher's arm. Robinson, however, hit more than any other of the eight sluggers, so the loot, according to agreement, was pretty evenly divided.

Apprehensive, perhaps, at the sight of all those pregame long balls, Hutch alerted the entire pitching staff—minus Henry, who stayed in bed with a bad cold.

"We're going all out for this one," said Hutch. "Day off tomorrow. You can rest then."

The Dodgers also sent their whole staff to the bullpen, and

for a while it looked like they'd be needed. Our first three men reached base and before the inning ended two runs had been batted in and a third run balked home by Stan Williams.

Dodger Manager Alston protested loudly to Plate Umpire Burkhart that he'd never seen such a mistaken balk ruling. Burkhart advised Alston to watch his insinuations, and when he didn't, threw the L.A. manager out of the game. Leo Durocher replaced Alston, demanding equal time to protest. Burkhart finally squelched Leo's spoken doubt as to Burkhart's ability by shouting, "I'm a hell of a lot better umpire than you are a manager!"

Durocher retreated, testily, and was heard no more except when he came out to change pitchers. Which he did four times, or enough to prevent any more Cincinnati runs.

In the seventh inning the Dodger bats woke up everyone who'd been dazzled by Joey Jay's pitching. Two walks and a single scored a run. Wills doubled home another but Robinson threw a third run-maker out at the plate to quiet the fans listening to the game in L.A.

With two out in the eighth Davis walked and Moon singled, so Hutch brought O'Toole in to pitch to Pinch-Hitter Aspromonte. Jim walked him on a 3-2 pitch and Hutch called me to pitch to Spencer.

"I told O'Toole not to give Aspromonte anything good to hit," he said to me. "You can strike this guy out."

Spencer took two low sliders for strikes, fouled one off that was close, took a high inside fast ball, and finally got a nice, fat pitch to hit. A high slider. Yummy! He swung hard, too hard, and missed it. Which excited the crowd to applause for the pitch instead of boos for the swing.

You're either a hero or a bum. That's what I like about my work.

Chicago — June 27

PITCHING wins pennants.

Pennant-winning pitching is good, usually; bad, occasionally. For pitchers are fallible human beings who have bad days no matter where they pitch. With pennant winners they have mostly good days. But when they're bad they look terrible.

As if to forestall any complacency the club might feel after the Big Series, Hutchinson made two changes in the roster. He replaced Bob Schmidt with John Edwards, a big, young catcher. And he sent Marshall "The Fox" Bridges to Jersey City for Sherman "Roadblock" Jones.

"We're makin' our move, Broz," said Whisenant. "You gotta make changes at the right time if you want to win. Schmidt wasn't hitting and Bridges wasn't pitching. Right?"

"I just work here, Pete. While they were at it they should have brought up some more pitchers. Nunn can't throw, Maloney's arm is tender, Henry's back in Cincinnati. What if we have a bad day?"

"What do you mean, 'Maloney's arm is tender.' What's 'tender'?"

"Stiff, sore, I don't know. He says he can't pitch."

"He can't get the ball over the plate, you mean!"

"Growing pains. He'll be all right. Hutch says he's going to be great in a couple of years."

"What's wrong with now?" he asked.

"Can't hurry greatness, Peter."

Edwards and Jones drew uniforms, meal money, and player passes; listened to Otero explain the signs he'd be giving as third base coach; and reported the news from the American Association (Edwards) and the International League (Jones). By the time the sixth inning started they both looked like they belonged.

The Cubs were not particularly impressed with Edwards or Jones, nor any other Red for that matter. They rocked Hunt for three in the third to take the lead, banged Hook for two in the fifth after we'd tied the score, and were swinging so viciously at every breaking ball that Hutchinson decided they must be stealing our signs.

"Nobody swings the bat like that unless they know what's coming," he concluded.

The obvious solution was to score more runs than they could. In the seventh, with two on, two out, Hutch sent four left-handed pinch-hitters to the plate. The first three reached first base safely, so Lynch hit a triple to score them all and we had a four-run lead.

Sherman Jones, although he'd pitched a complete game at Jersey City just two days before, agreed that he could get nine more outs as well as anyone. He gave up two home runs, both solo drives; but that was just good enough.

"That wasn't a very good start, was it?" he asked.

"What do you mean?" I said. "Welcome to the club."

"They *must* be gettin' the signs," Hutch said in the fourth inning of the first game of the next day's double-header. "They're just not that good."

"Never saw anything like it," said Coach Sisler.

"It's ridiculous," said Coach Otero.

"They're hitting everything we throw," said Coach Turner.

The Cubs, showing damn little respect for a league-leading club, swung the liveliest bats we'd seen all year. If the pitch was close, but not a strike, they'd take it. If it was over the plate, they'd hit it—past the infielders, between the outfielders, or over the fences.

"I've changed the signs three times!" said John Edwards, who was catching his first major league game. He might well have wished he were back at Indianapolis where he caught more pitches than were hit. A catcher, after all, must feel that he's helping the pitcher by calling the right pitches. He often gets blamed, facetiously perhaps, if a pitch is belted out of the park.

"Do you think John is ready for the big leagues?" asked Zimmerman, after the Cubs scored seven runs in the fifth inning.

"Don't laugh!" I said. "Hutch is looking down here."

The bullpen was equally as embarrassed as Jay Hook when Hutch refused even to warm up a reliever while the Cubs batted around and around in the fifth. Hook's neck was as red as his shirt when he finally reached the bench. Unable to relax, he refused to sit down and paced back and forth, mopping his face with a towel until it was time to go back onto the mound.

"He might as well finish it now," I said. "Good day to work."

"You're about as funny as a broken arm, Broz," said Zimmerman.

The lunch between games consisted of saltine crackers and stale cheese, which were consumed in a sort of nervous shock. Nobody complained. No one even said, "Let's get 'em the second one."

They weren't to be had in the second one either. Ron Santo, whose two home runs in the first game had shocked Hutchinson because "He hasn't had a hit in a week!" didn't get a hit in the second game. But Al Heist, who didn't get to the majors until he was thirty-four years old, drove in four runs, disgusting O'Toole, the pitcher, as much as it did Hutchinson.

"For Christ's sake," said Hutch. "———! Oh, what the hell!"

Purkey, who had started the first game at one o'clock, finished the second game at six o'clock, giving up a home run to Kindall as a parting concession to a Cub club that had hit five home runs, two triples, three doubles, and fifteen singles in five hours.

Purkey said, while shaving after the game, "I don't think we had it today."

Yeah, man.

"Guess what happened on the way to the park, Rooms," said Nunn.

"No. Anything that happens here is fantastic, anyway. You tell me."

"Okay, Rooms. Don't get pissed. The reason we were so late getting to the park was, the bus couldn't get under the overpass off the Outer Drive! We had to go ten miles to get off the expressway, then come back!"

"You weren't that far off, Howard," I said. "Couldn't be more than a couple miles out of the way."

Maybe they shouldn't have shown up at all.

The Cubs had obviously decided we didn't belong on the top of the league. Whereas they couldn't beat the Dodgers at all, they had no trouble scaring hell out of us. So:

Altman hit one out in the first; Williams hit one in the third; and Cardwell, the pitcher, hit another one in the fourth. That knocked Maloney out and Jones gave us five more runs in the fourth before he got the side out. His pride probably hurt more than his arm, which had to be a little tired after the work he'd had in four days.

"They're getting the signs from the scoreboard," Gernert confessed. "When I was over there last year that's how we got 'em."

"Why didn't you say something?"

"They're not doing it the same way," he said.

Whisenant draped a towel over a pair of field glasses, sat down on the dugout floor, and peered—spy-like—at the scoreboard.

"You're right!" he said. "That's where they're getting 'em."

"It might be we're hanging too goddamn many curve balls, too," said Hutchinson.

"I've tried thirty different combinations," said Edwards. "Maybe the pitcher should give his own signs!"

Bill Henry, having deplaned in the morning, dressed at noon, and warmed up in the sixth, shut the door on the Cubs for two innings.

"Right out of bed, Gab. Thata boy!" said Zimmerman.

Hutch asked me if I would like to pitch the eighth.

"It's only one inning," he said.

Sure.

The pitcher facing a batch of hot bats has more problems than his experience ordinarily generates. With three days' rest I felt *strong!*

Forget it.

The pitcher singled and the right-fielder lined a ball high off the top of the fence. It looked like a home run and the pitcher, unaccustomed to running the bases, sauntered around, slowing up the hitter, who stopped halfway between second and third. Robinson threw the ball back to the infield. I grabbed it, ran toward shortstop and tagged the man out for not moving. I needed that break. By the time I struck out

Santo there were more runners on base and I was so confused I had to ask Edwards, "Was my slider working or not?"

"I guess so," he said. "I never saw it before."

Hutchinson mumbled to himself as we climbed up the stairs to our clubhouse. "I never saw anything like it!"

The radio broadcaster of the Cubs gleefully reported that our league lead had been shaved to two games, and pompously added that he had told his listeners so. The Reds were just not good enough for first place.

Milwaukee — June 30

CHARLIE DRESSEN watched from the Braves' dugout as the Reds came into County Stadium for batting practice. Rubbing his hands together Dressen grinned maliciously as he described to the reporters what he was about to do to Cincinnati. The reports of our catastrophic Chicago series had bolstered Charlie's confidence beyond its normal stratospheric height.

"I figure we win at least three out of four in this series and we're just five and a half games out," he said.

The Milwaukee writers, famous for their *Gemütlichkeit*, or bad insight, confidently predicted that the Braves would probably win all four games and fold Cincinnati's pennant hopes before the weekend was over.

"I don't want to sound like I'm pushing any panic button," Hutch said in the clubhouse meeting. "But we're gonna play a ball club that I can *see* bombing us the way the Cubs did. Whether or not they were getting our signs from the scoreboard I don't know. But they were swinging those bats and I think we were giving them too many good pitches to hit. Or something."

He paused, tapped the score card twice, and said, "Well, let's forget about Chicago. Joey, get your good stuff over the plate. And let's rack somebody up ourselves."

The Braves had won eight out of their last ten games, three straight at St. Louis, and had placed four men on the All-Star team. Joey Jay couldn't have cared less, apparently, for he not only shut them out for eight innings; he teased them all the way. He allowed twelve runners to reach first, and several to reach third, but there he called a halt.

What's more he personally knocked Warren Spahn out of the box in the fifth, punching a bases-loaded single down the right field line.

"Joey's worth more money," I said in the bullpen. "Wonder if they gave him a bonus for his bat when they signed him?"

"How much bonus did he get?" asked Henry.

"About thirty grand. Or fifty. I don't know." I looked around the bullpen. "All we got out here, Gab, is bonus babies. Maloney a hundred thousand, Hook fifty, Edwards— how much did you get, John? Eighty?"

"Nowhere near it," he said. "I've seen about ten different figures in the papers since I signed and they're all too high."

"Edwards, you got money you haven't even counted yet!" said Hook.

"Atta boy, Jay. Give him hell!" I said.

Hook and Edwards had spent the first three innings discussing missiles and nose cones. Graduate students in mechanical and ceramic engineering, respectively, Hook and Edwards had solved the problem of atmospheric re-entry when Jay lined his single to right.

"When you two guys are ready to drop the bomb, aim it at Wrigley Field, will you?" I said.

"Don't remind me," said Hook. "My E.R.A. is in orbit now."

In the ninth inning Hutchinson phoned from the bench to have Henry and me heated up.

"He's not going too far with Jay," Hook reported. "Says he might be getting tired."

Sure enough, when Mathews came to bat with two on and two out, Hutch signaled for Henry.

"Go strike him out, Gabby!" said Whisenant. "Mathews can't hit you and he knows it!"

It took Henry longer to walk to the bullpen gate, climb on the motorbike, and ride to the mound than it did for him to retire Mathews.

"Nice pitch, Bill!" said Jay.

124

"Nice going eight and two-thirds," Henry replied.

"You old s.o.b.!" Jay said. "That's the bullpen for you! You know what Dressen is going to say now: 'Jay can't go nine innings.' "

And that's just what the morning paper reported.

"How come Turner never works with you and me, Brosnan?" asked Henry. We sat on the bench before batting practice watching Turner criticize Maloney's pitching stride.

"We're too old, Gab," I said. "Pitching coaches don't know you after you pass thirty."

Jim Turner had enough young pitchers to keep him busy for six months. Pitching faults often become bad habits if not detected and corrected immediately. The coach with a knack for explaining methods of modifying poor deliveries, wasted motions, and faulty pitching patterns is invaluable.

"It's tough to learn the tricks when you get up here, though, Gab," I said. "You watch Dressen today. If Hunt lets anybody get on base he can figure that guy's gonna steal the next base. Dressen takes advantage of every opportunity and Hunt just can't hold a man on with that slow delivery of his."

Hunt retired the side in order in the first, but Aaron led off the second with a double and stole third base on the next pitch. Maye then singled and stole second and third.

"Jesus, that's enough to drive a pitcher out of his mind," Jones said. "Poor kid."

Hutchinson walked out to the mound to talk to Hunt. Ken forced Torre to hit a ground ball to Kasko, but the ball went through Eddie for an error and Maye scored.

"Can't do anything right. It's contagious."

"How's your arm feel, Road?" I asked.

"Don't worry about ol' Road's arm. I can throw every day if I have to," said Jones.

"How about you, Roomie?"

Nunn wiggled his right hand, grimaced, and said, "Don't think I can throw any breaking stuff."

"Dazzle 'em with your footwork, Nunn," Henry suggested.

The phone rang, summoning Hook. Jay had given up

eleven runs in seven innings just three days before—a trauma-inducing experience. But he grabbed the ball and started throwing.

"Get naked, Jaybird," said Henry. "I think you're in there."

Post batted for Hunt in the fifth and Hook rode out to the mound, faced three batters, and fanned two of them.

"He's really throwing the ball today," I said. "That's the way to come back. Forget the cute stuff and let it all out!"

But Aaron and Adcock hit back-to-back home runs off Hook in the fifth and as Adcock circled the bases Hook crouched on the mound, hands on his knees, staring at the ground.

"Guess when you're having a bad week, nothing goes right," said Jones.

The phone rang.

"You're next, Road," I reported.

"He must have heard me," he said. He stripped off his jacket, held his right arm up and looked at it. "Well, let's go, rubber arm. It beats sloppin' hogs!"

"When you gonna work, Brosnan?" asked Henry. "You on a vacation?"

"Saturday's my day of rest."

Burdette had a five-hitter and a shutout as we started the ninth. A wet five-hitter.

"You could see the spit flyin' off the ball when it was half-way to the plate," Robinson complained after the game.

Maybe that's what Turner should be teaching.

"Milwaukee's got the best hillbilly music in the whole league, Broz," said Joey Jay as we took the bus to the park the next morning. We had packed and checked out of the hotel, expecting to fly home after the Sunday double-header.

"That's nice. Provincial but nice," I said. "Milwaukee's got some sportswriters that are slow to crib headlines, too. Look at this. Again: 'Are The Reds For Real?'"

"Dressen hasn't decided for them yet," said Jay.

"Nothing I'd rather do than beat that little Napoleon!" said Blasingame.

126

If his own players didn't like him, Dressen could rest assured that most of the other players in the league had a similar distaste for him. There are managers for whom players like to play; others whom players like to defeat.

"Let me tell you about Dressen," said Jay. "When he joined the club he said, in the very first meeting, 'I know you guys hate my guts. But I don't care! I don't care!' And he pounded his fists together to emphasize his point."

"That is what you call inspiring a club, getting the point across," I agreed.

O'Toole gave up three homers in the first three innings to give the Braves a 5-2 lead. It looked like another long day for the bullpen. Nunn volunteered to throw, just in case somebody had to take a beating. "I can lob the ball up there anyway" he said.

"Forget it, Nunn," Henry said. "Broz is about ready to work."

In the fifth O'Toole tried to score from first on Kasko's double, but slipped and fell halfway between third and the plate. Caught in a rundown he stuck his elbow in Mathews's face as Ed tagged him. Mathews jumped on O'Toole and they rolled over three times, headed down the left field line.

Both benches emptied and a pile of swingers soon formed around and above Mathews and O'Toole. A comprehensive report from all angles of the fight read like this:

"Hutch and Otis get there and start pulling guys off Tootie, *throwing* them out! . . . . Mantilla is lying flat on the ground and Otis yanks him by one leg and Felix *slides* ten feet! . . . . McMillan's running around holding his glasses in one hand trying to find the fight. . . . Elio Chacon is standing aside, peeking into the pile of players. . . . Adcock grabs Robinson and holds him while Robby's yelling, 'Let go, let go, Joe. I'm just tryin' to stop 'em!' . . . . The Braves are looking over their shoulders for Dressen. . . . Finally Hutch gets Mathews off to the side and asks, 'What you tryin' to do, Ed?' and Mathews says, 'But, Hutch, he tried to knock the ball outa my hands!' Hutch laughs at him and says, 'What's he supposed to do, give you a big kiss?' "

"It was a hell of a good idea, Tootie," said Whisenant. "Finally woke everybody up."

O'Toole left the game for a pinch-hitter when we tied the score and Nunn took over. But he threw a slider on his second pitch, hurt his arm again, and had to be relieved. Hutch called for Jones. Again. In seven days he'd been in five games, pitched seventeen innings, and thrown five hundred pitches. At least.

"Try to hold them, Sherm," Hutch pleaded.

Jones shut them out for four innings; and I did the same for four more. Finally Coleman hit a three-run home run in the thirteenth.

We had a picnic between games, feasting on barbecued spare ribs and great hunks of Wisconsin cheese. The photographers asked me to kiss Coleman on the cheek for winning the game, but the cheese was odorous and I didn't want to offend. His home run had been his fifth hit of the day and he deserved a sweeter reward.

After the four-hour first game we could see that catching the eight o'clock plane was out of the question.

"We may never get home tonight," I said.

"Let's win this next game and who cares!" said Whisenant.

Kasko led off the second game with a home run and the winning feeling was strong in every player on the field. Purkey rattled off six quick scoreless innings, then gave up three runs in the seventh and the score was tied. But Robinson smashed another home run.

In the clubhouse the photographers insisted he and Purkey do the kissing pose.

So they did. But don't print it in Mississippi.

Cincinnati — July 3

"You guys spoiled a lot of Sunday dinners last night," said my mother when I called to say Happy Independence Day. "They televised both games from Milwaukee and I'll bet there were a hundred thousand TV dinners served."

"Thirty thousand of those people showed up at the airport at midnight, too," I said. "Made me feel like a campus hero."

128

"You might as well win the pennant now," she went on.

"We've already won the first half," I said. "They should have a split season this year like they do in the minors!"

The crowd that had cheered our landing the night before showed up at the ball park for the game with Pittsburgh, some of them came carrying clippings from the afternoon paper.

Don Hoak, the Pirates' third baseman, was quoted as saying that the Reds couldn't win the pennant because the summer heat would burn up the young Cincinnati pitchers. Hoak, an ex-Red, was once quite popular with Cincinnati fans. As the National League's leading hitter of the moment his opinion was bound to be as widely disseminated as it was certain to be highly criticized. At least on Fountain Square and in Crosley Field.

"These guys think they can beat us," said Hutch as he reviewed the Pirate lineup. "We gotta scramble a little harder and prove to 'em—well, that they're no better than we are."

After the clubhouse meeting Hutch invited all the pitchers and catchers to his room, where we discussed the signs.

"We have to do something about the way other clubs are stealing our catcher's signs," said Hutchinson. "Anybody got any suggestions?"

There are as many pitching signs as there are fingers on the catcher's hand, areas of his body, and gestures of his arm. It is conceivable that a million different combinations of signs could be used during a season. Ordinarily a club likes to agree on one set of complex signs to be used only with an opposing runner on second base. Otherwise, one finger is used to indicate a fast ball, two or three fingers are used for breaking pitches; four or five fingers mean change-of-pace or knuckle balls; a closed fist asks for a pitch out; the right thumb being flipped up says, "Knock him down!"

With a man on second base where he can see the catcher's fingers, the sign is hidden in a succession of finger-flashings. The third sign seen may be the one desired; or the first sign to be flashed after an agreed-upon indicator. A more complex combination involves using an indicator (one, two, or three fingers) to be followed by a number of "pumps." That is, after the indicator (say, two fingers) the flashing of one finger three times might mean a slider—three pumps after the indicator. (The pumps could have been: one finger, then two fingers, then three fingers; or any combination desired.) Thus the indicator would appear within the pumps, making detection more difficult. Many clubs list on paper the number and order of finger-flashings in a catcher's signs and have a man on the bench decode information collected over a period of pitches.

Having rejected a wireless setup to be installed in the caps of catcher and pitcher with the pitch selection being made on the bench, we agreed to try the "pump" signs, and Maloney warmed up for the game. Jimmy swallowed his "bomber," a Dexedrine pill, and declared himself ready. "This thing makes me feel like I had fifteen beers—only real *strong!*" he said.

Post's two-run homer in the second made Maloney feel even stronger and he buzzed his hundred-thousand-dollar hummer right on by the Pirates for five innings.

Virdon hit a home run off him in the sixth, making him so mad that, after the inning had ended, he threw his glove on the dugout floor and stomped on it. Twice.

"Take it easy, Malone!" said O'Toole. "We're still ahead!"

We stayed ahead, and Maloney opened the ninth by fanning Clemente. His fast ball had lost some of its hum, however, and when Stuart hit one over the scoreboard Hutch called the bullpen.

"Henry and Brosnan hot?" he asked.

We both nodded and he said, "Give me Henry."

With Burgess, a left-handed hitter up next, to be followed by Hoak, a right-handed hitter, Henry was obviously due for a brief appearance.

"You get Burgess, Gab. I'll get Hoak," I said as he went to the mound.

"You got the save, too, you lucky bastard," said Henry as we took a shower.

On March 19, 1961, Sy Burick asked me, "Broz, what do

you really want out of baseball, besides money?" And I said, hiding my hopes behind a spray of tobacco juice, "I want to make the All-Star team and play in a World Series."

"Why don't you do both this year?" he asked, smiling to himself at the idea that we might win the pennant.

"One year at a time," I said.

Although Cincinnati had won the first-half championship the All-Star team selections excluded all the Reds but two, Kasko and Robinson. And they were on the second team!

"Coleman should be on it," said Robby. "He's hitting twice as much as any other first baseman in the league."

"Pinson deserves it," said Kasko. "Where would he be without him?"

The pitchers had not yet been announced. Ordinarily eight pitchers are selected for each team. Over and over, as the day of the All-Star game approached, I reviewed the statistics of the top pitchers, trying to figure if there were eight better records than mine. With five wins, thirteen saves, and a 2.25 E.R.A. I felt I'd done as well as I ever could hope to do for half a season.

"Jay or Purkey ought to make it," said Whisenant.

"Broz, you're a cinch," said Lynch.

"And you've got pretty blue eyeballs, Jerry," I replied.

"Isn't Broz a cinch, Pete?" Lynch insisted.

The holiday crowd that drifted slowly into the park looked like they'd lost their way. To somewhere else. Anywhere else.

"Lousy fans. Where are they?" asked Zimmerman. "Here we are leading the league!"

"It's a beautiful, sunny, holiday day. Would you go to a ball game?" I asked. "Besides, the game's televised. They're probably all at picnics."

"Where?" he asked.

"In the parking lot, stupid!"

The Pirates filed past our dugout, looking no more enthusiastic than the crowd. Hoak's appearance drew some expected booing. As Walter "Moose" Moryn walked by Freese yelled to him, "Hey, Moose, when you're done with that head I want to mount it!"

131

Joey Jay further dampened any Pirate holiday spirit by pitching a three-hitter. Freese hit a home run in the fifth to give Jay all the help he needed at bat. Jay failed to get any base hits himself, for which he was needled by Maloney, who had hit safely in each of *his* starts.

"I get 'em only when I need 'em," Jay said.

The trainer gave me a "bomber" to keep me awake for the bridge game on the long plane trip to Chicago and San Francisco; and we left by bus to the airport after the ball game. Just as we crossed over the Ohio River bridge to Kentucky Avery Robbins said, "Broz, you didn't make the All-Star team. I had to make travel plans for the guys that did. Don't tell anybody until they release it to the press. Sorry. You deserved it."

"Well, maybe we'll win the pennant," I said.

At the airport we had a forty-five-minute wait for the plane. I walked to the bar, ordered a martini—"Make it a double"—and drowned myself in self-pity.

I stared at the mirror. "With a head like that, how could you expect to make an All-Star team," I thought. My smile turned into a horse laugh. The horse sounded like a manager I played for ten years before. He had said, "Brosnan, you don't belong in baseball. Quit, why don't you!"

That's a manager for you. *They* pick the pitchers for the game. How could you expect to make it!

"So you rationalize" said the mirror me. "There are eighty pitchers in the league and you're making yourself out to be one of the top eight. Is that it?"

"You're goddamn right!" I said, almost aloud. "Let me have another martini, please," I said to the bartender.

He also poured me a glass of water and wiped the spillage of my last drink off the bar. Joey Jay tapped me on the shoulder.

"Partner," he said. "About the bridge game. You *going* to—"

"No," I mumbled. "Forget it."

I don't know why I should have been mad at him!

San Francisco — July 5

THE jet from Chicago to Frisco had, unfortunately, served more martinis during the three-and-a-half-hour flight. Pouring four of them on top of the six I'd gulped in Cincinnati, I dropped into a cataleptic daze. The All-Star team lost its appeal for the moment.

"Bross," said Whisenant the next day at the park, "you were a little gassed on the plane. I didn't think you'd make it! Don't take it so hard. We all thought you deserved it."

"Let's forget it," I said.

While we took batting practice I walked slowly back and forth across the outfield, just to keep moving. Hutchinson walked out to ask, "How do you feel today?"

I rubbed my stomach with my right arm, wondering which part of me he was concerned about.

"Look," he said, "all I can say is I'm sorry. We voted for you if that's any consolation."

"Thanks. I got it all out of my system last night."

"Well, that's one way," he grunted.

It was hardly the best way, of course, as my shaky nerves could attest. Nor had it assuaged my pride, which had counted on the extra reward for a job as well done as I could do it. All-Star recognition can be used to get a little more money at contract time.

The manager of the All-Star team makes the pitching selections. Hutchinson admitted that Murtaugh did not necessarily have to follow the recommendations of the other managers in the league. If I could focus my resentment on Murtaugh, my depression might turn into a simple determination to rip him or the Pirates every time I faced them. I'd know only when I got on the mound in another game whether or not I would feel the daily reward was worth the effort necessary to maintain my first-half record.

"If you need me tonight, I'm ready," I told Hutch.

"Of course," he said.

Ken Hunt was supposed to start, but he said his shoulder

felt tender, and Hutch asked Jones to pitch. With Nunn back in Cincinnati with a bad arm, we had just eight pitchers for the six games scheduled on the next five days. After the four-game weekend series in L.A. we had a three-day layoff. And a welcome one it would be.

Jones, traded by the Giants to Cincinnati along with Blasingame and Schmidt early in the season, had plenty of extra incentive to make him forget his tired arm.

"I never could figure out why they let me go in the first place," he had said when he joined us. "I thought I had done a good job for them last year, and I had as good a spring training with them as I ever could. But I guess they just didn't like me."

They liked him even less as the game progressed. Giant hitters managed to get just two singles in eight innings and we led 3-1 when the ninth started.

"We gonna give Roadblock a stripe, Captain?" asked Schmidt. "He's pitched a hell of a game."

"A stripe! If he finishes this inning we'll have to give him a silver bar, at least!"

Two Giant singles chased Jones, however, and Hutch called me.

"How's the slider?" I asked Schmidt as I passed him on the way from the bullpen.

"You'll be all right," he said.

"What the hell," I thought. "You do or you don't, I guess."

Haller struck out on three high sliders, Zimmerman catching a foul tip for the third strike.

Alou pinch-hit and lined a high slider past short to load the bases.

"Try and get the ball down, Broz," Zimmerman said.

"Sure, sure," I said, and threw four straight balls to Davenport, forcing in a run.

Hutch sent me to the clubhouse and brought in Henry. I did not even bother to watch him warm up. As I walked past our bullpen Whisenant said, "Hang with 'em, Bross."

"—— it!" I muttered.

Bressoud ran the count to 3-2, then fouled off two more of

Henry's pitches. Finally he hit a fly ball to left, ending the game.

Hutchinson smiled broadly as he came into the clubhouse. "Another laugher!" he said. "That's the way to go, men!"

On this club, it seemed, either you did or somebody did it for you.

"Did you know Rohde had a heart attack after the game last night?" Schmidt asked.

"No," said Henry. "Hope he's all right. How can we win the pennant without a trainer!"

"Otis can take over."

"Did you ever have Otis give you a rubdown? He makes you sore instead of just stiff!"

Douglas's right hand was minus parts of his thumb and index finger.

"He digs that nub of his halfway through your shoulder!" said Henry.

"How can you get a sore arm pitching to one hitter a game, Henry?" I said.

The tensions of one-run victories had had another significant, if minor, effect on the trainer. His supply of Gelusil, an antacid, had been exhausted in Milwaukee. Rohde could not get a new supply in Cincinnati because of the July 4 holiday, and some painful burping was evident on, and off, the Candlestick Park playing field.

"If we have another laugher today, Doc will probably collapse," said Sisler. "I can hardly take any more myself."

"Get some runs then, Sisler! You're the first base coach. Move 'em around!"

"I'll do that, Hemingway," Sisler told me. "And you put it in your book."

Making a note of it just in case we scored ten runs, I searched my duffel bag for the long underwear necessary to make the bullpen comfortable. How Arctic winds blow past the San Francisco Chamber of Commerce into Candlestick Park I'll never know.

Two of the best, and biggest, syndicated sportswriters in

the country strolled purposively through the clubhouse trying to find out why the Reds led the league by three games.

"Following the front-runners, eh?" I asked Jimmy Cannon.

"Partly. You guys are news," he said. "Besides, this is San Francisco. I come out here every chance I get. Great town."

"Yeah. Great town to win in."

The expression on Giant Manager Alvin Dark's face was positively unchristian as seen from our dugout. The potential difference between his players and the Cincinnati Reds should have made it a good bet that *his* club should be six and a half games ahead of *us*.

Dark had promised himself that he wouldn't take out his anger on his players, and after a particularly galling loss to Philadelphia he had thrown a clubhouse chair at his locker. Unfortunately the tip of his finger caught on a jagged tip of protruding metal and went the way of the chair. Further discipline, in the interests of self-preservation, might be expected to hurt some *Giant* feelings.

Jimmy O'Toole, who had received no batting supports at all from the Reds in three previous starts in San Francisco, welcomed two early inning runs as if they were the crown jewels. His pitching restricted any noise of Giant bats to those sounds made by Giant hitters ramming their bats into the bat rack after futile efforts at the plate. Six small singles had produced one lone run for Frisco as we started the ninth with a two-run lead.

Hutchinson phoned to tell me to warm up, but O'Toole was taking no chances. He hung one curve to Bailey, who hit it into the bleachers, but fanned the last hitter on a 3-2 pitch. It was the fifth straight game in which the final out had been recorded on a 3-2 pitch, with the tying run at the plate or on the bases.

It was too much for Doc Rohde. He was flown back to Cincinnati for a rest in the hospital. We flew down to L.A. for the Big Series.

Another one?

Los Angeles—July 7

THE Los Angeles baseball experts may have looked down their educated noses at Cincinnati from a position of pedantic subjectivity. But Southern California fans welcomed the Reds with that warmth of curiosity which is reserved for celebrity gate attractions. A record crowd for a National League night game was predicted by the Dodger front office.

On the bus to the park, Avery Robbins cautioned, "There are not going to be many good seats available for passes. So hold off the free-loaders tonight."

Hutchinson interrupted to ask, "Avery, why do you have so many passes on the Coast, do you think?"

"Guess these two towns really swing!" he said.

The Coliseum has a huge, horseshoe-shaped grandstand on which tiers of seats slope steeply into the sky. On a smoggy night fans in the last row are practically invisible to players on the field.

"There's my passes, Broz," said Zimmerman, pointing at the moon over right field. "They're really packin' 'em in here tonight."

"Hard to keep your head outa the stands tonight, right?" I said, admiring the gorgeous peacock-colored clothes brightening the gray Coliseum seat rows.

Ten thousand fans missed the first-inning excitement when the Dodgers attacked Hunt with three walks and a 250-foot pop fly double off the left field screen. Hunt then wild-pitched another run home. After facing four men he was behind 3-0 and had a runner on third. Hutch stayed with him, however, irritating a fan behind the bullpen who wanted to know if we had no other pitchers with guts enough to go out there.

Larker hit a fly ball to Pinson, who threw the runner out trying to score after the catch. The Dodgers attack subsided for three innings, and, when Pinson's three-run homer kayoed Koufax in the fourth, Cincinnati took a lead that they held all night.

It was a long night for L.A. and all the Dodger fans. Season attendance topped a million customers, the first major league club to reach that total for the year. But it was probably small satisfaction to either the fans or the management.

The fan who had questioned our bullpen pitching soon switched to Dodger-baiting.

"Why don't you bums go back to Brooklyn!" he yelled. "You don't deserve to win the pennant!"

But he still disliked our chances. "And you bums are just lucky!" he shouted at us. "Wait till the Cubs catch up with you!"

Word gets around.

Hutch's patience with Hunt's wildness gave out in the sixth. He sent me in to protect a three-run lead, but it soon was apparent that the Dodgers *liked* seeing the ball in the strike zone. Four of them reached base and two scored before Henry stopped them just short of a tie.

Walking back to the clubhouse after the inning, I pushed the game into the far recesses of my mind and memory. By the time the game ended I was halfway through the third chapter of Durrell's *Balthazar*. And, if the truth were known, I'd have just as soon continued reading while Purkey pitched the second game.

Freese, who had hit a three-run home run in the ninth inning of the first game, hit another one in the ninth inning of the second game. It was already past midnight but the loud-mouth behind our bullpen was still at it. He inquired, hopefully maybe: "Brosnan, why don't you warm up?"

Hutchinson, and I, didn't think that was a good idea.

The monumental pique into which my pitching had hurled me persisted. After the double-header I walked back to the hotel. Nothing should discourage self-pity more than an hour's exercise pounding the pavement of forty long blocks.

But a day at the movies and a meal at a Japanese restaurant failed to raise any glow of exhilaration that I should have felt as a member of a league-leading club with an eight-game winning streak.

"No," I said to a reporter who wanted to know if I thought

we'd sweep the series. "And at the moment I couldn't care less."

Fifty thousand more customers came to see if we could. Many of them crowded into the box seat sections; more than paid for box seat tickets.

The Coliseum is ideal for seat-stealing. Season ticket-holders who had bought box seats welcomed their friends to crowd into their purchased pews. The friends would buy general admission tickets, then flash old box seat stubs at the usher, who led them to the proper row. Crowding ten people into an area sold to six made for a degree of intimacy, but alternating thin broads with California cavaliers probably made even dull games worth enduring.

By the end of the fifth inning the game had lost most of its charm, at least to a good Cincinnati rooter. Jim Maloney had started for us, a gaggle of his Fresno relatives cheering him on from behind our bench. Their support did nothing for his fast ball, and when Roseboro hit one for a bases-loaded triple Hutch pulled him out.

Hook gave up four more runs in the fifth. Hutchinson, not wishing to see my depression deepened by further exposure to a Dodger clobbering, sent Sherman Jones in to mop up instead of me.

"Captain," said Jones, "I guess I'm back in the bullpen now. Do I get a stripe?"

"Sure, Road," I said. "You can be Colonel if you like."

Henry turned his back on the game, pointed at the dimly lit railing above the last row of seats, and said, "Think I'll fungo one clear outa here tomorrow."

"Impossible, Henry," I said. "Hundred bucks says you can't do it. In five tries."

"You ever watch me swing a bat?" he said.

"Yeah. So forget it."

"You're getting bitter in your old age, Broz."

That's the way life tasted all night.

The best way to get rid of the blues in L.A. is to rent a

car, drive to Malibu, stand on a cliff, and look at the sea over the top of a tall, cool drink. The Pacific Ocean waves have a discernible saline effect on the drinking (or mixing) water, making Scotch taste more nourishing than intoxicating.

Having arranged a postgame trip to Zuma Beach I drove to the park, perfectly content to lose, if necessary, the final game of the first half of the season. (We'd still have a three-game lead to take on our three-day vacation.)

Joey Jay had pitched eighteen consecutive scoreless innings going into the game, and he added another before Neal hit a two-run home run to tie the score in the second. Robinson had homered in the first, and planned to hit another later on in the game. So Jay's confident poise as he batted in the fifth was understandable, if you were psychic.

Jay lined a bases-loaded double off Don Drysdale to break up the game and smash hell out of Drysdale's disposition. Drysdale absorbed the shock of Jay's double numbly, but well enough to retire the side. On the Dodger bench, he fumed, burned, and blew up.

To start the sixth he threw a fast ball behind Blasingame's head. Blazer popped up the next pitch, so Drysdale knocked Pinson down with consecutive pitches. Pinson hit the third pitch to left for a double, and Drysdale threw the rosin bag into the air in disgust. When it came down he dusted his fingers and threw three straight pitches at Robinson. The third one hit Robby on the arm, and Boggess, the umpire, threw Drysdale out of the game.

"That's enough throwing," Boggess said to Alston and Hutchinson. "I've had enough."

Drysdale's tantrum had angered his own catcher, Roseboro, who said to Robinson, "You know I ain't callin' 'em." (The catcher is subject to retaliatory pitches from the opposing side, which often can't get at the pitcher.) Drysdale made it safely to his clubhouse locker, but his successors had their problems getting any more outs.

Hutchinson told Jay, "Lay off them now. We'll have our day. Don't wake 'em up today."

Jay laughed, and turned to Maloney. "*See* what happens

when I get my hits. See those R.B.I.'s? That's three times as many as I had all last year!"

Maloney's father, in his seat behind the bench, pounded the dugout roof and yelled, "Pour it on! Pour it on!" as the score mounted inning by inning. It was Dad's Day for the Reds, with Hunt's father in the stands to lend *his* support also. Drysdale's pique had evoked a general uproar in the Cincinnati dugout.

"Broz," said Jay in the eighth, "you want to finish this contest? In fact, you can go to the All-Star game in my place. I'd rather spend three off days with my family."

"Forget it, man. You deserve it. Endure it," I said, chancing a smile.

The shower room rang with raucous song after the game. The harmonizing was deafening if not melodic.

"I love singing," said Hutch, as if his ears had not really registered noise. "When you hear singing you know you're winning."

So I sang all the way to Malibu, and looked at the sea.

Cincinnati — July 13

FOR those men, husbands and fathers, who play major league baseball (but not well enough to make the All-Star team), the three-day vacation in July is a true blessing—if they like mowing lawns, painting eaves, washing windows, walking around the zoo, picnicking and shopping, and attending patio parties at odd, free hours around midnight. It would be un-American, of course, to dislike vacations.

It was probably unsportsman-like of me to ignore the All-Star game completely on July 11, but the sunshine on the patio had just the proper thermal strength to make gin and tonic an effervescent outdoor pleasure. While I didn't watch the game on TV, knowing I wouldn't enjoy it, I did reread the sports page several times, enjoying the National League standings more than somewhat.

Cincinnati's Reds had a five-game lead on the Dodgers and a ten-game lead on the Pirates and Giants. Milwaukee trailed us by thirteen and a half games, St. Louis and Chicago were fifteen games back, and the Phillies—they were so deep in the cellar you couldn't see them. At the halfway mark in the race we looked like bona fide contenders—at least.

Hutchinson snickered as he said in the pregame clubhouse meeting two days later, "Hope you all feel well rested now."

Window fans blew waves of hot, muggy air about the room. The humidity hovered near ninety, and spilled a puddle of sweat upon Hutch's forehead. He mopped his face with a towel and said, "I've had a couple requests asking if it'd be all right if some players' wives make the next trip to the West Coast. I feel like saying no, right off. But I'm going to leave it up to you.

"We're in this race now to stay. I think we've got a damn good chance to win it. I'd hate to see that chance disturbed in any way. You all know what happens when your wife goes on a trip to—uh, any big new town. She wants to shop in the afternoons and go out at night. You would be playing ball in between times.

"And that's not the way to win pennants. It takes even more dedication to your work than you've shown so far. And you've done a good job—so far. So I'll leave it up to you to decide, but you know how *I* feel about it. If we *do* win it, you can all afford to take a trip anywhere you like."

He raised a score card, frowned at the Cub lineup, and said, "Now. Anybody have any new ideas on how to pitch these guys?"

"Knock somebody on their ass!" said the hitters.

"Yeah. Ass," said Bell.

"They've been digging in, all right," said Hutch, half-smiling at the wishful vision of Altman or Santo lying on his back in the batter's box.

Well, after you knock a hitter down, you still have to throw strikes on the next pitches. Unless you hit him. And that's not the idea at all. No pitcher wants the hitter to reach base; he just wants to loosen him up a little with a judiciously placed scare ball.

Sherman Jones shook his head at the suggestion that he pick

the blue bill of a Cub's cap as target No. 1.

"I can't throw at a batter's head. What if you would hit it? And killed him? How could you pitch again? Or live with yourself?"

His remarks sounded as if they came from a pitcher less dedicated to Hutchinson than to his own conscience. Nice guys sometimes get hurt on the mound by line drives.

"I'm not worried about 'em," said O'Toole as a concluding comment on the Cubs' offensive threat. O'Toole, who'd started and won the first game of the first half of the season, was a natural, cocksure choice to start the second half. He asked earnestly, if not humbly, for a couple of runs to work with, and he got two in the second inning.

Pinson dropped a fly ball to help the Cubs tie the score in the sixth, and when Heist singled home the third Cub run in the seventh, the Cub jinx looked frighteningly, and continuingly, real.

Robinson's home run tied up the game in our seventh; and in the ninth Robby came to bat with nobody out and men on first and third.

"They gotta walk him," I said as the Cubs huddled on the mound to discuss the crisis.

"Tappe hasn't walked him all year," said Zimmerman. "Just keeps pitchin' to him and gettin' his brains knocked out!"

"You'd make a good sportswriter the way you second-guess managers, Zim," said Nunn.

"Broz does all the writin' for this bullpen," said Zimmerman.

I had hardly enough time to sharpen my pencil when Robinson bounced a curve ball slowly toward the second baseman, Bouchee, the Cub first baseman cut across the infield, picked up the ball, turned, and threw to the plate—too late to get Blasingame sliding home with the winning run.

We ran up to the clubhouse, trying to beat the coaches to the potato chips and sour cream dip that was spread on the table.

Robinson later accepted a handful of congratulations and a fistful of potato chips, but his composure turned sour when he learned that the official scorer had given him a fielder's choice

143

instead of a base hit on the last ground ball.

"You just *gotta* get those hits at home!" he screamed. "You sure as hell don't get 'em on the road! Whose side you on?" he asked the scorer.

Personally, I thought it best to be on Robby's side.

"Did you know," I said, as the Cubs came to bat in the first inning the next afternoon, "that there's a picture of Kasko and Pinson in the window of the building where the Waiters' Union is located?"

"So what?" said Zimmerman.

"Well, Vada's not a waiter, he's a swinger!" I said, trying desperately to make an odd point.

The blank expressions that greeted my *mot* made me realize I must sound as bad as I looked. I rubbed my eyes, blew my nose, ran ice water over my head, and asked Zimmerman for a towel.

"Been out with Howie again, huh?" he asked.

Nunn, a bachelor, was frequently blamed as the instigator of any exhausting pursuit of happiness. He once said that he needn't run with the pitchers before the game because he did plenty of running afterward.

"Did you know," I said, obliquely, "that in Cincinnati after two o'clock the only people you see are bartenders, ballplayers, and cab drivers?"

Nunn tried to explain his, or our, position but he obviously lacked sincerity and frankness.

"Nunn," said Maloney, "if bull—— were cement you could pave a highway from here to Fresno!"

The rain clouds that had threatened to postpone the game entirely dripped intermittently throughout the first four innings. Since the Cubs had scored three quick runs it would have suited us well if the clouds just burst and sent us all back home.

Those almost-postponements are bad news.

Glenn Hobbie, the Cubs' pitcher, knocked Purkey out of the game with a line drive that struck Purkey's knee and drove in the fourth Chicago run. But Hobbie was banged around in

144

the sixth, giving up four runs and the lead.

Sherm Jones protected the lead till the eighth, when Williams hit a home run and Santo doubled. Henry relieved Jones to pitch to the left-handed hitters, and after he'd failed to impress Hutchinson by retiring the two men he faced, was asked to let me pitch to a right-handed Cub pinch-hitter. Chicago then substituted a left-handed pinch-hitter and I struck him out to retire the side before the official scorer ran out of room to record all the strategical changes on his score card.

I had a two-run lead as the ninth inning started. And I had two outs, with one man to go, when the whole goddamn game lost its enchantment.

Altman came to bat, encouraged by some of the most raucous cheers I'd ever heard from an opposing bench. Truly, I was upset by the lack of respect! All I needed was to make three good pitches and the game was over.

Altman fouled off one good pitch, took another just inside for ball one.

"Guess I'd better waste a fast ball," I thought, "before I go back inside with the slider."

Altman took what I felt, instinctively, was a desperate cut at a ball six inches outside (but not *really* low, I guess). The sound of his swing was, instinctively, I felt, discouraging. And, sure as hell, the ball flew far and high, into the left field screen. Tie score.

Hutchinson was not discouraged at this lapse on my part, and he let me hit in the ninth. I took the only pitch I could hit for a strike; then waved at two knuckle balls and went back to the mound.

Two singles, both squibs, each breaking the hitter's bat, surrounded an error by Kasko on a double-play grounder, and the Cubs took a one-run lead. That was sufficient for an 8-7 win.

I didn't sleep much afterward. When I did my subconscious mind suggested I not forget the address of the Waiters' Union.

"Where's my score card?" I grumbled as I searched the

145

bullpen dugout. In order to note, and laugh at, the losing pitcher in other games posted on the scoreboard, we kept an old score card on hand. Few news items give a mentally depressed pitcher more pleasure than instant recognition that some other guy just lost a game somewhere else. The score of the Dodgers' loss to the Phillies was on the board when our game began.

"Who pitched for L.A.?" I asked.

"Koufax, I heard," said Henry. "He lost it anyway."

"Good," I said. "It's about time Philadelphia beat the Dodgers."

"Yeah," said Zimmerman. "They beat L.A. about as often as we beat the Cubs!"

"Don't remind me," I said.

"Boy, you're a grouch today," said Henry.

I sniffed at him, picked up a chair, and walked out behind the bullpen to sit privately, chew tobacco noisily, and watch disinterestedly as Joey Jay pitched his thirteenth win of the season.

It had become distressingly commonplace for the Cubs to bomb every pitcher Cincinnati used on the mound. Their own pitchers had not been too impressive, the Red hitters imploring, "Just hold 'em. We'll get the runs!"

Therefore it probably was as fascinating to the Cubs as it was frustrating to the Reds to watch Jackie Curtis shut out Cincinnati for seven innings. At any rate Chicago failed to score any runs either, and actually spent damn little time batting as Joey Jay threw cute, little ol' slop sliders on the first pitch and Cub batters popped them up, man after man. Jay's cuteness was not so baffling as Curtis and his changes of speed, however.

"He dazzles you with his footwork," said Whisenant.

"He couldn't break your jaw with his best fast ball!" said Robinson.

"He knows what he's doing," said Hutch. "You gotta give him credit, I guess. We sure as hell ain't doing anything with him!"

In the eighth inning Hutch went all out for one run. It

looked like that was all Jay would need.

Kasko doubled and Hutch had Pinson bunt him to third. Ordinarily Pinson swings away, since he hits as frequently as his .300 batting average would indicate. Yet, if he failed to move Kasko to third, Robinson would be walked intentionally, both to set up the double play and to take no chances with our hot bat.

"They'll still walk him," I said, bending over the water fountain to wash my mouth free of tobacco shreds.

"No, they're not!" said Nunn, paying attention as Curtis wound up.

"How stubborn can one manager get!" I thought as Robinson lined a single to center to score Kasko.

After Freese walked, Post singled Robby home from second with an additional run. Joey Jay welcomed it on the bench at the time, and treasured it on the mound ten minutes later when Santo hit a home run to lead off the ninth. That was all they got, though, and we replayed the game with smiles in the Rendezvous lounge for an hour after the game.

"Tappe says," I said to Howie Nunn and his brothers, "that he's going to bench Ernie Banks even if Wrigley sends him clear to Wenatchee."

"If he doesn't walk Robby next time he's in a jam, Wrigley will send him to Paul's Valley, Oklahoma!" said Nunn.

Howie's brothers alternated effulgent praise of Joey Jay's pitching with glowing descriptions of each other. It was apparent that any one of the Brothers Nunn, each of whom was big enough to make two of Little Brother Howie, had enough self-confidence to lick the Chicago Cubs singlehandedly. And, from the size of their hands and shoulders, I'd bet on them—in a brawl.

Little Brother Howie had made it in the Big Time, however, and their pride in him was as great as their protective attitude must have been when he was being reared on the Nunn farm in North Carolina.

"I like the Brothers Nunn," I said to Howie when we said good night and headed for our hotel.

"They'll tear this town apart," he said, proudly.

Why not? We won, didn't we?

On Sunday morning the sports section of any responsible newspaper prints a statistical record of most major league ballplayers, including games of the preceding Friday. *Some* players are excluded because they've made too few significant appearances at the plate or on the mound.

"Why don't you win a game once in a while?" my friends write when my record doesn't appear. "Or even lose one. It takes six decisions now, I see." (Or eight, or ten, depending upon the month of the season.) "I know you're pitching, because I follow you every game. If you'd just get your record in print on Sunday I could brag about you!"

Discreetly, your friends ignore you when your record is embarrassing. When your record is good enough for the top ten in the league, you often hope to hear from them. It is an important enough communication medium that, if you're on top on Monday or Tuesday, you hope you don't pitch on Thursday or Friday, just to maintain your position for Sunday morning.

I ignored the National League "pitching" statistics at breakfast on July 16, cursing the Cubs for being in the league. Had it not been for them in 1961 I'd have been so far in front that even Murtaugh would have had to pick me for the All-Star team. And my fan mail would fill the mailbox.

Turning to the theater section of the paper I noted that Chekhov's *Sea Gull* was playing at a local summer theater.

"That's where I'll go tonight," I decided. "Compare his pathos with mine. Wonder if I'll get a chance to ruin my day by pitching this afternoon?"

Hutch couldn't think of anyone better than me to relieve Hunt after we'd given the Cubs two runs to tie the score and Altman's homer had given them a sixth-inning lead. Hutch ranted up and down the dugout complaining about the poor fielding, lousy pitching, and lack of hitting, then yelled at me, "You go on down there and get warm!"

It took the Cubs fifteen minutes to get us out in our half of

148

the sixth, more than enough time for me to warm up. I sat down in the bullpen and a man leaned over the railing to say: "Broz, meet Janet."

He pointed to a cute broad sitting next to him. "She's the bartender at the Capitol. You know?"

I *didn't* know, but she was the best-looking bartender I'd seen in a long time.

"She wants an autographed ball," her friend said.

"What's it worth to you, chick?" I asked her, forgiving him his presence.

"The best martini you ever had, baby," she said in a husky voice.

"Rooms," I said to Nunn, "better check this out." And I went off to the mound as our inning ended, without any scoring on our part.

I walked Bouchee and hung a slider to Heist, who doubled a run home to make the score 4-2.

"Well, for Christ's sake!" I said to myself, undoubtedly echoing Hutchinson's reaction on the bench. The Cubs obviously loved to hit me so I had to get nasty.

Zimmer flipped away from a malice-directed fast ball, jumped back up, moved closer to the plate, dug in, and had to get out from under another pitch. His aggressive attitude changed slightly and he waved, feebly, at a curve ball that was the third strike.

My next two innings were scoreless, which may have proved a point about the efficacy of knocking batters down when they're beating your brains out. We damn near lost any chance at a pennant in the eighth inning, however. Pinson and Robinson collided, chasing a pop fly. Robby had the ball in his glove when Vada banged into him.

"Clumsy mother!" I muttered angrily, to myself. "I need all the help I can get!"

Pinson and Robinson lay sprawled in right center field for a few minutes while Hutch rubbed his hands and brow anxiously over them. They recovered quickly, although they both looked groggy and Robby limped back to his position.

They both finished the game, and so did I. But we, and

everyone else in the lineup, failed to get even one hit in the last three innings.

"We can't do anything right against this club," Hutch said after the game.

Maybe it was their multiple-coach management system. Wish they'd pick one man to run their team—say, Charlie Dressen. We could beat him.

The Milwaukee Braves followed the Cubs into our town. The Braves stayed at the Terrace Hilton Hotel in Cincinnati. Most clubs stayed at the Netherland Hilton, one block south, which had upper-floor windows offering an unimpeded view of the Terrace Hilton rooms. I could look into those Brave rooms that had a southern exposure. If Charlie Dressen had wanted to check on his players he could have rented my room.

Instead, he supervised his players' movements in his own subtle manner.

"I caught two of my players after curfew," he said proudly, "with a trick I guess they never heard of. I plugged the keyhole in their room door. When they went to the desk claiming they had the wrong key they found a notice that they had been fined!"

Which angered the kiddies no end. And they went to Crosley Field and beat hell out of the Reds.

Warren Spahn started, still looking for the 297th victory of his career. (Who *needs* that many? Most people don't win a hundred games in their entire lives!)

Almost a month had passed as Spahnie pitched unsuccessfully. He needed four wins to reach the "Three Hundred Win" mark, a symbol with as much practical definition as "A Billion-Dollar Deficit."

I couldn't have cared less, and Spahn didn't look too confident himself, when Post hit a tremendous home run over the parking lot beyond the screen behind the left field fence. Pete Whisenant pantomimed the motion of an angler casting for a big fish, aiming a line at Spahn on the pitching mound, and reeling him in as Post touched home plate.

Spahn shook the fantasy out of Pete's mind, however, retiring the side and doubling home the tying run in the fourth. Howie Nunn relieved Jones at this point. Howie's arm was still sore, but he was a bit self-conscious about the check he'd drawn the day before and said he'd better do something to earn his next one.

The Braves, as Charlie Dressen had publicly suspected, were a bunch of swingers, on and off the field. As much as they sympathized with Nunn, a mutual swinger, as he tried agonizingly to pitch, they gloated over the possibilities inherent in Howie's floating fast balls.

"Man, I thought you were gonna faint!" Adcock told Nunn after the game. "I don't see how you could get the ball to the plate."

Adcock's single in the fifth inning had made Nunn the losing pitcher, a fact noted by Paul Sommerkamp, the P.A. announcer, who reviewed the line score for the fans as they left the park, booing.

"Milwaukee 13, Cincinnati 4. Losing pitcher, Nunn," said Sommerkamp.

I bought Howie several postgame Scotches and watched Spahn celebrate, weakly. Spahn had staggered all the way to the win, and he said later: "I thought I might win my three hundredth around the middle of July, but if it's as tough to get as this one was, it won't be till the middle of December!"

Which would be a cold day in Cincinnati. Or any other hell.

Newspaper photographers prefer to cover any other event than a baseball game. Fires, murders, and accidents are much more dramatic. (They don't draw as many paying customers, though.)

Those camera-carriers who cover major league ball games often treat the ballplayers as if they were clay pigeons to be shot at whatever angle the photographer chooses. The results seldom justify the arrogance, but men behind machines often think they're superior to the men they're working over.

Vada Pinson is neatly, often impeccably, clothed. Even on the ball field. He shines his spiked baseball shoes before each game, a scene that captured one photographer's fancy as he prowled around the Cincinnati clubhouse looking for trouble.

"Don't let him do it, Vada!" said Lynch when Pinson asked why his shoeshining was worth shooting.

"They'll send it to Alabama, Vada," said Whisenant, mocking a racial reaction.

The photographer ignored the agitating, thinking it was all kidding, probably. He posed Pinson properly and when he was finished with him, packed his bulbs and film, irritating Whisenant.

"Hey, Smitty!" said Pete, "when you gonna take a picture of me? Ain't I good enough?"

Whisenant picked up the chair in front of his locker and threw it in the direction of the departing photographer.

"I'll show you someday!" he yelled. "Don't know when, though," he added, laughing at himself.

The relative public worth of ballplayers can be judged by the quantity and type of fan mail they receive as well as by their newspaper publicity. The clubhouse man who delivers the mail had dropped one of Robinson's many letters into my mail slot. Addressed to "Frankie, care of Crosley Field," it was as illegible as it was flattering. I laid the problem of answering it on Robby and went to the bullpen. The bench, with Hutchinson growling bearlike at our misplaying, was no place for a comfortable view of the game.

Howie Nunn, dragging his sore arm behind him, came out to the bullpen. Maloney, nursing his tender arm, stayed on the bench. Neither could hide from Hutch. He sent them both in to face the Braves, who batted around five and a half times in nine innings.

Milwaukee had a 9-2 lead in the fourth inning. Cloninger, the Braves' pitcher, could have been excused for taking it easy as we came to bat. He walked the bases loaded, a slipshod attitude that annoyed Charlie Dressen so much that he took Cloninger out of the game.

"That kid got a hundred-grand bonus," I said as Dressen waved for Nottebart in the Braves' bullpen. "He oughta kick Little Caesar's teeth in for taking him out of this game!"

Nottebart had trouble retiring the side and Burdette ran

from the Milwaukee bench to their bullpen.

"Look at Squirrel go!" I said to Henry. "Don't you know he'd love to get in there and suck this one up!"

Henry nodded his head half-sleepily. He was willing to concede Burdette, and Milwaukee, anything they were willing to work for. Unfortunately for his comfort he had to work also, giving up a run to Thomas on a double that smashed the clock atop the scoreboard.

I matched that easily enough, feeding Mathews a fat slider in the ninth inning that he hit into the thirtieth row of the right field bleachers.

Hutch was so upset that he picked a fight with Tom Gorman, the plate umpire. Gorman weighs 225, a big Irishman with a temper to match Hutchinson's. Mutual insults led to mutual threats and invitations to a fist duel.

"I'll be outside at twelve-thirty!" Hutch snarled. "If you got any guts you'll be there, too."

By twelve-thirty, of course, the park was cleared of fans, ushers, and Milwaukee players. Several Cincinnati players hung around, licking the wounds of a 12-8 thrashing, while Hutchinson paced back and forth in the clubhouse, still dressed in his uniform, still mad at umpires.

At twelve-thirty Tom Gorman sat on a stool in Jorge's, an all-night beanery, drinking a milk shake. Strawberry. Or raspberry. Whatever umpires drink.

With the Dodgers roaring in from the Coast, just three and a half games behind us, we might have been excused for nervous bickering in the clubhouse before the game. Fortunately the annual pension plan report had arrived, encouraging an almost complacent in-group atmosphere.

The major league ballplayer could, at one time, find nothing but frustration (or masochistic pleasure) in defeat. The modern player can, if he has a tendency to distemper, rationalize his loss and say, "Well, at least it's one more day in the pension plan."

Under the terms of their pension plan, ballplayers who serve in the major leagues for ten years may receive two hundred dollars per month for life, starting at the age of fifty. Few players last that long, but it's an encouraging prospect, one that might well spur the labor leaders of trade unions.

In addition to old-age income, the major league pension plan provides insurance payments in case of the player's pre-pension-age death, hospitalization benefits for his family, and generous maternity benefits. The latter are most welcome, since ballplayers, at least during the off-season months, are famously procreative.

Gus Bell, the Cincinnati Reds' player representative to the pension committee, smugly detailed all the benefits to be enjoyed by players who had at least five years in the majors, and we all went out to see if we could play well enough to merit the privilege of staying around to collect.

The Dodgers presented a picture of determined aggressiveness as they took the field in the last of the first inning. The mosquitoes in the bullpen were equally aggressive, and we called the clubhouse for a can of pest-control spray. They sent us a noxious bug repellant that we had never used before.

"Try it on that son-of-a-bitch behind us who wants to know what's wrong with us," I suggested.

The s.o.b. ignored the hint and persisted in his annoyance. "Isn't Drysdale pitching?" he asked, his blood lust showing.

"No," I said. "You want your money back?"

He ordered some beer from a passing vendor, just to tempt us, I'm certain. He was a ginger-ale man for sure, according to his attitude.

As the game progressed, inning by onerous inning, it became increasingly apparent that however we had offended the gods, our expiation was not satisfactory. Every break in the Book went the other way. Our line drives never fell in; theirs were never caught. Their bloops frequently dropped safely, just out of reach; ours were ridiculously easy outs. Their hanging curves were popped up; ours disappeared over the fence. We made an error, they made a run; and they didn't boot a ball all night.

The Dodgers won, 8-3. It wasn't that close.

"It's just a phase, isn't it, Hutch?" the sportswriters asked.

"I sure as hell hope so," he said.

Some ballplayers shave after the game and get in the way of those other players who want to comb their hair and leave the clubhouse. Some players shave in the morning when they get out of bed. They look sleek at home, a little fuzzy-faced at the ball park during night games. (Some players shave so infrequently that they don't count, statistically.)

The shaving clique often starts dissecting the game ten minutes after the last out. They continue in the shower room, replay the last few innings over a final can of beer, and carry lingering impressions to bed and dream time.

Four losses in a row had shaved our league lead to two and a half games, and nobody could figure out why the skid should stop.

"We oughta all talk it over—everybody on the team—have a meeting. No coaches, no manager, just us," said Whisenant as he lathered his face.

"Good idea," said Lynch. "Everybody speak up. Anybody got any gripes, we oughta hear about 'em."

Hutchinson agreed that it might very well be a good idea, so he took the coaches and the trainer outside while Bell explained that we were all gathered together to talk it out.

"We gotta kick ourselves in the ass," said Whisenant. "Nobody can do that better than us."

"We oughta be more aggressive," said Robinson. "We got up here by takin' chances, takin' the extra base, stealin' runs, takin' charge."

"We're letting them run the game," said Purkey.

I stuck my hand up to get in a word.

"I've been pretty lousy—lately," I said, "and I'd appreciate somebody tellin' me why. The pitching coach has done a good job so far as he goes but he hasn't said twenty words to me all year about my pitching. Anybody want to kick me in the ass I'd welcome it."

"All of us have been horse, Professor," said Robinson.

"Broz has a good idea, though," said Whisenant. "We gotta help each other out on the field. Everybody makes mistakes that he's not conscious of sometimes. Tootie blows his stack when somebody makes an error behind him. If all the infielders blew their stacks when he made a bad pitch, he'd see how silly it looks."

"That's not gonna bother me any more," O'Toole said. "I made up my mind."

Whatever therapy the general confession afforded us, we *looked* more like a team the next day, grimly contented despite our misfortunes of the moment.

Sherman Jones observed, somewhat quizzically, "I've heard Hutch talk about panic. Well, this is what I call pushing the panic button."

"Don't be a cynic all your life, Road," I said. "I think I'll sit on the bench tonight."

Joey Jay threw harder than I'd seen him all season long as he warmed up. Ordinarily Jay is a breaking ball pitcher with a good fast ball that batters must look for. It's not quite good enough to sustain him by itself, however. The Dodgers hit it as hard as he threw it, and when Jay switched to the curve ball he couldn't get it over for a strike.

Four home runs helped L.A. score nine runs and I had to give up spectating and start working in the sixth.

"Why don't you try out that fork ball?" Whisenant suggested.

When Hutch added, "I think you might as well finish up; it'll help you get your rhythm back," I agreed with Whisenant and warned Kasko I had a new pitch.

"Good," he said, enigmatically.

The Dodger batters didn't like the fork ball at all, which pleased Whisenant as much as it did me. Plate Umpire Ed Sudol asked me, when I went up to hit in the seventh, "You got a new pitch, huh? It's a good one. Throw it. I'll call it."

Elated, I got a base hit, first of the season. I broke my bat, and then was almost picked off first base by the catcher. It would have made little difference in the score. L.A. won, 10-1.

Although we'd now lost five games in a row, there was a strangely confident air in the clubhouse.

"We played good ball, boys," said Lynch. "Just got the

—— kicked out of us. Get 'em tomorrow."

Maybe our luck would change and it would rain.

A reprieve from the good god Jupiter Pluvius helped us weather the seventh day of the second half of the season. We were down, and the Giants, clodhoppered and merciless, were anxious to kick us right in our pitching staff, which hurt the most. A brief but violent thunderstorm presented the Cincinnati front office with a chance to cancel the July 21 game. A sellout crowd was advised at six o'clock that there would *be* no game. At eight o'clock the skies cleared, the moon shone, and the Giants screamed.

"Yellow!" the Frisco writers called the Reds.

Almost as though this natural reaction deserved emphasis a bolt of lightning struck one of the pennant flags that flew above the façade of the grandstand roof. These eight flags stood in an arc behind home plate, representing each National League team's place in the standings. The toppled flag read "Cincinnati" and it had been knocked out of first place.

To add further to the unpropitious outlook, *Life* magazine sent a writer and photographer to record an expert's prediction that Cincinnati's balloon would burst for good over the weekend just like the Zeppelin *Von Hindenburg*. This hot-air theory failed to take into consideration that the Giants might get gassed in premature celebration.

"This is the best little ol' town in the league," said Ed Bailey. "After the game, of course."

To the resigned dismay of our pitching staff the sun shone brightly on Saturday. The high winds continued to blow, moreover, and we bet, masochistically, on the number of home runs that could be expected to sail out of the park.

"Four at a minimum," I predicted, dolefully.

"You're a pessimist, Broz," said Jones.

"I'm a realist. An experienced realist," I insisted. "And my arm's tired."

"I'll pitch," said Jones.

Hunt started, and kept the ball inside the park. But he walked one batter and gave up singles to four of the other five men he faced before Jones relieved him in the first inning. Hutchinson was booed for sticking his head out of the dugout, and the fans applauded derisively when Jones finally got the Giants out.

Jack Sanford practically ran to the mound to face us with a five-run lead. Sanford is a big, heavy-set right-hander who works strenuously on the mound. His shirt was soon thoroughly soaked in the heat and humidity, both reading ninety.

"He'll never finish," said Zimmerman.

"You're on," I said, in a betting mood. "A beer he goes nine."

"What's Road betting you on home runs?"

"Five Popsicles to a beer. He doesn't like beer."

"I like beer," said Zimmerman.

"So does Sanford, but he'll still finish."

"You're a pessimist."

Out from the dugout came Ken Johnson, a new pitcher signed when Howie Nunn was placed on the disabled list with a bad arm. Johnson declared that he was glad to be with us, and Hutchinson suggested that the best way for him to show his gratitude would be to pitch the ninth inning.

Johnson warmed up. He looked fairly fast, had a fair slider, and sweated a lot. Wiping his face with his shirt sleeve he signaled to Zimmerman that he would like to throw a knuckle ball.

"I can see why they got him now," I said to Henry. "That's a hell of a good bug!"

A good knuckle ball is a pesty pitch to catch, and Zimmerman had trouble stopping it in the bullpen. Johnson took it to the mound, where the Giants had just as much trouble hitting it.

San Francisco had hit one home run, off Hook in the sixth. But Sanford gave us nothing until the ninth, when he served one to Robby before finishing the game a winner, 8-3.

"We're even," I said to Zimmerman and Jones in the clubhouse.

"Yeah," said Zimmerman. "Hey, that Johnson's got a good one!"

"Best thing to happen to us all week."

"You don't have to catch it," he grumbled.

"I love to watch it, though. Hope he throws a lot of 'em in the next two months."

"You're a sadist," said Jones.

True. I'd rather beat than be beaten.

As our losing streak stretched to six straight, our league lead dwindled to one game over Los Angeles.

The first really hot summer day greeted us as Nunn and I stepped from the air-conditioned Jet Chef, where we'd decided after all not to ruin the night by having breakfast.

"We can eat between games," I rationalized.

"I'll bring you a hot dog in the fourth," said Nunn.

"That's right, you can't stay in the bullpen, can you? We'll miss your snoring, Roomie!"

"The rubbing table is more comfortable."

"Live it up. You get paid, anyway."

The disabled list looked like a good place to be during the game. The sound and sight of home runs became numbingly commonplace. Robinson hit one for us in the first, to give us the lead for the first time in a week. But Ed Bailey, straight from the Rendezvous lounge, where he'd told everyone who'd buy a round that he was happier to be with the third-place Giants than the first-place Reds, hit two home runs. Cepeda also hit one for San Francisco and they led 5-2 in the seventh.

"Do many balls go over that center field fence?" Ken Johnson asked us in the bullpen.

"Is the Pope a Catholic?" I said.

"Watch," said Zimmerman.

Jerry Lynch, who had started the game so Hutch could get more than one swing from his big bat, slammed a home run to lead off our seventh. After Freese walked, Cardenas, subbing for Kasko in another part of Hutch's lineup shaking, hit a high fly ball that blew over the center field fence to tie the score.

"See what we mean?" Zimmerman said to Johnson.

Jay Hook plugged the drain in our dugout and laid the hose

on the floor.

"Let's make a wading pool," he said, turning on the water faucet.

The flowing water cooled the dugout, but the rising water drove us out into the sun, where we could appreciate why Purkey was staggering through the ninth inning. He retired the Giants, and as we came to bat, Lynch was the first hitter.

"Hey, Hook," I said. "You got a B.S. in mechanical engineering. Figure out why a curve ball can be hit further than a fast ball."

"Like that one," said Henry, pointing to the fly ball that jumped off Lynch's bat.

"Oh, hell!" said Zimmerman. "It ain't got enough."

"Oh, yeah!" yelled Henry. "Yes, it has!"

Lynch's drive dropped just over the center field fence and we ran to lunch. Nunn had beaten us to the table and was well stuffed when our twenty-five-minute break had ended.

"How'd it look from the stands, Howie?" I asked him.

"Terrible. They sell three-two beer only, on Sundays!"

Blasingame's uniform was completely soaked with sweat. Hutch said he looked tired and told Chacon to play second in Blazer's place. Cardenas, who weighed only 150 anyway, had a jubilant confidence that was practically inspirational.

"You're in there, too, Leo," said Hutch. "Hit us another one."

Chacon and Cardenas led off the second game with base hits and everyone else in the lineup but Zimmerman followed, noisily. Six Red runs in two innings discouraged the Giants, who allowed Loes to pitch the last four innings of the game.

"I've got a new pitch," Loes had said the night before. "But I'm saving it for next season."

He'll need it.

Milwaukee — July 24

OUR arrival in Milwaukee failed to excite the good burghers of Beer-Town. They had lined the airport to greet the Braves the night before. Milwaukee had just won four straight from Pittsburgh and had returned to the first division where they belonged (said their writers).

Charlie Dressen confidently predicted (again?) that: "Now we'll take three out of four from the Reds and be right up there where we belong."

The Braves players did not evince any such confidence about where they belonged. Warren Spahn, the Milwaukee starter, had a slightly perplexed look on his face as he stared at Gordon Coleman. According to the Book, Spahn, a left-hander, should not have too much trouble pitching to Coleman, a left-handed hitter. However, Coleman had hit Spahn's variety of pitches safely eighteen out of twenty-eight times with disastrous results for Spahn. Over the years, Spahn had made it a habit to beat Cincinnati four or five times a season. So far in 1961, partly due to Coleman's bat, Spahn was one and four against Cincinnati.

Coleman singled in the third, after Spahn had retired six batters in a row. He got the next two men also, but Elio Chacon bunted toward first and beat Spahn's late throw as Coleman scored from third. Spahn's eyes followed Coleman all the way to the dugout and he lost his concentration on succeeding hitters. Wally Post homered in the fourth, when we scored two more runs.

Dressen took Spahn out in the fourth when Milwaukee scored a run off Joey Jay. They got another in the fifth just before the rain started.

"Come on, Jupe!" we implored, in the bullpen. "We could use a break and win a shortie!"

The rain failed to stop the game, and Charlie Dressen had to endure it at third base. The regular coach, George Myatt, had been ejected for complaining that Aaron's foul ball had cleared the left field fence just inside the line. It was, apparently, fair; but that's just the wrong time to insist on justice. Umpires are most vigorous when defending their miscalls.

In the seventh inning, the Braves' rookie pitcher, Tony Cloninger, brushed Robinson back with a fast ball.

"He should have hit him," I said. "Robby's liable to hit the next pitch outa here."

BAM!

"Thata boy, Broz," said Jones. "Way to call 'im."

Four more Cincinnati runs scored before Dressen could retire to his manager's room and figure out how he got beat, 9-3.

In our clubhouse Blasingame pointed to Turner's locker, where our esteemed pitching coach was rubbing his jaw.

"I'm trying to catch the infield ball, see," said Blasingame, "and it bounces over my hand and hits the Colonel. I get one play all night and blow it!"

Fortunately for us, Chacon had played second base.

The visitors' dressing room at Milwaukee's County Stadium is, by far, the best in the league. Spacious, comfortable, deodorized, it offers individual lockers with brightly colored name cards designating each man's place. (The better tippers, or highest-paid players, are nearest to the shower room.) Some of the names are misspelled, but the thoughtfulness is evident and spelling has always been a problem in the major leagues.

Engrossed with the spectacle of all the shirts, shoes, and gloves that I'd collected over the years and carried with me on road trips, I failed to notice a Henry-disturbing feature.

"Your shoe's torn, Broz," he noted. "Why don't you get it fixed?"

The leather toe plate had been ripped at the sole of my right-foot shoe.

"I see," I said. "I'll just trim it up. You got a knife, Gab?"

"No. Can't carry knives on the mound."

"What if a batter charges you?" I said.

"How about a scissors?" he responded. "It's okay to carry scissors."

The afternoon paper had revealed the fascinating information that Charlie Dressen had asked Mathews to report early for batting instructions. Hutch couldn't resist yelling, "Hey, No. 41! I understand Dressen's teaching you how to hit!"

Mathews blushed.

"Charlie never hit .220 in his life!" Hutchinson told our bench.

Mathews fielded the first ground ball of the game, gripped it twice for a firm hold, then threw it to first.

"Get a towel, Ed," yelled Bell. "The spit's still on it!"

"That Burdette throws spitters all the time," Hutchinson complained. "Nobody does anything about it. They oughta legalize the damn thing."

At the end of our futile first-inning attempts to score, the bullpen crew ran out to the bullpen to talk about jazz and other forms of Negro music.

Sherm Jones tried to explain the meaning of certain musicians' language, while we expressed doubts that Jones knew who and what he was talking about.

"Hook," said Jones, exasperated. "You're a college boy and you don't know who Marian Anderson is or what 'funky' means!"

"Do I have to?" Hook asked.

It didn't really seem necessary, but Jones worked on the theme while the game flashed by, quickly. Hunt gave up a home run to Aaron in the fourth, and Burdette singled home an extra run in the seventh. The Braves managed to get just five hits but they were plenty. Burdette gave up only two.

"Here it is the eighth inning," I suddenly realized, "and we've already hit three balls out of the infield!"

"We gotta save ourselves for the stretch drive," said Zimmerman. "Get a good night's sleep."

"Is this where all the Braves stay?" my wife asked me when I returned to the motel from the ball park.

"There are a couple of them here, I guess," I said. "It's better living for the single guy than staying at a hotel downtown."

"They've got the swimming pool surrounded," she said. "Them and the 'girls'!"

She shuddered as she said the word.

"What's wrong with the 'girls'?" I asked.

"Ooh, they're awful-looking. Real pigs!"

"Must belong to the bonus babies," I figured.

163

We had decided to stay at the motel because of the pool. Of all the things I miss in the baseball season, swimming on a hot summer day is the most tantalizing. Major league ball-players are usually discouraged from such muscle-tiring exercise. Especially in the enervating heat of a July sun.

I stayed in the air-conditioned room, reading Henry Miller's *Tropic of Cancer* while my wife swam and stared.

"There are two girls to each player!" she reported later in the afternoon.

"No wonder they can't win."

Jim Maloney's tender arm continued to irritate him the following day.

"I need another starter," Hutch said, and picked Ken Johnson.

Johnson's knuckle ball was so obviously effective that Zimmerman put on his mask to warm him up. I put a copy of *Newsweek* in my shirt to carry to the bullpen. If Zimmerman thought Johnson's knuckler was so dangerous, then the Braves weren't likely to knock him about too much.

"President Kennedy says he needs the reserves, Road," I read from the magazine.

"So, I'm ready," said Jones. "Unwilling but ready. What can you do?"

"That's the spirit, Road."

"Don't let me kid you," he said. "Personally I think this country's being run by a bunch of amateurs."

"You a card-carrying Red, Road?" I asked as the bullpen phone rang.

Jones knew I was just agitating him, but he urged me to get hot because Hutchinson was using a pinch-hitter for Johnson and I was the next pitcher.

Bell batted for Johnson and homered; Robinson then hit a two-run homer with two out to give us a 3-2 lead. I jumped on the motorcycle and rode out to the mound.

Thinking it was the seventh inning, I decided to use my fork ball, hoping to hold them to no more than one run. Aaron popped up my first fork ball, but as I threw the second one I heard Myatt yell from third base, alerting the batter. Apparently my grip was visible when I took the ball from my glove during my pitching delivery.

"I'll need a bigger glove," I said to Whisenant on the bench after retiring the side. "Myatt can read the pitch."

"You only need three more outs. Forget it," he pointed out.

"Is that right?" I said. "Christ, I thought it was only the eighth!"

Happily I walked back to the mound in the ninth certain that I had enough to get me through one more inning. Milwaukee got one man on base but he never got past first, surprising me, delighting my wife, and satisfying Hutchinson.

"Your wife gets kinda nervous during a game, doesn't she?" he asked.

"Let me tell you," she said afterward. "There were two blondes in the box behind me. All they said was: 'Maybe we'll see Jim.' Now, buster, who were they? Just good fans?"

She described them for me. They *sounded* pretty good.

All season long Charlie Dressen wanted to win "three out of four" from Cincinnati so he could get back into the race. Every time he opened his mouth Robinson or Jay or Purkey or Lynch shoved a loss down his throat.

All season long the Milwaukee management hoped their fans would buy beer and *Bratwurst* at the concession stands so the Braves could make another million dollars to give to bonus babies. The Braves had banned picnic hampers and carry-in six-packs from the park, thus discouraging the fans to the point that paid attendance was half a million below any other season in Milwaukee.

Once upon a time visiting clubs took an attendance check from County Stadium that paid the salaries of the entire bullpen—and the pitching coach, too. On sunny summer days the noise, pro-Brave, was often deafening in the visitors' bullpen.

"Wonder if these fans don't like Charlie either, Road?" I asked as we pushed through the gate into our bullpen.

"Where are they?" he asked.

"Gone bowling," I guessed.

Spahn and Burdette greeted us as we passed from the ramp under the bleachers.

"Charlie send you down here to get some work?" I asked.

"——— him! You know he put detectives on us!"

"He must suspect you really do wet one up now and then, Squirrel."

Burdette smiled. Cynically, I thought.

Jones had forgotten his sunglasses, which made his view of the game a squinty hardship. I caught a two-inning nap behind my prescription dark glasses, barely acknowledging Jones's requests for sympathy in his income tax problems in Atchison, Kansas.

"They're segregationists, probably," I suggested as the ninth inning began.

Purkey and Willey had pitched eight impressive innings in less than two hours, hardly time to sell any profitable amount of *Bratwurst* to the twenty thousand fans.

Willey had a four-hitter as he made his first pitch to Pinson. Vada singled. So did Robinson.

Dressen called the bullpen and Spahn warmed up. Coleman grounded out, but Bell walked to load the bases. Hutch sent Lynch up to hit for Freese, and the chant, "Lynch in the pinch!" echoed throughout every responsible Red fan's head.

Willey wound up to pitch and Pinson broke for home.

"Good God!" I thought. "What the hell's he thinking about!" With the best pinch-hitter in baseball batting, the runner on third does *not* try to steal home!

Willey's pitch beat Pinson to the plate and White, the catcher, tagged him. But Vada kicked the ball from White's hand and Umpire Dascoli changed his signal from "out" to "safe."

During spring training Hutch had decreed: "Anybody who pulls a 'rock,' makes a mental error, is going to be fined twenty-five dollars."

"Was that a rock, Broz?" asked Zimmerman.

"Depends on whether we win or not, I guess," I said.

Purkey held the lead in the ninth and declared in the clubhouse, "I'll put our room up against any other in the league!"

He and Joey Jay, his roommate, had twenty-seven wins at that happy moment.

My wife had a nervous comment on Pinson's dash.

"I had taken a histamine tablet for my sinus and was pretty dizzy. When Vada started to run I leaned over the railing along the first-row box seat, jumped up, and nearly fell onto the field when White dropped the ball!"

"What a way to get your name in the paper," I said.

Chicago — July 28

ALTHOUGH they must have known we were coming to town— hell, they must have been anxious to see us!—the Cubs had not yet mowed the outfield grass by the time we got on the field. The addition of flying grass pollen to the Wrigley Field air didn't help my sinuses, Maloney's asthma, or Hutch's disposition.

Fortunately, as we pitchers started our pregame running, a summer shower cleared the air. It also delayed the game for fifty-six minutes, giving us a little more time to breathe freely in what was still for us a catastrophe-haunted ball park.

Hutchinson had not bothered with a clubhouse meeting. No matter how we'd decided to pitch the Cubs in the past, they had bombed us regularly. With O'Toole pitching for us, the Cubs' left-handed big batters figured to be less noisy. That left Banks to hit the long ball for them.

He hit one in the fourth and another one in the sixth, although O'Toole insisted that he was pitching Banks the same way he always had done.

"And he *never* hit me!" O'Toole claimed.

Hutchinson raised doubtful eyebrows at O'Toole's confident assertion, but he excused Jimmy—mostly because Robinson had hit two home runs also, and Post had added one to give us a 4-2 lead.

The bullpen debate over who had more power, Banks or Robinson, reached a grammatical impasse at the same time that Robby's second drive cleared the left field screen.

"See," said Jones. "Neither of 'em is best."

"Neither is better," I insisted.

"Lay off, Professor!" said Jones. "This is baseball not grammar school."

O'Toole seemed to get stronger after Banks hit his second homer. The names of other power-hitters received favorable mention on our bench when we weren't holding our breaths with each Cub swing.

"That Leon Wagner was somethin' else," said Jones.

"Best pair of wrists I ever saw," I said. "But he was the worst outfielder I ever saw, too."

"Leon couldn't care less about fielding," said Jones. "All he wanted to do was swing the bat. And drive in runs. They'd send him up to hit with men on and he'd say, 'There's a couple young'uns I gotta bring in out there,' and he'd smile as if that was the best job in the world and he was the best man to do it."

Henry and I started to warm up, just in case, as the ninth inning started. I thought I had it made, myself, especially when O'Toole got Altman for the first out.

"They've got nothing but left-handed pinch-hitters left, Gabby," I told Henry. "Guess you're it if he gets in trouble."

With two strikes on Williams, O'Toole went up inside with a fast ball, to brush the batter back and satisfy Whisenant's code on how to pitch with a 2-0 count.

Williams didn't get out of the way, though, and the pitch hit him in the head.

"That dumb kid!" I said. "Why didn't he duck?"

The Cubs carried Williams off and put in Rodgers, a right-handed hitter that I'd forgotten about, to run for him. Santo then came out to pinch-hit, and tripled to drive home the third run and raise some throat lumps on our bench.

"Now I *know* they can't have any more right-handers to hit," I said. "Get hot, Gabby. Hutch is going out."

Hutchinson waved me in and said, "You have to pitch to Will."

Will was left-handed, and had driven in the winning run in the last two Cub games.

168

"I *won't* pitch to Will," I said, and I walked him on four pitches. Henry came in to pitch to the next two left-handers.

I was certain that Will somehow would score, giving me another loss, so I went to the clubhouse, shaved, and showered. As I came from the shower, toweling my head, I heard the clubhouse man say, "It's all over," and saw him turn off the radio. That usually means a loss for the visiting club because grave silence is their just due after a bad game.

Suddenly, the burst of joy that Bell and Kasko brought with them as they bounded into the dressing room hit me in the right ear and wiped the frown from my face.

"Nice goin', Broz!" said Kasko. "You set 'em up just right for ol' Gabby!"

"Atta boy, Prof," said Whisenant. "Stay away from that hot bat!"

"That's what you call thinking, boys!" said Lynch.

"I didn't know I *was* thinking, Jerry," I said. "Thought I was lousy, as usual."

Henry congratulated O'Toole for the win, and O'Toole was mutually praiseful. Henry smiled and said, "That was the best pitch I ever made when I struck out Bouchee."

"Sorry I missed it," I said, smiling with him.

One of our jolly sportswriters pessimistically reported that "The Reds have the worst record for Saturday games of any club in the league."

All of which he could have kept to himself but for the selfish desire to append a line: "Which only proves that every dog will have its bad day." Twisting a cliché for his own perverted use would be permissible, even in our clubhouse, but twisting it into our nervous systems was a bit too much.

We'd disregarded the sign-stealing spy-in-the-scoreboard in O'Toole's win. Probably because the Cubs had scored just three runs instead of the six that they'd averaged against us in Wrigley Field. When they bombed Joey Jay for nine hits and six runs in five innings, however, suspicion raised its field glasses again on our bench.

"I don't know how they're doing it for sure," said

Whisenant, "but watch those red exit lights. They keep flashing on and off."

Ray Shore was dispatched from his seat behind our bullpen to the center field bleachers. Shore stripped to the waist to disguise himself as a bleacher fan, and draped his shirt over one of the lights. A man in the scoreboard leaned out, pointed to Shore and his shirt, and yelled to a park policeman.

Shore took off, shirt in hand, but returned minutes later, drinking beer from a large paper cup. He walked over to the other exit light, drained his beer, reached up, and hung the paper cup over the light.

The Cubs failed to score in the next two innings.

We still trailed by five runs, but Jerry Lynch had not yet appeared to pinch-hit. When he did we had a rally going and the Cubs changed pitchers.

Lynch hit a two-run home run anyway to put us just one run down. Hutch kept Jerry in the game. Lynch had now hit three pinch-hit homers off Chicago and had driven in seventeen runs against them. He didn't say whether or not he was getting their signs.

Henry relieved for us, and Ray Shore, overexcited probably, ran to the uncovered exit light and threw his shirt over it again. Santo hit a home run, anyway, because Henry hung him a curve and batters don't really need to know that that is coming.

Kindall booted two plays in the top of the ninth to give us one run before Lynch came to bat with two men out. Jerry drove a knuckle ball toward right center, but the wind, which was blowing in from right, kept the ball down and Altman leaped against the fence to catch the third out and save the game for the Cubs.

My wife, who claimed she had a headache from the sun but who was probably hung over from the party the night before, said the Cubs were just lucky.

They were lucky they didn't have to pitch to Lynch all day.

Sunday morning is the popular time for church going, prayer-making, and wishful thinking. Every one of us Reds was probably willing to try anything to change our luck and stop the deterioration of our spiritual welfare. (Being in first place makes a man somehow *feel* good. To stay there even *I'd* consider going to church.)

It was probably improper, if not sacrilegious, to light a votive candle for the demise of the Dodgers as individuals or a team. What we needed most was a voodoo priest to cast a spell or put a hex on the Cub bats. Had it not been for Chicago, the Reds would have clinched the 1961 National League pennant in July. A pox on them!

In eighteen games the Cubs had hit thirty-three home runs off Red pitching. Hutchinson alternated praises of Altman's swing and Williams's wrists with profane damning of our pitching mistakes. Jim Turner searched his black book and old pitching charts to see what we pitchers were doing wrong. He tried to tell Joey Jay where he'd made his mistakes against the Cubs.

"*I* know what I did wrong!" Jay said, irritated. "I know it better than you do."

Turner patted him on the shoulder. "That's all right, Captain. Just so you remember next time, you hear?"

Jay shuffled slowly around the outfield, pretending he was doing his running.

"The Colonel and his damn book!" he grumbled. "You'd think it was worth keepin'."

"The record of our games will go down in history, Joe!" I argued.

"They oughta bury 'em," he said. "Especially the ones we played against this club."

The Cubs ran from their dugout at one o'clock with a hell of a lot more spirit than the weather and their position in the standings should have decreed. They were seventh, and unless the Phillies bought nine new major league ballplayers, the Cubs were going to finish the season seventh. Why didn't they act their role against Cincinnati?

The umpires looked even less enthusiastic than usual, strolling to their positions behind each base. Shag Crawford looked thin and pale as he approached our bullpen along the first base line.

"Hey, Shag!" said Bell. "Doesn't Giles give you guys any meal money?"

Al Barlick, umpiring at second base, explained that Crawford lost weight working double-headers.

"They ought to be banned!" said Barlick. "Especially in this hot weather."

"Wait till next year, Al," I said. "They'll add eight more games to the schedule, cut out all the off-days, and play double-headers every Sunday!"

He shuddered at the mere idea.

Neither umpire had a tough play to call in the first game, which started out in a frighteningly familiar pattern. Bouchee accepted Hunt's challenge to a first-pitch duel and hit a two-run home run in the second inning to give the Cubs a permanent lead. Bouchee is a notorious first-ball hitter and the patiently compromising pitcher will throw him nothing to hit on the first pitch. Hunt looked exceptionally fast but his reasoning wasn't any better than his luck of recent games, and Bouchee bombed his high hard one over the right field fence.

Hunt had been unable to encourage any batting support for some time, and this game was no exception. The Red batters couldn't even coax a base-on-balls from Cardwell, the Cub pitcher. Leo Cardenas, who had hit so well in place of Kasko that Ed couldn't get back in the lineup, banged two singles and scored a run.

Cardwell knocked Cardenas down for getting so uppity, a gesture that received almost as much attention *in* our bullpen as the broads were getting *behind* it.

Two girls, who probably were regular bleacher fans judging from their bared chests, simpered and grimaced so much that they hardly had time to keep score. If the game had been more interesting we couldn't even have paid attention to them, of course.

"Real mullion, Road," I said.

"Yeah. They're so bad they'd draw flies."

Nine innings were completed before we could get anything

172

going. The scoreboard showed that L.A. had beaten Pittsburgh and now had a full game lead on us.

"We could use a win," Whisenant pointed out as we ate lunch between games.

"I'll be glad when we get out of this damn town," I said, not really meaning it, or even intending to, since the second All-Star game gave us the next two days off. I had planned to stay over while the team went back to Cincinnati. If we lost the second game, however, Hutch was likely to call a workout for the next two days.

The Cubs had the bravura to start Brewer in the second game. Brewer had never won a major league game, nor was he impressing anybody but the Cubs with his general ability. Ken Johnson started for us, and his pregame knuckle ball was so good that it bounced off the mask Edwards insisted on wearing while he warmed Ken up.

For six innings pregame form reversed itself and the Cubs hit two home runs, while Brewer struck out six men and gave up just four singles. Hutch looked mad enough to pitch batting practice all day Monday and his comments on our hitting were uncomplimentary, to say the best.

We still had Jerry Lynch, though. He hadn't started because Brewer is left-handed. When we rallied for two runs in the seventh, the Cubs foolishly brought in a right-hander. Lynch then pinch-hit another two runs home to give us a one-run lead, 5-4.

Whisenant, who had walked as a pinch-hitter off Brewer, scored the tie-breaking run. He insisted that everyone on the bench shake his hand and Blasingame said, "Nice going, Pete. You can be my coach any day."

"See me use my line-drive stance?" said Whisenant. "Brewer was scared to pitch to me when he got to 3-2!"

I pitched two innings, breathing hard and hoping that the Cubs had had enough of me for one season.

In the ninth Hutch said to me, "Altman and Williams are leading off. Let's let Henry finish up."

Gabby retired them both, and Hutch decided to go all the way with percentage. He brought Sherm Jones in to pitch to

173

Santo, but Santo singled. Then Hutch asked O'Toole to pitch to Will, who batted for Bertell.

The Cubs substituted McAnany, who'd just arrived that day from Houston and wasn't even on the score card but was right-handed, to hit for Will. O'Toole asked Hutch how to pitch McAnany but Hutch didn't know anything about him. McAnany singled, and the last Cub right-handed hitter, Kindall, came out to hit for the left-handed Bouchee. The crowd loved it. All the wild strategy of their fanatic dreams was on display.

Kindall struck out and we all went home.

Cincinnati — August 2

HAVING broken even with the Bad Guys in Chicago, we heartily welcomed the Good Guys from Philadelphia two days later. The pressure of consecutive double-headers can often crush a ball club's stamina, but the Phillies *knew* they couldn't beat us. The *Sporting News* said so.

Art Mahaffey, their best pitcher, hadn't worked against us since the first series of the season, when he threw at Robinson for divers and malicious ends. His pitch had prompted a revengeful response. His manager, Gene Mauch, had finally, three months later, reported, "They popped off about my not pitching Mahaffey. All right! I'll pitch him tonight!"

Mahaffey was so enthusiastic that he singled to help the Phillies score their first run. And he got Robinson out.

But Pinson and Coleman hit home runs and Mahaffey left in the sixth inning, doomed to his ninth straight loss. Mauch had explained his star's bad showing in an interview.

"Art's trying to pitch like Christy Mathewson instead of Art Mahaffey."

Mahaffey didn't look even as good as John Buzhardt, much less Christy Mathewson. Nor was he even as effective as his relievers, who shut us out without a hit the rest of the game.

O'Toole had had enough runs, however. In five days he'd won two and saved one game. We'd won three in that time.

Even Whisenant admitted that Tootie was doing his bit.

Joey Jay started the second game but he looked logy, as if he'd eaten too many of his kid's jelly rolls. Or you might say he looked horse—as if he shouldn't get anybody out. The Phillies punched ten hits around the park while Jay stood on the mound wearing a superior smile. The hits produced only two Philly runs, and we had three.

In the bullpen Sherm Jones leaned back over the railing and asked Howie Nunn to go get the iron ball from the clubhouse.

"The humidity makes the baseball seem heavy tonight," Jones explained.

"I don't run errands," Nunn said.

"Do *something* for your pay!" I urged.

Nunn grinned. "Y'know, I got a month's pay for two-thirds of an inning last month!"

Jones couldn't wait for Nunn. He was summoned to Jay's aid in the sixth inning when the Phillies threatened, weakly, to tie the score.

"Now watch Road work," I said. "He'll probably strike out four or five and maybe give 'em one hit. He needs the save."

Sometimes my intuition pleases me no end.

In the Rendezvous after the game Darrell Johnson, the Philly catcher, explained his team's position:

"This club's in the cellar 'cause too many guys are giving seventy-five percent instead of a hundred. The only player on the club is Ruben Amaro. He's the first Latin I ever saw who thinks like a winning ballplayer."

I agreed that Ruben was a gentleman.

"We had three runners tagged out at the plate tonight," said Johnson. "They all should have scored. Changes both games."

I nodded. "You're last, we're first."

Los Angeles had lost to Frisco, 6-0, according to the bartender who bought us both a drink.

When Doc Rohde heard that we were back in first place he rose from bed, said he was needed, and returned to the trainer's room at Crosley Field.

"Don't worry, Doc. We'll vote you in!" said Post. "You just take it easy."

"Like you always do," said Henry, greeting Rohde left-handedly.

Gene Freese lay on the rubbing table and said, "Hutch says I'm tired." So he went to sleep, and Kasko played third. It was the first game Freese had missed all year. His bat had hurt the Phillies all season too, but Hutch figured Robinson had enough power to carry us.

"He'll be even better than last month," Hutch said.

Robby had hit .409, driven home thirty-four runs, and already cinched the Most Valuable Player award so far as most of us were concerned. Without him we might be challenging the Cubs instead of the Dodgers.

The Topps Chewing Gum Company had sent its president to talk the ballplayers into signing with them. Another gum company had also solicited us for the right to enclose flattering picture records of each major league player in a package containing gum for the bubble-blowing youth of the country.

Leo Cardenas blew a record-breaking bubble for Sy Berger, the Topps man. He used the other company's gum to do so, but who can tell the difference?

"Let 'em fight it out between themselves," advised Gus Bell when Berger asked us to choose which gum was worth endorsing.

Ken Johnson pitched the game against Philadelphia. He had three balls and two strikes on half the Philly hitters.

"He can't pitch like that!" I insisted.

"He's winning, ain't he?" said Henry.

"Wrong way to do it," I mumbled, and turned the page on the first pro football forecast of the year. (I'm a fan.) My magazine said the Green Bay Packers would win the pro title, which I could believe even if I'm a fan of the Chicago Bears.

The evening paper had said that Robinson had the hottest bat in the league, which Buzhardt, the Philly pitcher, apparently believed, wholeheartedly. He gave Robby nothing to hit but low curve balls, normally a wise move.

176

Robinson, however, had made up his mind to hit anything he could reach. His thirty-third home run of the year deflated Buzhardt's confidence, and gave Johnson all the lead he needed to make magazine reading a pleasure in the bullpen.

The only thing that could have interrupted me was a blonde asking me to autograph a copy of my book. Most book readers have less pleasing smiles.

"That's all right, Broz," said Jones. "You go first-class, man!"

"But, Road, I don't even know her!" I protested.

"Cool it. Thirty thousand people seen it."

Why don't they pay attention to the game?

Don Hoak's late June prediction that we would fold in July had not yet come true. We still led the league, although Milwaukee and San Francisco now looked like additional threats to the Dodgers. I would have figured fourth place was reasonable, considering our potential and the other club's pretensions.

"There's no such thing as a jinx!" said Whisenant, not believing it but ever striving for the positive approach to the Pirates.

I might have argued with him in the first inning when Virdon and Skinner blooped a couple of base hits to give Pittsburgh a run. And, when our base runners (we had eleven of them in seven innings) stumbled all over the base paths to prevent us from taking a lead, I might even have said what Blasingame said:

"We got the *awkwardest* team in the league, anyway!"

Whisenant managed to tie the score in the seventh while running for Zimmerman. But Post dropped a fly ball in the eighth and Stuart hit a home run on a high, inside pitch to plunge us into anxious review of our pitching strategy.

"We been pitching Stuart up and in for two years and he's killing us," I said.

"What do you suggest, Professor?"

"Call time. I don't know."

Fortunately, the Pirates changed pitchers and brought in

177

the wrong man so we soon tied the score, pleasing Hutchinson so much he brought me in to pitch. The 28,000 fans thought this was hardly worth applauding, but I wound up anyway and threw a fast ball to Burgess. It was only the first one I'd thrown in three games, but Burgess hit it like he knew it was coming. Smugly, he perched on first base.

Groat tried to sacrifice but bunted the ball directly to me. That was one indication that the Pirates weren't playing as well as they had done in 1960 when they won the pennant. In '61 they made as many mistakes in the late innings as everybody else.

Except Cincinnati. We didn't make many errors after the other team gave us a chance to win.

Pinson singled to start the ninth. And Robinson's double off the center field fence scored Vada.

"Suck up those easy ones," said Nunn, as we walked into the bar where our favorite trumpet man blew.

"There aren't any easy ones, are there?" asked the horn man later.

"You'll make a ballplayer yet," I told him.

"Who do you like to win it, Broz, Milwaukee or Frisco?"

Ray Shore's impertinence had more than a little significance for anybody who had read the paper every day for two weeks. The Braves and the Giants both had moved up as the Dodgers came up with two broken fingernails and a case of schizophrenia to halt their winning streak.

"Who says we can't win it?" I asked, holding up my hand before he read me the list of doubters. We still had a two and a half game lead over the second-place Dodgers.

"*Cherchez les Braves*," I muttered.

The CBS-TV network had selected our game with Pittsburgh as "Game of the Week." Fred Hutchinson had selected Ken Hunt to pitch against the Pirates. Hunt's father, in Ogden, Utah, may well have thanked both network and manager for their combined efforts to help him further his son's career.

It was the impassioned, parental, and self-appointed obligation of Mr. Hunt to supervise Ken's major league pitching.

When the kid lost a game his mail was filled with Utahan advice; when Ken won, he patted *himself* on the back. The elder Hunt, of course, is the elemental fan.

"Hunt's real pert today," said Zimmerman when he came out to the bullpen. "If he just forgets about his blister now . . ."

"Nice to have your report," I said, and handed him a seat cushion. "Sit down, and rest your predictions."

Hunt was less pert when Plate Umpire Steiner told him it was all right to make the first pitch. Virdon hit it for a single and before the inning was over Pittsburgh had four runs, Hunt was in the clubhouse, and his father was probably writing a letter.

Clemente had helped knock Hunt out with a single.

"That's Roberto's one thousandth hit," I said, when Steiner called time and gave the ball to Clemente.

"Did he get 'em all off us?" asked Henry.

Ridiculous, of course. Even at two hits a game, he couldn't—

"Have you appointed a finance officer, Cap?" asked Jones. "We need peanuts today."

"The way things have been goin', I think we ought to consider this an open mess. Everybody buy his own," I said.

"You've lost your spirit, Broz," said Jones, searching my eyeballs for life.

"Road, I tell you. You win this game and you can be Captain. Okay?"

"Don't do me any favors," he said.

The Pirates dribbled eight singles through the infield, agitating Jay Hook, who had relieved Hunt. Pittsburgh managed to maintain Hook's record of giving up at least a run per inning that he pitched. But they broke a lot of bats to do it.

"They look more like last year's team now, Gab," I suggested.

The Pittsburgh pitcher, Alvin O'Neill McBean, a native of the Virgin Islands, hit a home run in the fifth to satisfy the millions of TV homer-lovers.

"Why doesn't it rain on Saturday?" I asked Henry.

He didn't even bother to answer. Probably because Hutch told him to finish the game. Henry hadn't allowed a man to reach base in his last four games. That record should have gained him better status than "Mop-up Man."

"You hired out to pitch, didn't ya!" I yelled at him as he walked down to the mound.

Grumpy Texan.

The Pirates—at least those who didn't like the Rendezvous —stayed at the Netherland Hilton Hotel. So did the general manager of the Reds. And Hutch kept a room there. It was often hard to stumble into the elevator without bumping into a National League ballplayer.

Danny Murtaugh, my favorite All-Star manager, blew cigar smoke into my face as I stepped on at the twenty-third floor, headed down to the coffee shop. Murtaugh's smoke didn't make me feel any better after a short night, but he had more attentive eyes for his pitcher, Wilmer "Vinegar Bend" Mizell, who got on the elevator at the nineteenth floor.

"What kind of hitter are you?" Murtaugh asked Mizell.

"Ah'm a pretty fair country hitter at six o'clock," drawled Mizell, who lives in St. Louis but acts like he's just out of Alabama.

"By six," said Murtaugh, "I'll probably be out of the game."

Murtaugh's pessimism could be attributed to a season-long frustration, both from his team's playing and from the National League umpire's optical illusion—they thought Pittsburgh really *looked* like a sixth-place team instead of a world's champion.

Mizell started pitching at one o'clock on the Sunday afternoon, and had his chance to hit at one-thirty-five. Joey Jay struck him out, but Virdon bounced a single through Jay's legs to give Mizell the lead in the game.

He didn't lose that lead, partly because Murtaugh took him out of the game in the sixth and let Clem Labine save the win.

Whisenant complained loudly that he should have started the game. His reputation as a Mizell-hitter had been established years before when Pete played for the Braves and the Cubs.

"Hell, when Mizell heard I was back in the league he panicked!" Whisenant said. "Lost seven straight, didn't he?"

Hutch didn't put Pete in in time to keep Mizell from breaking his losing streak. In fact, he didn't put Pete in the game at all. It wasn't necessary. We lost without him.

"Pete's really poppin' his bill," said Zimmerman. "Thinks he's a coach or something!"

The bullpen during the first game of the double-header was less noisy than sometimes, thanks to a beauteous broad who, uncomfortably, I'm sure, sat next to the railing behind us.

"Aren't those the loveliest green eyes you ever saw, Road?" I asked Jones, staring into them until they shifted desperately toward their nominal lessee. The husband drank his beer and yelled at the Reds in the field. Silly ol' fan!

Jones insisted on talking to keep me awake, although I'd lost whatever energy Nunn's pill had given me after my postgame depression and pregame celebration the night before. At heart, I'm an optimist.

"Road, I can imagine you and Bridges in the same bullpen. Can you envision that, Hook? I mean, can you hear that?"

Hook brooded, silently, ignoring ol' Green Eyes, who ignored her old man eventually.

It was almost six o'clock and, sure as Irish hell, Murtaugh was thrown out of the game by Ed Sudol, the plate umpire. Murtaugh had complained about a "strike" call that Sudol had made. Such a complaint is a grievous sin, according to the commandments of Warren Giles, the president of the National League.

I was sorry to see ol' Dan go. Especially when Hutch asked me to relieve O'Toole. We were down 2-1 at the time but I could hardly stand up, much less pitch. Only the chance of beating ol' Dan kept me moving out to the mound.

Sudol helped me strike out Stuart in the ninth inning, giving me the benefit of the doubt on a pitch right on the black. What the hell! I wasn't going to give their big man a chance to beat me.

In three misty innings I'd faced nine hitters—the minimum. Pinson hit a home run in the tenth to give me the win, which kind of flabbergasted me.

"I mean, why train, Howard?" I asked Nunn. "I could hardly stand up on the mound!"

"So take another pill," he said. "I get 'em from a doctor. They take 'em all the time, y'know."

They don't have to win, though.

St. Louis — August 7

WHEN the Cincinnati Reds 1961 schedule was released in the spring my wife and I scanned it speculatively, eying possibilities for family living. Since my home is in Chicago I can use it as a residence instead of a tax deduction only on days when the Reds play in either Chicago or Milwaukee. This arrangement saves wear and tear on the master bedroom, but is a compromise at best—even considering the size of the mortgage which makes the sight of the house a cynical pleasure on the first of the month.

The "Games Abroad" section of the Reds' schedule included a promising listing of two consecutive series in Chicago and Milwaukee, the last ending on August 1. From then on, only one bright day was in prospect—the twenty-sixth of September. (Had I but known, that date might have made me more nervously expectant than usual, just looking at it.)

I had ignored, in February, the prospective road trip that was scheduled between August 7 and August 16. When the itinerary for that trip was passed out to us in the clubhouse on August 6 I said, "I don't want to go!"

The schedule decreed that we play ten games in ten days in five different cities ten thousand miles apart—as domestic airlines fly. From Cincinnati we were to fly to St. Louis for two games, to Philadelphia for one, to Cleveland for an exhibition game, to San Francisco for a weekend series, to Los Angeles for the West Coast showdown with the Dodgers, and thence back to Cincinnati for a night's sleep.

"I'm not going," Nunn said.

"Sorry to hear it, Rooms," I said. "Have a good time resting your arm. Stay out of the places we usually go to. *You'll* be dead by the time we get back."

He grinned, rather confidently, I thought.

Avery Robbins looked like a man with an impossible mission when he checked us onto the plane to St. Louis. A rookie traveling secretary, Robbins could see nothing but trouble getting us in and out of the right hotels, and on and off the right airplanes, on time.

"Please try to follow the itinerary," he pleaded.

"We will if you will, Avery," Robinson said.

No ten-thousand-mile tour works out as scheduled, of course. We made it to St. Louis all right, but the Hotel Chase did not have enough rooms for the players. For the writers and broadcasters, yes—for the players, no.

"The reporters need their rest," I explained to my new roommate, Ken Johnson.

"But I'm pitching tonight!" Johnson protested.

"We'll have rooms for you by tonight," said the desk clerk, a Cardinal fan who couldn't have cared less whether the Reds' pitcher got his pregame nap.

"At least Avery could have got rooms for the regulars," Coleman complained.

The American Bar Association had convened, with one hundred thousand members, and had liked St. Louis so much they didn't leave when they had promised. Avery Robbins couldn't stir them either, nor could he get much sympathy from the hotel manager, who insisted, "Yes, you *will* win tonight, Mr. Robbins!"

Sleeplessness produces lethargy, and "lethargic" is probably the word Hutch was after while describing our hitting against Larry Jackson at Busch Stadium. Few members of the Bar Association showed up for the game. Lawyers are not, at heart, likely to be baseball fans. Baseball is not subtle enough a game for anyone who deals with the complexities of justice.

"Cocky" Jackson, a polished professional with as much confidence in himself as he has stuff on his pitches, had more than enough for our weakly swinging bats.

183

"There's a pretty good pitcher," I said to Jay after relieving him of a wad of chewing tobacco. "Cocky knows where to throw the ball and he dares you to hit it."

Jay shook his head. "Do you believe in percentage on your stuff? Really *believe* it so you *dare* 'em to hit you?"

"Of course," I said promptly.

Of course, when I don't think I have good stuff—and there are such days—I don't see how I can get anybody out.

Usually I don't.

It appeared that Jackson would get enough hitters out in our half of the ninth inning. Whisenant stopped rooting for runs and said, "Bross, do you get pissed off when you lose?"

"Only on Mondays, Peter," I said.

Avery Robbins bade us all to check our bags out of the hotel before leaving for the ball park on Tuesday. In some cases it was unnecessary, for the bags had remained in the lobby for twenty-four hours after we'd arrived in St. Louis. Having lost a game, and dropped out of first place, who needs to change clothes?

Any red-blooded professional ballplayer can find a place to sleep after a game, even if there are no rooms at the inn. Still, everybody showed up in our clubhouse to play the concluding game of what seemed like the longest two-game series of the season.

I walked into the anteroom behind the Cardinal dugout thinking about the joys of batting practice just ahead, and bumped into Ernie Broglio, the Cardinal starting pitcher.

"Listen," Broglio said, "my wife wants an autographed copy of your book."

"So does mine, Ern," I said.

"I'll buy one," he said.

"That's the best offer I've had in weeks," I assured him.

"How much do you get per book?"

"Two cents in paperback."

"Why don't you give me one then?"

Broglio will never understand how to make a million.

The Cardinal dugout is ninety feet long. I walked the

length of it, staring at Joe Cunningham as he stared at the bat rack. His concentration could not have been so intense that he couldn't hear me clumping, spike-shod, on the dugout floorboards.

"Joey," I said as I passed him, "you looking for a base hit?"

Cunningham giggled to himself, not even looking up to see if I were serious or not.

But then, he didn't really need a base hit because he didn't get into the game. And neither did I.

Purkey pitched the entire game for Cincinnati. He also hit a home run, an extraordinary feat which kept him in the game after Lynch had hit a pinch-hit homer and tied the score in the ninth inning. Perhaps Hutch thought Purkey could hit another homer and shock the Cards into insensibility.

The Cardinals had hit two home runs to make the game an even match as St. Louis batted in the last of the ninth. Ken Boyer was listed to hit against Purkey.

"How much is Boyer making?" I asked Whisenant.

"More than you and me combined," he said.

"Funny," I assured him. "He really hasn't had that good a year, y'know. No home runs to speak of."

Boyer then hit a home run to win the game.

"You and your big mouth," Whisenant mumbled.

Another big mouth accosted our bus after the game, waving his hands and yelling, "See you guys after L.A. cinches it, you bums!"

Freese yelled back at him, "Your alarm goes off at six A.M. Get your lunch pail ready!"

The drunk staggered back into the bar at the very thought of it.

Philadelphia — August 9

AMONG other unenforceable rules of conduct for major league ballplayers is the one that bans fraternization on the field after the park gates have opened to the public. The Commissioner even insists that an umpire be present to monitor any overtly friendly relationships evident before each game.

Unenforceable laws of conduct usually stem from a lack of

human understanding on the part of the rules-makers. It may seem possible to a peculiarly prejudiced mind that a player in a white uniform might give more than an even break to his friend in a gray uniform. On the other, more practical hand, it is more than likely that I'd knock my wife down with a fast ball if I thought she was thinking about hitting a line drive through my legs and beating me a ball game. That's pro baseball, both sides.

Frequently, therefore, there are groups of mutually friendly players from each club gathered behind the batting cage while the home team is hitting before each game. Inevitably a coterie of Cubans—or, better perhaps, a lobby of Latins—convene wherever there are several Caribbean natives on the two opposing clubs.

As a minority group in a Caucasian world, they stand out, with hand gestures hypnotic and lip movements unintelligible. I surprised even myself when I found myself surrounded *en conclave*.

I had walked out to the batting cage to talk to Ruben Amaro, the Phillies' Mexican shortstop. Ruben and I had played together at St. Louis and had traveled throughout Japan together. He had once said to me, "I don't mind the way some people treat me up here because I know there are others who like me for what I am. And so all those other people really don't understand."

Because he's dark enough to be a Negro "all those other people" probably gave him a rough time while he learned English and other useful American philosophies. Fortunately the social pressures had not prevented him from becoming an exceptional professional shortstop.

Pancho Herrerra, the huge, happy-go-lucky Cuban first baseman, interrupted my conversation with Amaro to say, "Jeem, Rube, he talk about you all de time!"

"That's because I think he's the best shortstop in the league. Right, Rube?"

Amaro blushed—I think. It's hard to tell.

Pete Whisenant followed me to the outfield, where I took up my position as ball retriever for our hitters. Whisenant feigned interest in my desultory conversation for a moment, but finally admitted, "Bross. Something's bothering me. I been getting on these young players and I think they resent it. Do they?"

"Sure. Wouldn't you at their age?"

"Maybe. I don't know. All I'm thinking about is winning the pennant."

"Well, keep it up, Peter. I can't think of anything you do better. Let 'em learn now how to take it. You have to take a lot of criticism in this game before you find out what you can do."

"And what you can't do," he added.

Since we were playing Philadelphia neither Whisenant nor I figured we could lose. And neither did Joey Jay, who knew a sixteenth victory when he saw it.

The Phillies started Ferrarese, which is a hard name to pronounce but whose pitches weren't hard to figure out.

Hutch started Elio Chacon, who certainly couldn't pronounce "Ferrarese" and didn't even try. Elio did hit a home run, walked three times, and started a double play, all of which made it easy for me to sit back in the bullpen and read *The Realist*, an off-beat magazine published in Greenwich Village.

Among other insights into his personal philosophy the editor of *The Realist* offered a most reasonable suggestion. Let everyone pledge allegiance to the democratic organization, Union of Non-Joiners for the Use of Creative Kinetic Energy to Resist the System—a capitalized Utopia.

San Francisco — August 11

THE cab ride to Candlestick Park from downtown San Francisco is expensive, but it seemed more reliable than the scheduled bus that the traveling secretary had arranged. Our trip from Philadelphia, via Cleveland, where we'd played a completely unnecessary game, had been hectic. As we deplaned in California Avery Robbins was halfway inside a bottle of Scotch, trying to elude questions like: "When do we leave for Honolulu?"

If we all were headed for as bad a road trip as Robbins had had so far, we might just as well fly to Hawaii. The Dodgers couldn't lose for winning, and even the Cardinals, who had won eight in a row, didn't look like they could help us by beating L.A. while we played Frisco.

"Whaddya mean?" said Whisenant. "Who care what St. Louis does! We can't wait around for somebody to do it for us, goddamn it. Let's win!"

"You sound more like Hutch every day, Peter," I warned him.

Candlestick Park is the grossest error in the history of major league baseball. Designed, at a corner table in Lefty O'Doul's, a Frisco saloon, by two politicians and an itinerant ditchdigger, the ball park slants toward the bay—in fact, it *slides* toward the bay and before long will be under water, which is the best place for it.

One architectural expert, writing for *Harper's Magazine*, called the park a "monstrosity," but he was obviously a baseball fan, a Giant rooter, and genteel.

Nevertheless, a million fans had paid to get into Candlestick Park as we started the August 11, 1961, game with the Giants. Their dogged devotion was enough to rekindle man's faith in Barnum and Bailey, and other sporting promoters.

Our bullpen was empty except for Henry, Jones, and Zimmerman. Henry had refused, for the seventy-fourth time, to sit on the bench where he could stay reasonably warm. (Otis Douglas and Pete Whisenant could keep a bench warm just by the force of their cheerleading personalities.)

"Gabby," I told him, "you shouldn't even be out here tonight. You look so bad you oughta be in a hospital. At least your glove should. Look at that thing!"

Henry blushed for his glove, which had served him well for many seasons—how many he wouldn't say.

"Go —— ——" he urged me, and I ran on up to the dugout. Elio Chacon had joined the chorus of bench jockeys. Elio's accent and choice of epithets were better for laughs than agitation.

"Call de ball right, Chocko!" he yelled at the plate umpire,

Augie Donatelli. Jocko Conlan was behind first base, shivering, but he would hardly have been offended anyway. Donatelli looked over at our bench and laughed.

Chacon urged Gus Bell to "Come on, Guz. Two for one, two for one!"—a cheer that probably puzzled Bell as much as it did me. I asked Elio for some chewing tobacco and Bell struck out trying, maybe, to respond to Chacon's request.

"Wonder if Spahn got No. 300," said Gernert in the corner of the bench.

"Hope so," said Post.

Warren Spahn, pitching against Chicago for his three hundredth major league win, had everyone's sympathetic support. Except Whisenant's, apparently.

"Christ, let's root for Tootie!" said Pete. "To hell with Spahn!"

Pete had us all wrong. We were for O'Toole, too, and applauded him when he drove in our two runs. But he allowed San Francisco four runs. That was one more than enough for them to win, but hardly so many that it should have taken nearly three hours to complete the game.

Conlan noisily objected to the length of the game as he blew on his hands before opening the door to the umpire's dressing room.

"When I was playing, if the game lasted three hours, we scored thirty runs!"

Those old-time ballplayers were something else.

One of the substantial reasons why we were in the pennant race was the pinch-hit record of Jerry Lynch. His four-month total of eighteen hits in thirty-seven attempts was almost good enough to warrant his claim that he was the "best hitter in the majors now that Musial has had it."

Lynch offered one explanation of his record: "The good pinch-hitter is the guy who can relax enough to get the pitch he can hit. You almost always do get one pitch to hit every time you bat. So you have to have the patience to wait. And then you've got to be able to handle the pitch when you get it."

His explanation probably left the bat on the shoulders of most pinch-hitters, who don't know which pitch they can hit and which ones they can't, nor did it reveal any useful information to pitchers who had to face Lynch. It *did* suggest that Lynch knew what he liked and what he didn't like.

He didn't care for the Sheraton-Palace hotel.

"We check in yesterday and our room isn't ready. So Augie, my roomie, gets on the phone and bugs 'em about it. They hang up on him. Ha! So Freese *really* lets 'em have it!

"Eventually they send around a little-bitty maid about four feet tall. We stand around watching her clean up the room so we can go to bed. Half an hour later a dog starts barking next door! *He* shuts up and five minutes later a *duck* quacks! In a hotel! To hell with 'em."

Avery Robbins promised to put us up at another hotel in 1962 "if you win some ball games." For some reason or other this produced laughter in the clubhouse and a subsequent outburst from Whisenant. Pete's pique reached Himalayan heights as he stormed back and forth.

"Goddamn it, how can you laugh when you lose! Why aren't those outfielders out there takin' fly balls off the bat during batting practice? And why do the pitchers talk puss instead of working off the mound before the game? I'll tell you why. They don't care if they win the pennant or finish in the second division! Second division clubs never work at their trade. L.A. will. You watch them before we play those games next week!"

Whisenant picked up a baseball that had been laid out on the table to be autographed. He wound up, threw it into Otero's locker, and shouted, "—— on this ——!"

Hutchinson walked out of the clubhouse with a smile on his face. And Whisenant trailed after him as Lynch said, "Pete has to work it off, get it out of him, or he goes batty. We do it different."

"Maybe we need ten more Petes," said Kasko.

After the sixth inning we needed five more runs because Mays and Cepeda had hit two of Purkey's sliders out of the park. The wind currents that swirl around the Candlestick

Park pitching mound make the slider undependable. Sometimes it breaks, sometimes it doesn't. When it doesn't the sad slider pitcher may just as well take a warm shower, and Purkey did so. I pitched an inning and worked on my fork ball, which is an eccentric pitch, well suited to Candlestick Park. It worked well enough and when Pinson hit a three-run home run in the eighth inning we were down by just one run, and Whisenant's optimism returned. Briefly.

When Stu Miller relieved Sanford and retired the last five Red batters on eleven pitches Whisenant grabbed another ball and carried it purposefully toward the clubhouse. I thought Otero's locker would catch it again but Pete couldn't wait. He threw the ball far over the right field bleachers.

Which still left us short—and two games behind Los Angeles.

"Sy, don't look so downhearted," I told Burick when he came into the clubhouse. "I've just received virtual assurance that Cincinnati will win the pennant."

He eyed me with so much cynicism I thought I was looking at a mirror.

"Look," I said, and held up a small brocade silk bag and a wooden tablet. "These are *ofuda*. They were blessed by a Shinto priest at a rite performed at the inner sanctuary of Fudo shrine. We will now win or the gods will hear about it back in Kyoto."

Burick looked hopeful, I thought. "You don't think they came too late, do you?" he asked.

Having lost six out of seven games we needed some change of luck. The Japanese gentleman who had offered his prayers sent congratulations in advance. We were an off-beat choice to win the pennant anyway. Maybe we needed off-beat help. The Japanese gods might just be baseball fans; everyone else in Japan was. I stuck the small bag in my pocket, nailed the tablet to my locker, and walked out to the field.

Sherm Jones and I warmed up during batting practice by discussing etymology, specifically the derivation and usage of such words as "ofay," "spade," and "nigger." Jones admitted to a burning sensation in his pride while I prattled on about words not being things, and so who could take offense?

He said, "There was a time, if you asked me if I disliked the word 'nigger' I'da hit you. Now ain't that a bitch? That stupid reasoning is why this country's in the fix it's in!"

Politics leaves me cold. So we ran back and forth across the outfield in a parallel course with three Giant pitchers who must have forgotten to run during their batting practice.

"There's a big spade," I said, pointing to Sam Jones, "who is a hell of a pitcher so long as you don't call him a 'nigger.' "

"Sam's all right," said Jones.

"He's feelin' sad, I understand. Dark won't use him any more and he says he's looking for a job. As groundskeeper."

"Sam's all right," Jones insisted.

Jerry Lynch claimed it wasn't Sam's ears that bothered him.

"He's not thinking any more. Now I'm the hitter, see, and Sam has to throw me his best pitch to get me out. And that's Sam's curve ball. So he throws me four straight fast balls!"

Sam's last pitch to Lynch had gone for a pinch single to drive in the big run in our seventh inning rally. For six innings I'd squeezed my *ofuda* in vain while Ken Johnson held the Giants to one run. Vada Pinson had tied the score with a long home run to left center field off Mike McCormick.

Mike had claimed that moving pictures of his pitching motion had revealed to him an error in his technique.

"I wasn't getting on top of the ball," said Mike.

All season long it hadn't mattered to Pinson how McCormick threw the ball, just so it got to the plate. Vada then hit it as hard as he could and ran around the bases.

"See how easy it is?" Whisenant said, demonstrating Pinson's swing to the bench.

"Go get a fungo bat, Pete," said Gernert. "You're a coach now. Let the good lumber alone."

"Yeah, Coach," said Bell.

Hutchinson had announced that Whisenant had been taken off the active player roster and been made a coach. An extra catcher, Darrell Johnson, had been signed to a Red contract to take Pete's place.

"We'll miss you, Pete," I told him. "Now nobody will have

to pay any attention to you."

"Someday I'll be a manager," he promised, an inspirational thought almost worth celebrating. We also won the game, 8-1.

"We won the big ones all year, boys," Lynch said as we sat in the trainer's room waiting for Hutchinson to open the meeting.

"No use stopping now," said Kasko.

"The Dodgers have been playing good ball," said Hutch quietly. "They're hot, but they can be beaten. All of you who saw last night's game know that."

Many of the Reds had watched, on their night off, as Ernie Broglio shut out the Dodgers on five hits. I had watched *La Dolce Vita* myself and had left the theater happy I wasn't a winner because the sweet life looked a bit gamy. Hutchinson continued to recommend it, however.

"We *haven't* been playing good ball," he said. "You know it as well as I do. Don't you want to win? Don't you like money? There's five thousand dollars staring you in the face. Are you too lazy to pick it up?

"All year long they've been counting you out, and all year long you've kept coming back. Don't pay attention to them that are saying you've had it. Most of them never played anywhere before and they don't know what they're talking about.

"*I* know what you can do, and you do, too. Now let's go do it."

Hutch forgot to use the word "panic" but it must have occurred to him in the last of the first inning when the Dodgers put their first four batters on base off Joey Jay. L.A. had a two-game lead over us already. Give them two or three more games and they might disappear.

Jay convinced Hutch that everything would be all right when Hutch went out to talk to him. And, after calling Plate Umpire Pelekoudas a "big-nosed Greek" for not judging the pitches correctly, Jay retired the side, having given up just two runs.

Hutch expressed additional doubts as to Pelekoudas's competence when Chris called Pinson out on a high curve ball; but that didn't help us score any runs. Pelekoudas warned Hutch that he "would take just so much," an unfortunate phrase that evoked mutual words and gestures, such as graphic imitations of a benchload of ballplayers puking into a large bucket.

Pelekoudas, in the fifth inning, missed a strike on Robinson, irritating Dodger Pitcher Koufax, who hung a curve ball that Robby hit against the screen to drive in two runs and tie the score. It gave Robinson one hundred R.B.I.'s for the season.

"He had ninety-eight ten days ago," said Henry. "If he'd been hitting we wouldn't be in second place."

"Maybe that'll get everybody started," said Zimmerman.

Koufax pitched out the inning but embarrassed himself at the plate when he lined a clean single to right field and loped so slowly to first base that Robinson threw him out. Koufax never quite recovered.

Post homered in the sixth to break the tie. It gave Post a record of having hit a home run in each park in the league, remarkable for a man who played only against left-handed pitching.

Even the veteran Dodger players made mistakes. Whereas Koufax had run too slowly, Duke Snider ran too far, futilely trying to stretch a single into a double. L.A. was three runs behind at the time and Snider was just as valuable on first base. Pinson threw him out by ten feet and the crowd booed him back into the L.A. dugout.

"That's a 'rock,' right?" asked Zimmerman. "Should cost him twenty-five."

"In this series it might cost you a bill," I suggested. "Nobody can afford to make any mistakes now."

"Don't you try stealin' bases, Zimmerman," said Henry.

"What's a rock?" asked Ken Johnson.

"Any time you do something the manager knows you know you shouldn't, you pull a 'rock,' " I explained. "Hutch said in spring training that it would cost you twenty-five dollars."

"Any time Zimmerman tries to steal a base it's a 'rock,' " said Henry.

"Forget it, Gabby," said Zimmerman. "You should be glad Hutch doesn't fine you for hanging curve balls."

"You don't call 'em, I won't throw 'em," Henry said.

"Let's go!" I said as Jay retired the side in the ninth. "First man in the shower gets to sing tenor!"

In the Los Angeles Coliseum beer is not served in the visitors' clubhouse. Song-singing hardly matches beer-drinking as postgame refreshment, but that's all we had for the celebration.

A Bible preacher harangued the crowd gathered around our bus after the game. He turned his megaphone toward us just as we pulled away, entreating us to repent our sinful ways. . . . Another Dodger fan! Gene Freese advised him, loudly, to "Give it a rest!"

Why do they always pray for *winners?*

"Nobody Likes the Dodgers" was the title of a magazine article that I wrote on August 3, 1961. Written in fervid, perhaps fevered, ambition to prove a point which I lost in composition, the article purported to reflect the general opinion of millions of baseball fans and hundreds of ballplayers, some of them wearing Cincinnati uniforms. One specific complaint revealed in a phantom quote (a type of journalistic curve ball) that the Dodgers were a bunch of dirty ballplayers. And I didn't mean they neglected to use shaving cream or deodorants.

"Dirty" play is unsportsman-like, of course, but not unprofessional. It *sounds* derogatory, however, and a dedicated L.A. sportscaster asked the Dodgers to defend the charge.

"We asked Leo Durocher to answer you," the man told me, "but L.A. says Leo doesn't speak for the club. Alston does. And you know Alston. He won't say anything!"

Jim Gilliam, the L.A. utility man, said, "I've been playing for the Dodgers for ten years and nobody ever liked us." But he was feeling depressed at the time because of his batting average.

Facetiously I insisted that my motive was to help Dodger home attendance, since they were down some half a million from 1960. Dodger business manager, Harold Parrott, admitted that business picked up after the L.A. press printed various cries of indignation from those wounded who couldn't feel the difference between a needle and a knife.

At any rate, 72,000 customers attended the Big Double-Header. Some of them sat behind the Cincinnati bullpen and prepared epithets for my ears—when I showed up. One of them called Ken Johnson, who looks like me without glasses, a "Big Mouth." Johnson thought it was funny, because he doesn't wear glasses. I offered him my uniform shirt and a bottle of bourbon but he didn't want to play pretend so we both sat on the bench, out of sight. I never did get down to the bullpen.

Purkey and O'Toole pitched in two games, gave up just six hits between them, and allowed only ten Dodger batters to reach base. For eighteen innings the Dodgers looked like the Phillies, and we *knew* we could beat *them*.

Purkey had warned Doc Rohde before the first game that "My arm's sore. I don't know how long I can go. Give me some Capsolin every inning."

He had a four-run lead to work with before he made a single pitch. And in the third inning, after Larry Sherry had decked Robinson with a fast ball and Robby had hit the next pitch for a home run, Purkey echoed Lynch, who said, "There goes the Jolly Jew!"

Sherry was relieved by Alston, who brought in Perranoski.

"Let's see Whole Staff!" said Purkey, unnecessarily.

Stan Williams, the next L.A. pitcher, hit Vada Pinson on top of the head with a curve ball, and Vada was taken to the hospital.

"They'll probably send him to the San Fernando Valley Hospital so he misses the second game," said Lynch.

Pinson lay on the dressing table between games, however, insisting that he was all right. Hutch told him to rest.

"We're in good shape," he said.

Freese hit a low curve ball over the screen in the fourth to give O'Toole a one-run lead over Podres. That was all Jimmy really needed, but Freese hit another one in the eighth, with two men on, to make it look easy.

O'Toole bore down all the way, and his two-hitter was rewarded by Vin Scully, who declared him "Player of the Day."

O'Toole said, afterward, "I needed that twenty-five dollars

196

they gave me for the interview. I was right on E."

"You were a gas," he was assured.

Joey Jay stuffed six telegrams into his duffel bag as we packed for the trip home.

"That's a new personal record—six in two days. It's my birthday, of course."

We all had something to celebrate. By sweeping the series we'd regained first place, a full game ahead of L.A. The Reds were for real.

Cincinnati — August 18

"ALL you bullpen pitchers weigh in before you suit up," said Otis Douglas.

"Hutch wants to know if we're getting fat sitting around watching the starters go all the way," I said to Henry. "You look a little flabby Gabby."

Henry, lean and lithe, had maintained the same weight for seven years. "Picked up three ounces this month, I think. Gotta get more work. Let's pitch batting practice, Broz," he said.

"Save it. I've already worked five innings since the first of August."

"At a grand per inning, huh, Broz?" said Zimmerman.

"Only Musial makes that kind of dough."

The Cardinals were cheerful and chirrupy when they came from their dressing room. Since changing managers, St. Louis had played the best baseball in the league. And since they had four series with the Dodgers to play we welcomed the improvement. A nice long losing streak for L.A. would help make first place more comfortable for us.

"How's Musial hit the knuckle ball?" I asked Joey Jay as we watched Ken Johnson warm up to start the game.

"If Ken throws it in this game the way he is now, Musial and nobody else will hit it," said Jay, enthusiastically.

"Kenny's got it tonight," I admitted. "He ate the same meal, wore the same clothes, and took the same route to the park as he did the last time he won. How can he lose?"

"Are you superstitious, Broz?"

"Not as much as the fans who write in. I've received two lucky pennies, a double acorn, a real rabbit's foot, and a buckeye in the mail. With my Japanese charm I've got so much stuff in my pocket there is no room for chewing tobacco."

"Here, try mine," Jay said. "Did you hear where they're thinking of knocking down the left field wall and putting up temporary grandstands for the World Series?"

"If they'd just move that fence back sixty feet we might have a chance to get into the Series," I said.

"Maybe they're hoping Robby and Freese and Post will knock the wall down with line drives."

"Good idea. File it."

Gordon Coleman chipped a hunk of brick from the center field fence in the first inning, driving in three runs to give Johnson room to throw his knuckle ball. Musial liked it so little that he watched one third strike and waved at another.

"Ken's got a dandy bug tonight," chortled Edwards, who had trouble catching it even when it was a strike.

"Imagine Kansas City sending him to the minors this spring and telling him to forget about his knuckler," I said.

"Probably Charlie Finley's idea. He's telling everybody in the American League how to run their business. Wonder why fans always think they know more about baseball than the pros?"

St. Louis almost got back in the game in the seventh when Johnson tried to mix in some sliders and fast balls. Maybe his fingertips were sore. He gripped his knuckler with his fingernails. When Musial saw a fast ball instead of a bug, his eyes lit up, and his old reflexes reacted in a youthful and dangerous manner.

But Johnson held them to two runs and Robby got one back in our half. For the sixth straight day there were no phone calls in the bullpen.

"It's beginning to get lonely down here," I said to Henry.

"Hutch is gonna have an intrasquad game tomorrow and let us pitch it," he said.

198

"Do you remember where the mound is?"

My wife had suggested that we stay at a hotel with a swimming pool in order to get a sun tan before the summer ended. We found a beautiful pool, with a room attached, and bought bathing suits, beach robes, and sun-tan lotion. Naturally, it rained for three days.

"I thought you were having a good year," she complained.

"Look at it this way. It keeps the heat down."

It also kept the crowds down.

"The bullpen boxes should be filled already," I said to my brother when he'd finished throwing batting practice. "Lousy fans."

"Don't worry," he said. "You'll draw your million."

"Jeez, what a hell of a raise!"

"Maybe you'll be able to afford a new pair of shoes," Pat said, pointing at my slipshod feet.

"Those are the same shoes we've won with in the last five games," I said. "So long as I wear 'em I don't have to work."

"How *can* you lose then?" he said.

"Go peddle some insurance," I retorted. "Try Robby. After the season he's had he'll be worth a fortune."

Speculation on Robinson's prospective salary increase soared to a financial peak as the game progressed. He hit two singles and a double, drove in two runs, made a running, one-handed catch, broke up a double play with a shortstop-jarring slide, shrugged off a spike wound, and was showered with applause for nine innings.

Joey Jay did his best to match Robby's heroics. Jay gave up a triple and a single for the Cardinal's first inning run, but then allowed just two more singles the rest of the game.

"The big men are makin' it easy, Meat," I said to my wife as we drove back to the hotel.

"You're gonna have to back up to the pay window yourself if this keeps up," she said.

"Wonder if they'd let me sell hot dogs in the stands just to keep busy during the game."

"Relax and enjoy it," she insisted.

We pretended a lack of concern while the bartender fiddled with the radio trying to find out how the Dodger-Giant game was going on the Coast. L.A. had lost their fifth straight to Frisco the night before.

"They lost again!" the bartender said, smiling. "You guys are in. Where can I get some Series tickets?"

"What am I going to wear?" asked my wife.

"Don't count your furs till we get the little buggers skinned," I warned her.

The tremendous momentum which the Dodgers had built up in winning nineteen out of twenty-three games before we hit town had apparently left them in a rubble heap when Purkey and O'Toole stopped them cold. The double shutout was the first such calamity suffered by a Dodger club in twenty-five years. The effects were still showing for they'd scored just one run in losing two games to the Giants.

"Funny how a ball club suddenly can't do anything right after doing no wrong for so long," I said.

"Funny! I think it's hilarious!" my wife said. "Laugh, why don't you!"

"The Dodgers shouldn't feel so bad," my wife said as she read the sports page. "Philadelphia lost their twenty-second straight game yesterday."

"They don't have anything to gain even if they do win," I said, pouring my third cup of coffee. "Why do we drink stingers anyway?"

"To feel good," she said. "Those Philly players must feel awful. Don't they?"

"It's almost as bad as being in a long winning streak. The tension gets you more when you're winning. You almost feel relieved when you finally lose a game. In a losing streak you just don't want to go to the park. You *know* you're gonna lose, some way or other. I'd rather win no more than four in a row, and never lose more than two in a row. That's the easy way to win a pennant."

"You're still leading the league in E.R.A.," she pointed out.

"I haven't pitched in a week!" I said, forcing a smile.

"You sure don't look like it!"

"It's those damn stingers, I tell ya!"

The venerable cab driver who drove me to Crosley Field made more noise than the taxi meter, and less sense.

"Some of these hackies you'd think they'd played baseball all their lives the way they talk. Just 'cause our Reds are on top that's all ya hear, baseball! Why I never been to more than two games in my life—twenty-six years I been hackin'— and believe me, mister, I know more about baseball than any of 'em!"

"It must be an easy game to learn," I said.

"Your first game?" he asked. "You're gonna be early."

If I didn't look like a ballplayer at the time, I soon felt like one. The clouds that had covered Cincinnati for days pressed moist air over everything that wasn't refrigerated. A damp jockstrap is almost doubtfully utilitarian. I debated taking a chance—forget it. And the condition of my lucky shoes made them unwearable. I dressed, feeling clammy, signed a dozen baseballs, left passes for ten people, tore up all the fan mail in my locker, and trudged out to the field. It looked like a bad day.

"Why doesn't it rain and get it over with?" asked Zimmerman. "When's the last time we had a day off?"

"Tomorrow," I said. "Hang in there."

The Cardinals scored runs in the first, fourth, and fifth innings, while O'Toole griped about his support, the batters bitched about Plate Umpire Venzon's decisions, and 27,000 fans drank beer. Three-two beer. Nauseating.

Coleman tied the score in the last of the sixth, but Sherm Jones gave up four more runs in the next three innings to allow the Cardinals a 7-4 win.

"I didn't throw one pitch all day where I wanted to," he said, after the game. "You can't win like that, Road!"

I sympathized with him. In the bullpen, pitchers complain when they get too much work because their arms get tired; and they complain when they don't get enough work because their timing goes awry.

"All pitchers will work out at eleven tomorrow morning,"

said Jim Turner.

That killed the off-day. When you're having a bad day, it never rains.

The Giants had beaten the Dodgers three straight times to help us gain a three-game lead on the rest of the league. Both San Francisco and Los Angeles then headed our way for the last time in 1961. There were reports that Willie Mays was glad to get out of town.

"How can anybody spend four hundred thousand dollars in four years?" Nunn asked.

"Budget. You gotta budget," said Zimmerman.

"Mays's lawyer says Willie's broke and his wife is misrepresenting his net worth," I recalled from the paper. "I wonder if the judge would grant Mrs. Mays the right to sell Willie's right arm, or his bat? That would be better than alimony."

"How can anybody spend four hundred thousand dollars in four years?" Nunn repeated.

"You're just jealous 'cause you haven't figured it out, Howie," said Zimmerman.

"Mays's wife paid four hundred dollars for a pair of shoes, according to Willie," I said. "Maybe she thought the *Giants* were gonna win the pennant."

San Francisco's doughty sportswriters were, indeed, predicting a pennant. Alternating juicy gossip from the Mays divorce case with glowing reports of Giant triumphs, the sportswriters had taken over the front pages of the *Chronicle* and other Frisco fish-wrappers. In seventeen days the Giants had gained three games on Cincinnati and Los Angeles. At that rate they were a cinch to take over first place by October 5, four days after the season ended. There's no substitute for imagination in vivid journalism.

"I'd feel a lot better if we had a three-game lead when this week is over," Sy Burick said in the dugout before the double-header.

"Can you pitch, Sy?" I asked him.

"What's wrong with our pitching?"

"Nothing. Couple of tender arms is the only problem. We've got eight games in the next six days, though."

"Purkey says his arm's not tender, it's sore," Burick said.

"Yeah, but he's pitching, not sitting on his ass."

Purkey started the first game but his slider was as sick as his elbow and he had to leave in the third inning, trailing by five runs. The Giants batted around in the third and took so long doing so that a fan behind the bullpen said, "Come on, get 'em out. There's no room left on my score card!"

His humor regaled the customers around him and we had to listen to him all night long—those of us who didn't have to pitch. Even Maloney joined us, for the first time in two weeks. He warmed up for fifteen minutes to see if his shoulder tenderness would subside.

"Is she all right?" Henry asked, when Turner called from the bench to check on Maloney. Jim said he'd try it, which is akin to volunteering. He pitched an inning, then gave way to a pinch-hitter.

"The way he swings the bat Hutch oughta let Maloney hit," I said, knowing that if he had I wouldn't have to pitch the last two innings.

"Maybe his bat is tender, too," Henry suggested.

I had trouble staying on my feet in the next two innings but managed to maintain the *status quo*. (We trailed 5-3, and I had visions of winning, considering my luck.) Mays had knocked me over on a play at first base, but didn't hurt me. He *could* have. I was half-sprawled over the bag when Mays came roaring down the base line. He yelled in his high, squeaky voice, "Look out, man!" but slowed down just before bumping into me.

"Why didn't you tag him in the eye!" my wife asked me after the long night ended with the Giants on top twice, 12-2 and 5-3.

"I was lucky he didn't kill me!"

"That was the rowdiest crowd I ever saw at a ball game," she continued. "One loud-mouth criticized the Reds all night for their fielding and when a foul ball came near him he ducked away from it and let it hit a little old lady behind him!"

"Happens all the time," I assured her. "Little old ladies should wear baseball gloves at the ball park."

"Then there were two Detroit Tiger scouts here to look over you and Henry and Pinson. Is Detroit going to be in the World Series?"

"Maybe *they* will and *we* won't? What did they have to say?"

"I didn't hear. Two men started a fight and their language was so bad I couldn't listen."

"What were they fighting about?"

"They wanted to see Henry pitch. So did the scouts."

"Henry didn't," I said.

"Who could blame him? The only time you all looked good all night was when the scoreboard said the Cardinals beat L.A. You lose only half a game, right?"

It *seemed* like we'd lost two.

The next night, when Joey Jay threw a second strike to Amalfitano, leading off the game, Darrell Johnson, thinking it was strike three, threw the ball to third base.

"He'll probably hit one out now," said Henry.

When Amalfitano did line a ball against the left field screen, Hook said, "You dumb Texan! Don't anybody talk to Henry all night!"

Hook had no idea how long the night was going to be or he'd have considered a lesser punishment.

The game was a bit dull for eight innings, if you like hits and runs. Joey Jay gave up just two more hits and one of them was a cheap double that Freese should have caught inside the third base line.

Meanwhile, Marichal, the Giant pitcher, allowed only two men to reach first, a feat that so impressed Henry that he yelled—to himself—"Let's *never* score another run!"

"Shut up, Grumpy, you're interrupting our game," said Zimmerman. He and I were playing a game called "boats" in the corner of the dugout.

"Boats" is played by two persons, each of whom has a graph

of one hundred squares, ten of them shaded to symbolize a battleship (four dark squares), a cruiser (three squares), a destroyer (two squares), and a submarine (one square). Alternating calls, or shots, each player tries to detect the other's boats, isolating them as each series of calls hits or misses a shaded square.

Zimmerman led, two naval triumphs to one, as the ninth inning started, Joey Jay trailing, 2-0.

Willie McCovey doubled and Willie Mays popped to Blasingame in right field. When McCovey tagged up and headed for third Blasingame threw the ball on a bounce to Freese. The ball hit McCovey and Willie scored. Cepeda and Alou then hit home runs and Hutch brought me in.

Orsino hit a hanging slider as far as he could without getting a base hit in Crosley Field. Pinson caught it against the fence. Pagan singled through my legs and Marichal bounced a hit off my glove. I started to sweat.

Amalfitano grounded to third and I thought we were home free, but Freese juggled the ball, looked at second in time to see he couldn't make a play there, then threw to first too late to get Amalfitano. When Pagan tried to score all the way from second Coleman threw wide to the plate and Pagan slid home safely. The official scorer gave Amalfitano a hit.

Davenport hit a high slider off the top of the center field fence, where it bounced along the wall long enough for Davenport to circle the bases while Lynch and Pinson chased it. When McCovey singled Hutch took me out.

Henry relieved. Mays hit a home run. Cepeda singled and Alou grounded to third. Freese booted this ball, and left it lying in the dust while he prayed for surcease from the plague. Orsino hit a home run and Pagan struck out.

The Giants had set a record for scoring ninth-inning runs, and tied a record by hitting five home runs in one inning. (They had once before hit five home runs in one inning, against Cincinnati in 1939, the year the Reds won the pennant.)

Marichal had no trouble getting us out in the ninth, but the writers had a hell of a time getting in to ask Hutch what he thought about it all. Hutch had locked the door, called a meeting, and said, "Go get drunk or something! Try to do *something* right! You look awful!"

"I'm glad you're still alive," my wife said, when finally we got away from the park.

Our pitching staff had been mauled so badly in the last four games that Hutchinson decided to shake up the batting order. He benched Kasko and replaced him with Cardenas, a move that had paid off well the last time our pitching had looked so bad. Gernert replaced Coleman at first, and Whisenant, noting Coleman's depression, handed him a book: *How to Think Big.*

"This oughta help," said Pete.

"I've read it," said Coleman. "Also *How to Stop Worrying.* Neither of 'em helped."

Doc Rohde inadvertently disclosed that the bullpen might be shaken up for the night's game, too.

"Maloney took another 'bomber.' Is he pitching?"

"No," said Turner. "But he's in our bullpen."

Someone had killed the cricket that had sung in our latrine for a week. Some people get shook up about things like that, but we'd used up seven years' bad luck in one inning the night before.

"Things go bad just so long, then they have to get better," Rohde assured me as he oiled my arm.

"The worst already happened, before the game. Pinson's wife and Freese's wife both wore the same dress for the Family Night program."

Family Night is a Crosley Field feature in which the wives and children of the players parade to home plate to honor domesticity. Mrs. Pinson said she wouldn't walk out of the dugout. Mrs. Freese said she had to go home to change before the game.

The chances for a nice Family Night squabble looked promising.

Chico Cardenas posed with his cute young daughter for a Family Night picture album, and Post said, "Spider, your bambino looks like her momma. Pretty. Not like you, a mullion! Ha, ha!"

Cardenas forced a grin, the kind that small boys wear just before the Family Night squabble.

The ball game was anticlimactic, even though we won, 8-5.

Cardenas took it out on the Giants, hitting a single and two doubles, scoring three runs, and driving in three. Gernert also batted in one, and Maloney saved the win for O'Toole by retiring the last four Giant batters.

To cap it, and make every fan in the park feel like part of the family, the Cardinals beat the Dodgers 10-1, a score that was posted just before the ninth inning.

Suddenly everybody was happy again. (We were still three and a half games ahead.)

The Dodgers crawled into town August 25, dragging their ten-game losing streak behind them. They complained that they weren't ready for the final Big Series of the season.

"We can't do anything right," said Manager Alston. "And my bullpen is overworked."

Hutchinson played the same tune. "Robby isn't hitting and I've got just two starters for the four-game series."

What might have been billed as a headlong meeting of tough, young, would-be champions looked like it might degenerate into a waltz of punch-drunk old pros.

Desperately, General Manager Bill DeWitt of the Reds pointed out that a total eclipse of the moon was scheduled for ten o'clock, or just after the seventh inning of the ball game. Crosley Field was filled with fans who knew a bargain when they saw it. Waving thousands of red and white pennants that read "Root The Reds Home," the crowd clambered into the stands and clamored for Dodger blood. They looked a lot more excited than the players. Hutchinson dispensed with a reading of the Dodger lineup and advised us, merely, "We have a day game tomorrow. On day games following night games we all have looked logy, tired, dead-ass. The Dodgers have been playing worse than we have recently but they're not going to give us anything. So try and get some extra sleep after tonight's game."

"Let's grind it out, boys," said Whisenant.

Skies were clear, the night air was cool, a slight breeze blew in from right field as Bob Purkey opened the first inning with a pitch to Maury Wills. Wills singled and Gilliam promptly scored him with a triple.

"Perfect night for an eclipse," said a fan behind the bullpen.

We never did catch up, although Koufax, the Dodger pitcher, tried his best to help us out in the fifth inning. He walked two men and hit another to load the bases with none out. His wildness so disconcerted him that he stomped around the mound looking for his control. Alston came out to pat him on the back and assure him that the crowd was yelling not at him but for Pinson and Robinson, the next two Red hitters.

"We haven't had a big inning in a long time," Henry said, thoughtfully, in the bullpen.

Pinson and Robinson then hit the next two pitches, one straight up, the other on two hops to Wills, who started a double play to retire the side.

"Don't you think they should have to take a strike with the pitcher so wild?" asked Hook.

"They're the best hitters we got," I said. "They hit strikes, both of them."

"That's the ball game right there," said Henry.

The Dodgers hit three home runs just to make sure. In the seventh inning Henry had to warm up to pitch and he missed the eclipse, which wasn't total, after all. The fans booed, stowed their pennants away, and filed grumpily out of the stands.

"Why do we always look so lousy on Saturday?" Blasingame asked me as we sat at our lockers before the second game of the series.

"I didn't think I looked so bad," I said. "Too much sleep, probably."

"Look at John."

Edwards sat before his locker, his mouth swollen, his lower

208

lip cross-stitched to close the cut that had been inflicted by a bouncing curve ball.

"They give you an anesthetic, Big John?" I asked him.

"They're gonna give me a mask to wear when I warm you guys up," he muttered.

"Keep a stiff *upper* lip, anyway," I said.

"The paper calls us a bunch of ragamuffins," said Sisler.

"They should call us 'The Unpredictables,'" said Otero. "One day we play so lousy I can't sleep at night, then next day we play like champions."

"What's wrong with Hook?" I asked Joey Jay.

"Hutch just told him he's starting today."

"Well, they won't *kill* him. He looks like he's going to a funeral."

"What's Hutch tryin' to prove?" Jay asked.

Jay Hook hadn't started a game in two months, nor had he looked too good in relief.

"Well, he pitched some damn good ball last year," I said. "He ought to have *one* good game in him this year. It's worth a gamble, I guess."

"Great time to gamble," Jay grunted.

Hutchinson had predicted on the day before the season started that "Our young pitchers would carry us as far as we could hope to go." He had explained, during the All-Star break, that it was a matter of "everybody's doing his bit that is keeping us in the race." If Hook could, possibly, win this one big game, the psychological lift in team spirit might just carry the team all the way.

"Who's starting for L.A.?" I asked Jay.

"Podres. We haven't had a loud foul off him all year."

Whisenant insisted that I sit on the bench during the game. "The last time you did, we won. Where were you last night?"

"I'm not superstitious," I said. "Where, exactly, was I sitting? Did I have my legs crossed?"

"I don't know. But cross 'em, anyway. And your fingers, too. We're gonna need all the luck we can get today."

Hook's luck ran out in the second inning when the Dodgers punched five singles through and over the infield for four runs. Hutch took him out and tried five other pitchers. Four of us had reasonable success but Maloney had a rough seventh inning, giving up the last four Dodger runs. That gave L.A. a 10-1 lead.

Podres was so anxious to go out and celebrate the win that he forgot how to pitch in the last of the seventh. Three singles loaded the bases and Pinson cleared them with a grand-slam home run. Alston took Podres out, but we were still five runs behind.

"Now," said Waite Hoyt, the Cincinnati broadcaster, "if Hutchins had had a little pitching today, the Reds would still be in the game. Those four runs Maloney gave up look mighty big."

Maloney threw his wet sweatshirt at the clubhouse radio.

"That second-guessing old s.o.b.!" he yelled. "I guess he could do any better!"

My wife complained that her hands had turned ice-cold after the eighth inning. "I think I'll go back home tomorrow morning. I can't stand any more of this."

"Don't give up," I said. "Remember Scarlett O'Hara's famous line: 'Tomorrow *is* another day.'"

"That was the end of the movie, wasn't it?"

Pessimist.

Fred Hutchinson looked like a man with a problem almost too hard to solve as he sat at his desk in the manager's room before our scheduled double-header with L.A. A box of fan mail on his lap, two lineup cards in his hands, he seemed loath to make a decision. For seven days the Reds had looked like anything but a first-place ball club. A double loss could put Cincinnati in second place by nightfall. He looked out the window at a blue sky, full of sunshine, promising no rain. There was no getting around it. He had to make out a lineup; we had to play.

When he finally walked down to the dugout, he forgot the lineup cards and had to send the batboy back to the clubhouse so that the umpires could read the cards and officially start the game.

Among other changes he had decided to put Coleman back at first base and have Freese lead off the batting order.

Joey Jay wiped sweat from his face while the umpires huddled at home plate. "Get me some runs. I'll hold 'em," he said, half-audibly.

For six innings the game followed an inexorably anti-Red pattern. The Dodgers scored three runs off Jay and we could get just one back. Stan Williams, the Dodger pitcher, struck out ten batters and looked better every inning.

"Best slider *he's* ever had," Robinson muttered after Williams threw a third strike past him for the second time.

Joey Jay became increasingly depressed with his support and when Lynch let a fly ball drop for a double in the top of the seventh Jay's composure split. Hutch had to call for Henry to get the third out as L.A. went ahead, 5-1.

"Well, we'll beat Drysdale in the second game," said Whisenant. "He's never finished a game here."

Williams lost control of his slider in the last of the seventh. He had kept it low and away all day. When he hung the first one, Cardenas doubled. And after Kasko had walked, Freese hit another hanger off the left field screen to cut the Dodger lead to one run.

"Remember, boys. We won the big ones all year. And this is a big one! Right, Bross?" Whisenant said.

I nodded, picked up my glove, and pitched a scoreless eighth. The nervous despair that had gripped our bench all game changed to nervous excitement as the Dodgers took the field.

With one out Lynch hit a ground ball to second and Charlie Neal booted it. Cardenas tripled off the scoreboard and Post, batting for me, doubled down the left field line to put us ahead by a run.

O'Toole threw just four pitches in getting the last three outs. The Dodgers looked a little shocked as they filed down the ramp to their clubhouse. Whisenant took it all in stride.

"That's the way to come from behind, boys. Now let's rack Drysdale."

Pinson hit a two-run home run in the first inning of the

second game and Drysdale walked the next two batters. His temper threatened to get completely out of hand as his pitches strayed farther and farther from the strike zone. Alston had two pitchers warming up, and three minutes of fatherly advice for Drysdale. Alston's words calmed Drysdale sufficiently for him to fan Bell, and when Lynch tried to steal third, Roseboro caught him for the third out.

"Jesus, you can't have Jerry running in that situation!" Whisenant whispered at the north end of the bench. Five heads nodded agreement as six pairs of eyes looked southward at Hutchinson, who kicked the bat rack.

"We're all a bunch of second-guessers," I mumbled to O'Toole.

We'd lost a chance at a big inning, and Drysdale settled down for five innings until Ken Johnson hit a bases-loaded double to finish Drysdale for the day.

"First time I ever knocked a pitcher out of the box!" Johnson crowed when the inning had ended.

"Just don't get knocked out yourself, Rooms," I encouraged him as he headed back to the mound.

Leo Durocher, the Dodger coach, who had led all the bench jockeys when L.A. led by four runs in the first game, retreated to the back of the Dodger dugout. The Dodgers were doleful, but not dead. They knocked Johnson out in the eighth, and, after I stopped them there, they loaded the bases with two out in the ninth.

Hutch came out and said, "Why don't we let Henry strike Moon out and get this over with?"

"Why not?" I agreed.

Pittsburgh — August 29

TWENTY-FOUR hours after the Dodgers had crawled back out of town still three games behind, the Reds' general manager, DeWitt, announced that he had signed Hutchinson to a new, two-year contract.

"Hutch received a substantial raise," said DeWitt.

"Do you think DeWitt will give everybody who has a

good year a two-year contract?" I asked Joey Jay.

"Did Hutch have as good a year as Robby?" Jay countered.

"There may not be enough money left for us," I said.

"You can't have a much better year than you're having," he said, graciously.

"Neither could you," I responded in kind. And, patting each other on the back, we walked into the Pittsburgh clubhouse.

I undressed, put on a jockstrap, and lay down on the rubbing table. Robinson was two steps behind me and tried to push me off.

"Regulars first, Professor!" he said.

"Bird seed! You've been on this table more than you've been on base lately," I said. "I just got hurt. Doc's tryin' to figure out what's wrong."

"What did you do?"

"Slipped off the side of the swimming pool and hurt my neck."

"Fell off a *bar* stool more likely!" he said.

"Never happen," I assured him.

Rohde examined my neck, spine, and shoulder but could find nothing out of place. Otis Douglas watched Rohde probe and tug.

"Maybe it's just contracted," Douglas said. "Why don't I put a little pressure on it and see if I can't pull it loose."

Douglas gripped my head firmly by the jaws and pulled, steadily, for several minutes.

"Look at Broz!" said Bell. "His neck's a foot long!"

I felt the muscle spasm relax slightly but when Douglas released the pressure I still couldn't turn my head more than three inches.

"It's no use, Doc. I can't pitch tonight," I said. "Besides, I can't get the Pirates out anyway."

Turner told me to rest, sit on the bench, and keep the pitching chart. For the first time all season I was free to relax during the game knowing I was unable to work and so couldn't be asked.

I didn't know whether to cry or laugh it up. The injured

professional frequently is uncomfortable. His job is more in jeopardy when he can't work at all than when he's working badly. While I made out the pitching chart for the night's game I wondered who Hutch would use in my place if O'Toole got in trouble late in the game.

For five innings neither O'Toole nor the Pirates' Bob Friend were in any trouble to speak of. Still, the Red batters complained:

"Alice ain't got a thing!"

"I don't know how Friend gets away with that crap!"

"She's not throwin' hard enough to bruise your eye!"

The protests did more harm to Friend's psyche than to his E.R.A. But his luck wasn't anything to bet on. It just wasn't the Wonderland of 1960, where Friend and the Pirates were big winners. In the sixth inning Pinson reached third on an error, scored on Coleman's single, and represented the winning run when Friend left the game for a pinch-hitter in the seventh.

"Poor Alice," said Purkey.

"To hell with him. He didn't have a chance," said Whisenant. "This is our part of the game, boys. Let's grind it out!"

Robinson tripled home an eighth-inning run and scored himself on an infield out. We needed the extra runs in the ninth when the Pirates loaded the bases with two out. Hutch took O'Toole out and waved to the bullpen for Maloney.

"How are you going to pitch Nelson?" Hutch asked Maloney.

"I'll get ahead of him, then give him my good curve," said Maloney, breathing deeply.

"You better throw him your good hummer," Hutch warned him. "Forget the curve ball."

Nelson ran the count to 3-2, hit two foul balls high into the right field stands, one of them just a few feet outside the line, and then struck out.

"I let it *all* hang out on that last one!" Maloney said.

Hutchinson laughed. Weakly.

Les Biederman, the Pittsburgh *Press* sportswriter, said, "I've just made my plane reservations to Cincinnati for the third game of the Series. You're in, aren't you?"

"Sure, Les, why not?" I said. "What did L.A. do today?"

"Podres won it, 5-2."

"That means if we lose we're only two and a half games ahead, right? With twenty-two games to go. Right?"

"Yes, but you've got everything going for you. Just like the Pirates did last year. That's the way it goes in the National League. Each year there's a team that's just bound to win. This year it's Cincinnati."

"Let's start the Series next week then. This tension is getting to me," I said.

Turner gave me the pitching chart again, partly because he's just as superstitious as the next pitching coach, and partly because I still couldn't turn my neck.

"Stay out of swimming pools," said Rohde.

"Let me stretch it one more time," said Douglas.

"Why don't we let it rest, Otis?" I said. "We got two off-days in a row comin' up and it's taking ten minutes now for each Scotch to reach my stomach."

"The boys suggest you don't read so much and hurt your neck some more," said Whisenant.

"Tell the boys to get some goddamn runs and they won't have to worry about it," I bristled.

Robinson insisted that we weren't going to have any trouble with Tom Sturdivant's pitching because "All he's got is a knuckler and you can see that comin' and still hit his fast ball."

After the first inning it looked like an interesting evening for knuckle-ball students. Purkey gave up a single to Virdon and a triple to Groat, the first two men in the Pirate lineup.

"Both pitches were sliders," Purkey said after the inning was over. "I guess I'm going to have to be a one-pitch pitcher tonight. I'm going to throw my knuckle ball till it kills me."

Purkey's knuckler, when it's working, is even more difficult to catch than Ken Johnson's. In four innings Purkey made three wild pitches and Darrell Johnson, the Reds' catcher, was charged with two passed balls as Purkey's knuckler danced wildly.

"Toughest four innings I ever caught," Johnson said. "His ball moves three ways."

Whisenant had suggested an unorthodox move to guard against a wild Purkey pitch when Pittsburgh put men on second and third with the pitcher, Sturdivant, hitting.

"Why not bring Lynch in from left and put him behind the plate? Throw nothing but hard knucklers. He ain't gonna hit the ball anywhere."

Just then a pitch bounced off Johnson's glove and Burgess scored from third.

"See. It would have worked!" Whisenant said.

"I think it's against the rules, Pete," Sisler told him.

"I think it's too late," said Jay.

Eleven thousand women attended the Ladies' Day game. Ten thousand of them didn't know a passed ball from a sacrifice fly but they shrieked heartily for each Pirate put out. Three of them were struck by line drives hit foul by Cincinnati batters.

We didn't hit many line drives fair, and had just two hits as the ninth inning started. Robinson pinch-hit for Chacon to get things started but was an easy out, just like the rest of the lineup had been all night. Pittsburgh won, 3-1.

"Hang in there," Biederman advised me after the game. "Next time you come in here you'll have it cinched."

We were scheduled to play in Pittsburgh on the last weekend of the season.

"What else is new?" I asked.

Philadelphia — September 2

AFTER an early evening supper on September 1 I was sitting in my Philadelphia hotel room, counting my current blessings. Avery Robbins had passed out the pay checks after the morning workout on our second straight off-day. My neck felt so much better I could almost look over my shoulder to see if the Dodgers were catching up to us. And the 1961 season had just entered its last month.

A sheet of Hotel Warwick stationery on the desk before me was covered with mathematical formulae. Just as I had figured out how many games L.A. would have to lose in order for us to win the pennant by playing .500 ball the rest of the month, the phone rang.

"Honey," my wife said, "I just decided how to fix your neck. Tell Hutch to get you drunk."

"I can do that myself," I insisted. "Besides, he's in New York for the Yankee-Tiger series. Scouting future opponents or something."

"Reason I mentioned it," she continued, "Kimberlee is walking around with my robe on and she looks pregnant."

"She's only fourteen months old!" I said.

"Yes. Well, remember when I was carrying her I had a muscle spasm like yours and I fixed it with five martinis? When I woke up, my neck was fine."

"Everything's going to be all right," I said. "Incidentally, I'm reading Lawrence Durrell. He says that sex is the only proper field for the deployment of man's talents. Do you think I'm in the right profession?"

"You're in the right town right now, you bastard. It's your muscle spasm I want cured. Did you hear that Milwaukee fired Dressen?"

"Yes. How about that? Milwaukee must figure they're out of it. The Giants blew their chance, too. It's us and the Dodgers."

"Hurry up and get it over with," she insisted.

Hutchinson listed Jerry Lynch in the starting lineup for the first game of the Philadelphia series. Lynch's chances to break all the pinch-hitting records seemed remote so long as Robinson's slump continued. Although Lynch's big bat is not as potent when he plays regularly, it was sorely needed. (And Jerry had decided to think of himself as a pinch-hitter every time he came up with men on.)

In the fourth inning Pinson homered to tie the score and, after Robinson walked, Lynch lofted a curve ball over the right field fence. Joey Jay had a permanent lead for the night.

Jay was after his sixth straight win from the Phillies and they made it as difficult as possible. For them. They seemed determined not to let us sweep the entire season's series of twenty-two games, and we had just six more games to play together. For a young club that looked so good they couldn't be all that bad.

Jay staggered into the ninth, his curve ball hanging. Dalrymple singled and, with two out, Herrerra batted for the pitcher. Jay quickly threw two strikes to the big Cuban.

"Come on Joe, let it all hang out," I said as Henry and I watched from the bullpen where we had been throwing.

Jay reached back for a little extra, wound up, kicked his leg so high he almost fell back off the mound, and threw his best hummer. It hit Herrerra right in the ass. Taylor doubled home one run and Hutch called Henry in to save the game. Gabby threw three straight balls, then three straight strikes.

"I think you're getting the feel of this thing, Gab," I told him in the shower. "Drama. That's what we want."

In losing seventeen straight games to Cincinnati the Phillies had done everything but forfeit a win. Each day they showed up, swung the bat (wildly, at times), threw the ball (wildly, at times), and ran the bases (infrequently). Inevitably they trailed by one or more runs in the late innings.

"And they never come from behind to win," said Larry Merchant, the *Daily News* sportswriter. "I don't think they've won ten games all year after the sixth inning."

Hutchinson explained that there was nothing unusual about the way in which the Reds beat the Phillies.

"It's the same reason why we're leading the league," he said. "We've got pitching and hitting. That's all baseball is—pitching and hitting."

It all sounded so easy. The drizzle that prevented us from taking batting practice added to the stifling humidity. Baseball in the fall usually has a crispness that often has seemed muffled by summer heat. But whereas the 1961 summer had been pleasantly cool, September had arrived in a cloud of steam.

"Summer's finally arrived, Joey," I said to Jay. "We

shouldn't run too much then. Save ourselves for the stretch."

"How many miles have you run this season, Howie?" Jay asked Nunn.

Nunn claimed that he counted every one of his steps from spring training till October. "I've got more miles run than innings pitched, I know that," he said.

Philadelphia started Jim Owens, a right-hander whom we hadn't faced all year. He didn't look any better than the others. Lynch tripled in the second inning and scored on a fly ball.

"There's your lead, Tootie," Lynch said. "Hold 'em."

The Phillies' batting order looked the same and swung the same as always. O'Toole breezed into the fifth inning, heading for a quick win. He walked Amaro to start the inning, and Dalrymple bunted. O'Toole ran off the mound, reached for the ball, slipped on the wet grass, and fell down.

His *faux pas* apparently embarrassed O'Toole for he then walked the pitcher to load the bases. Taylor hit into a double play, Amaro scoring to tie the game. It looked like we were out of the inning, for O'Toole normally has little trouble with Callison. But Tootie hung a high pitch in Callison's eyes and he hit it off the scoreboard.

"Look at Tootie!" Zimmerman said. "He's so mad he could spit!"

"Hutch is li'ble to chase him into the stands if he has another inning like that one," said Nunn.

"Let's get it back," said Maloney.

Owens wasn't giving anything up, though, and when the rain halted play in the seventh inning, Philadelphia still had a 2-1 lead.

Maloney warmed up just after the umpires decided to continue the game. Forty-five minutes had elapsed and O'Toole's arm had apparently stiffened. Hutch decided to change pitchers and use a pinch-hitter for O'Toole when he led off the eighth. Hutch phoned to the bullpen, asked if Maloney was ready, and called him in to bat for O'Toole.

"Jesus. Tits is a pretty good hitter but that's a bit much, Hutch!" I thought to myself.

"We sure as hell got better hitters than him, Broz, haven't we?" asked Zimmerman.

"Maloney's just cocky enough to hit one outa here," said Nunn.

He didn't. And when Freese popped up, the situation looked a little desperate. Our seventeen-game winning streak was on the line. But Chacon doubled and Pinson, whose bat was as hot as Robinson's was cold, singled Elio home with the tying run.

"Now, hold 'em, Tits!" yelled Lynch.

Maloney retired just two men in the eighth, however, as Philadelphia scored the tie-breaking and eventual winning run.

"That's the way it goes," said Maloney after the game. "Did you dig that new wrestling hold on TV last night?"

Get 'em tomorrow, Scarlett O'Hara.

"What time do we get into St. Louis tonight?" Nunn asked before our final game in Philadelphia.

"About midnight, I guess. If we get these two games in," I said. "Why?"

"I'll be glad to get outa here."

"Don't be in such a hurry. We're playin' the team that's last in hitting and pitching. The Cardinals are leading the league in pitching and hitting. Wouldn't you rather play Philly the rest of the year?"

"Not in this town."

"I hear that Detroit is rootin' for L.A. to win the pennant," said Zimmerman.

"Best the Tigers can hope for is second-place money anyway," I said. "That's a pretty good chunk if the Dodgers and the Yankees get in."

"*We'd* probably be just as well off finishing second to L.A., wouldn't we?" asked Zimmerman.

"Somebody figured out that second place is worth $3,500 in a New York–Los Angeles series," I said. "We'd get more than that if we get in the Series against New York."

"Not much more," Henry said.

"Don't be such a grouch," said Zimmerman.

Our chances remained good only so long as we won. The Dodgers hadn't quit yet, and some die-hard experts who had made Cincinnati a preseason pick for sixth place insisted that the Dodgers still had the better players.

Kasko smiled for the first time in a week when Hutch told him he was starting the first game of the double-header.

"I must have impressed him with that fly ball I hit yesterday," said Kasko. "Maybe I'm out of my slump."

With Chacon on first to lead off the game, Kasko hit a home run into the left field stands, which proved Hutch's hunches were still hot. Ken Johnson needed no more help than that except for twenty-seven put-outs. He got them, three at a time, and made it look easy.

"I never thought I'd last," Johnson confessed between games.

"Is that right? It looked like such a breeze we let the fans come in the bullpen," I told him. "Two broads. Pigs is what they were."

"You guys got it made down there," he said.

"If Hunt goes all the way in this next game we might just!"

Hunt's blistered finger pained him in the fourth inning, however, and Hutch took him out after the Phils scored two runs on three walks, a stolen base, and a wild pitch.

Mahaffey, the Phils' pitcher, worked confidently from then on, as if he needed no other help. When Sherman Jones gave up three more runs the Philly fans above our bullpen crowed loudly, "You bums! If it weren't for the Phillies all year Cincinnati would be in sixth place!"

There might have been a sportswriter among them, come to think of it.

In the ninth inning Robinson doubled and Coleman singled him to third. On the throw in from the outfield Mahaffey fumbled the ball when Catcher Clay Dalrymple yelled to him to cut it off, and Robinson headed home. Mahaffey turned to throw the ball to the plate but Dalrymple was looking for his teeth, which had fallen out of his mouth in the excitement. Robinson slid under him safely.

That was good for one run and one laugh and wasn't enough to keep us from losing 5-3.

St. Louis — September 5

ALTERNATING days of delight and despair we bumped along, winning one then losing one. The day after winning was full of anticipation—World Series loot, pennant raises, champagne. Only to be followed by a loss and subsequent black moods when each player looked back on those particular games in which his error or failure had cost a ball game. Had *I* just, for instance, not blown those two leads to the Cubs, we'd be four games ahead, not two.

My concentration drifted from the cards in my hand and I said, "Two spades" instead of "Two clubs." Joey Jay raised to game and went down two tricks, vulnerable.

"What were you thinking about, partner?" asked Jay.

"Champagne. Let's eat. Bus leaves in an hour for the park."

Hutchinson chased the sportswriters, glove and shoe salesmen, and other hangers-on from the clubhouse before the game and suggested that each player pay close attention to what he had to say.

"Apparently there are some guys on this club who can't, or aren't, taking this thing seriously. They know who they are because I've already talked to them. And they know now what it costs not to take this seriously. We're fighting for a pennant. And we've got eighteen games left to play. I don't think I'm asking too much for you to bear down for eighteen more games.

"There's five thousand dollars at stake for each of you. Don't you guys want money? That's what you play for! It means a lot to win a pennant. A lot to me, to you, to your family. You won't always get the chance you've got this year. So make the most of it."

The Cardinals, as a hitting club, didn't seem to interest him. He waved the score card away and said, "You know how to pitch to these guys by now."

I ran out to the outfield and looked around for soul-pained

faces and empty pockets of the guilty night owls.

"Who was it, Pete?" I asked Whisenant.

"I can't tell you," he said. "But I'll say this. Hutch told me there's two things a young ballplayer has to learn early in baseball: Never borrow money from your club, and never try to fool your manager!"

"There's another thing you might add," I said. "After you get your ass chewed go out and beat the hell out of somebody."

For four innings we didn't even get a hit and I walked over to the bat rack to see if the bats had been left out all night. They looked a bit logy so I shook them up, banging them back and forth in their slots, and yelling: "Wake up!"

"The Professor's flipped, Robby," said Pinson, nudging Robinson and smiling till Hutch stared him down.

In the fifth inning we scored one run, and in the sixth Pinson and Robinson both scored on Lynch's double.

"That's the way to shake 'em up. Right, Hutch?"

Purkey never looked better, and the Cardinals never even threatened to score until the ninth. Musial twice took third strikes, attesting to Purkey's good stuff. Musial did not complain. He never had to. The umpires never missed any pitches on him. Great hitters always get the benefit of any doubt.

"I had the best slider I've had all year," Purkey told the reporters after the game. "And a great knuckler."

"How'd they get six hits?"

"You didn't *have* to say that, Broz!"

Apologizing, I handed him a beer.

Avery Robbins pulled back a chair from our table in the Hotel Chase dining room. He sat down, sighed deeply, and said he was too tired to eat.

"What's the matter, Avery?" I asked. "You've got it made. One more road trip is all that's left."

"I'm tired," he said.

"Relax. We've all got it made. Nine days off in the next three weeks. The Dodgers play every day but two."

"They should have my problems," he insisted. "Listen, you

know how many requests for Series tickets I've had? Fifty. And they're not even printed yet. Why, I had a phone call from the surgeon that operated on my father-in-law's nose! He wants six Series seats! I hardly know the guy. It's ridiculous. I think I'll go hide somewhere if we win this thing."

Robbins shook his head at the horrible thought of it, and ordered a bowl of onion soup. Nibbling a round of Melba toast he stared at another group of ballplayers who gabbled noisily at the next table.

"Tie a ballplayer's hands and he'd never be able to carry on a conversation," said Robbins.

Joe Nuxhall, the indicated talker, ended his story and laughed heartily. He waved at us and at every other ballplayer who came into the dining room. Nuxhall had spent two years in the Cincinnati bullpen moaning about how nice it would be to be somewhere else, "suckin' up a couple of Hudies," a beer brewed in Cincinnati. Hutch had reluctantly sold him to Kansas City during the winter of 1960; Nuxhall played baseball with hearty, aggressive enthusiasm.

"You got away just in time, Nux," I said.

"Suck it up, Prof!" he said. "I come all the way from K.C. on my day off just to see you all."

My last recollection of Nuxhall watching a ball game in St. Louis included the painful memory of my being bombed off the mound by the Cardinals. It wasn't his fault, of course, but it was the kind of coincidental omen that stuck in my augury-oriented mind.

The Cardinals quickly quashed Joey Jay's ambition to pitch his twentieth win of the year. Flood doubled and, after Jay retired Javier, White singled. Flood tried to score from second and Crawford, the plate umpire, called him both "out" and "safe," finally settling on "safe."

After Musial and Boyer singled, Jay was relieved by Maloney, who retired the side. Freese doubled home two runs in the second to tie the score and Larry Jackson then threw thirteen straight balls and forced home a third run.

"Cocky's pitched five complete games this year and walked nobody," I recalled. "Never saw him so wild. How can he stand himself?"

"How can Keane keep him in there?" said Whisenant.

Cardinal Manager Johnny Keane didn't even come out of the dugout to talk to Jackson, who retired the side with no further scoring.

Kasko booted two ground balls to give the Cardinals the tying run in the last of the second. Jackson gave back the lead in the third, and Maloney let St. Louis tie it in the fourth. Lynch homered in the sixth, but Blasingame and Coleman booted two ground balls in the last of the sixth as St. Louis went ahead, 6-5.

"*Nobody* wants the damn game!" Gernert complained. "This is ridiculous."

Jackson, deciding he wanted the win, shut us out in the seventh and eighth, just before the Cardinals blew the game wide-open. I got the first man out, but Musial, who had by now learned how to hit my slider, doubled down the line. Boyer walked, James doubled, Grammas and Sawatski singled to right, and Jackson doubled to right center. I hadn't given up an earned run in over six weeks, but when Flood hit Nunn's first relief pitch for a single I was charged with five big ones.

What the hell. If you're going to have a bad day have a *bad* one.

Cincinnati — September 8

AMONG other interested gamblers who appeared on the Cincinnati side of the Ohio River during the weekend series with St. Louis were fifteen hundred members of a cavalcade assembled to "Root The Reds Home."

We still had a one-game lead, despite the Dodgers' luck in drawing San Francisco as an opponent for the previous four games. The Giants had lost all four and then had flown back home, with the Dodgers in hot pursuit. While we had to fight off the Cardinals, San Francisco hosted L.A. in a weekend series. The Giants had lost pretensions to pennant glory and now were battling the Cardinals for fourth place.

"We should offer to do the Giants a favor by taking two

out of three here while they win two from L.A.," I suggested to Nunn.

"Why don't you dream at night?" he grumbled.

The waitress at Caproni's restaurant beamed at us when we ordered a pregame bowl of clam chowder.

"I've become a baseball fan again now that you fellows are in first place. You sure are bringing us plenty of business."

"Would you call her a front-runner, Rooms?" Nunn whispered.

The caravan of Red rooters marched around the stands, scaring up more laughs than cheers as the Reds took the field at eight o'clock. An airplane boomed across the sky, its jet speed breaking the sound barrier.

"You know what'll happen, Road," I said to Jones as we sat down in the bullpen. "We'll win the pennant and Khrushchev will drop a bomb on New York and ruin the Series."

"We wouldn't have to play the Yankees then, would we?" he noted.

Hutchinson had his pitching lineup in its most effective pattern for the three games. Jim O'Toole, the best pitcher we'd had for the last two months, led off against Ernie Broglio.

O'Toole gave in first, the Cardinals scoring two runs in the fourth inning. Jimmy had been consistent in his pitching in his last seven starts, giving up no more than two or three runs in any of them. Unfortunately he couldn't get any runs to work with.

Broglio shut us out for seven innings, and should have weathered the eighth except for an error. Given one break we looked for another. Broglio hung a curve to Robinson and he hit it off the top of the scoreboard to tie the score.

I had warmed up, ignoring the boos of the crowd and the advice of a fan who suggested I give up five more runs and "look more like yourself, you bum."

Hutch put me in anyway and I worked two scoreless innings. Boyer did dribble a hit through my legs, causing Hutchinson extreme pain.

"Don't we have one goddamn pitcher who can field a ground ball?" He yelled from the dugout.

226

The ball had been hit more softly than I was used to and I had flinched when it came my way. Musial hit the next slider with more authority, the line drive bouncing off Coleman's glove before Gordy had a *chance* to flinch. That break helped me settle down and Schoendienst popped up to end the inning.

Gus Bell led off the tenth inning with a single off Broglio, so Keane brought McDaniel in to pitch. Blasingame bunted Chacon (running for Bell) to second base, and Kasko singled to left. When Charlie James fumbled the ball in left field Chacon scored easily and I tripped on the dugout steps in my haste to shake everybody's hands.

Hutchinson helped me to my feet and patted my back.

"Don't get hurt," he said. "You're gonna win some more before we're through."

That was a pleasant prospect. I'd already won nine, lost three, a winning percentage that I knew was worth a raise for '62.

A sheet music publisher had printed copies of two songs written by competing Cincinnati band leaders. The lyrics celebrated the cause of the Reds, and a hundred requests were made to working musicians by the thousands of Red rooters who infested the town. The musicians were understandably offended by both the saccharine music and the off-beat renditions. But then, heat and humidity may have had something to do with their pique.

Cincinnati's summer weather, a combination of high temperature and higher humidity, annually makes a mockery of the weather bureau's Comfort Index. The warmth generated by night-long celebrations of our Friday night victory over the Cardinals was emphatically exaggerated by the next morning's sun. Panting groups of sweating humanity crowded into Crosley Field for the afternoon ball game.

The first order of the day in the bullpen called for a general hosing down of the roof, steps, and floor before the game. Some of our pitchers wore their thin cotton undershirts for the first time all season. And Doc Rohde placed a bottle of salt tablets on each water fountain, in the bullpen and in the dugout.

Jim Turner came out to the bullpen to urge Henry and me to sit in the air-conditioned dugout for six innings.

"Can't do it, Colonel," I said. "There aren't any tobacco chewers up there. Can't enjoy a ball game without a chew, can I?"

"We'll get you a carton," he assured me and led us to Hutch's lair, where Otis and Pete growled and roared in our ears for the next seven innings.

Ken Johnson and Curt Simmons shut each other out until the fourth, when walks to Robinson and Gernert and a single by Post loaded the bases with one out. John Edwards then took a called third strike, annoying Hutch and enraging Whisenant.

"If Edwards comes back here and says 'Pick me up' to Johnson, I'll club him!" said Whisenant. "He's been doin' it all year long!"

"Forget it, Whiz," I said. "Watch my Roomie rack up a couple of runs."

Johnson blooped the first pitch for a two-run single, and Whisenant yelled in Edwards's ear, "That's the way to pick everybody up!"

Sawatski hit a home run for St. Louis in the fifth inning, and in the seventh we gave the Cardinals two runs and the lead. With two out and two on, Schoendienst hit a pop fly up over the mound. As the wind blew it back toward the plate, Gernert charged in from first base, lunged for the ball, got a glove on it, and dropped it. One run scored. Johnson then struck out Cunningham but the pitch went through Zimmerman and the tie-breaking run scored.

St. Louis gave us a run back in the seventh on two walks, a bunt and a long fly ball; and the game remained tied until the twelfth.

We had one chance to win in the ninth after I had pitched two scoreless innings. With two outs Bell singled Cardenas to third and Kasko fouled off seven pitches with the count on him 3-2. I groaned aloud after the seventh foul ball skipped

228

just outside the left field line.

"Why not win another for Ol' Broz, boys?" said Whisenant. "You don't mind, do ya, ya big dummy!"

"You da babe, Pete," I said, sweating.

Kasko finally struck out, and Henry pitched three more scoreless innings. In the twelfth Cardenas led off with a double. Henry batted for himself with a ton of pressure riding on him. He was after his first hit in two years and his first win in four months. A little-bitty single would do it.

He struck out. And so did Kasko. But Freese walked and Robby singled to end the game.

"Nice sucking up those easy wins, Gabby," I said in the clubhouse.

Henry frowned, unhappily. "I *know* I'm a better hitter than that!" he said.

Texans are never satisfied with a *little* glory.

Coupled with the Giants' two straight wins over L.A. in San Francisco our latest winning streak (two games) gave us a lead of three games and made the weekend look like the Big One worth all the celebrating.

The rooters brought along a Dixieland band, a line of chorus girls, and an acrobat to entertain themselves. Their pregame show put everyone in a festive mood. Hutch smiled. Bill DeWitt sat with his family in a front-row box next to the dugout and beamed. Whisenant passed out dark glasses to the benchwarmers.

"We're gonna wrap it up today, boys," he insisted. "The Dodgers have had it."

Bob Purkey explained that his slump was over and he was ready to win again.

"All those home runs they were hitting off me," he said, "didn't come off bad pitches. The hitters were looking for certain pitches so I changed my pitching pattern. Now I've got my knuckle ball working and I'll use those other pitches to get ahead, and get 'em out with the knuckler."

The Cardinals managed to get just five men on base off Purkey, and made just two hits, both singles. Purkey threw just ninety-five pitches, making my job easy keeping the pitching chart.

"Get it over with quick, Purk," I said. "I got a plane to catch after the game."

Wally Post hit a three-run home run in the sixth inning to clinch the win.

"Did you see that stroke!" said Lynch, as Post trotted around the bases. "I'd give a hundred grand for his stroke and I'd hit seventy-five homers a year! I tell him and tell him, 'Quick hands, short stroke, Wally,' but he doesn't always do it. Stubborn Indian."

Post's homer knocked Sadecki out of the box and Whisenant yelled to Johnny Keane when he went out to relieve the young left-hander, "Keep those kids out of the Rendezvous, Keane! They ain't old enough to live that good yet!"

"Sadecki's gonna be a hell of a pitcher, Peter," I said. "He has really come fast for a kid. Kept his confidence. Didn't get beat too often when he first came up. You got to have that early success in order to develop fast in this league."

"Let him beat L.A.," said Whisenant.

Purkey retired the last ten batters in a row, flourishing an infectious air of confidence that precipitated an extra-loud roar of applause when the first-inning score of the Giant-Dodger game was posted. San Francisco led 2-0 as we filed down the ramp toward our clubhouse.

Larry Jackson tapped me on the shoulder, held out his hand, and said, "Congratulations. Good luck in the Series. You guys ought to do it now."

I showered, dressed, took a limousine to the airport, and flew home to tell my wife.

The Cubs arrived in town September 12, knowing exactly where they stood for the 1961 season. Picked to finish seventh the Cubs surprised no one, except the Cincinnati Reds.

"What have they got against us?" Nunn asked. "They're the only club in the league that beat us more than we beat them."

Hutchinson pondered this paradox before picking his

pitcher for the penultimate game in the Cincinnati-Chicago season series. Since the leading Cub hitters were both left-handed, percentage decreed that O'Toole pitch instead of Joey Jay, who was still looking for his twentieth win.

"You can beat the Braves tomorrow," Hutch told Jay.

O'Toole had an ugly fever blister on his lip, and Doc Rohde shook his head at the sight of it.

"If you win tonight you'll have to pose for pictures. Ugh!"

"Don't worry about it, Doc. Just get my arm ready."

I stood on the scale, half-afraid to look at the results of two days of relaxing. Two hundred and fourteen pounds. Complacency setting in, making me fat.

"As soon as I finish this book, I'd better do some running," I thought. I went into the gym room, lay down on the slant board, and turned a page of *The Devil's Advocate*.

Avery Robbins hung up the phone, stared at me, and said, "Broz, someday I'm gonna catch you reading a book standing on your head like a Yogi!"

"Cool it. Get me twenty tickets for the Series, will ya?"

"Forget it. I don't know you."

The Cubs looked different from the dugout than they had from the bullpen. God knows I needed a different view of them.

"If it weren't for those guys, I could get a raise next year," I complained to Whisenant.

"Win a couple more games and I'll get you one, personally," he advised me.

O'Toole handled the Cub batters as easily as if they were Phillies for five innings. Post hit a home run to give him a lead and O'Toole broke three Cub bats with fast sliders. His pitching pattern had the professional touch of a veteran.

"Whiz," I said, "Tootie has finally made it."

"He's come a long way," Whisenant admitted.

Santo bounced a two-hopper to Kasko for the third out in the sixth inning.

"Look at that July hop!" Blasingame said. "Breaks are goin' our way, boys!"

In the seventh inning Turner sidled up to me and said, "Bet-

231

ter meander on down to the bullpen, Captain."

When I reached the bullpen Henry greeted me: "Whaddya say, Lieutenant! We just took a vote and demoted you. You been spending too much time in the dugout."

"I was just checking the Philly pitcher in the L.A. game, Gab!" I protested. "Look. Buzhardt's got a two-run lead in the first."

"Come on, you old roomie!" Henry said.

But when Buzhardt was bombed out by the Dodgers, Henry said, disgustedly, "Ol' Roomie, you ain't worth a ———!"

Fortunately the Phillies scored nine more runs in the second inning.

"That oughta do it!" said Nunn. "Figure it out for us, Broz."

It figured to be easy, if we kept winning.

A young business executive gets no more pleasure seeing a title on his door than a young pitcher feels winning his twentieth game of any season.

Joey Jay, who hadn't pitched well for two weeks, had been assured of several chances to get his twentieth win.

"Hope Jay isn't waiting to clinch the pennant with No. 20," I said to Whisenant as we watched Jay warm up to start the next night's game.

"It's time for him to have a good game," said Pete, as the Milwaukee Braves' lineup was announced.

"Look at that lineup!" said Nunn. "How can they be behind us!"

Elio Chacon held out his hand to me and said, in his curious José Jiminez accent, "Professor, you got tobacco?"

I watched Chacon stuff half a pack of my Beech-Nut into his mouth, then turned back to the game.

"Watch Joey throw Mathews high sliders and get him out," I said.

"Maybe that's how to pitch him," said O'Toole.

Mathews popped up to end the first inning.

"It just ain't right!" I said.

Carlton Willey, the Braves pitcher, matched Jay's effectiveness for four innings. He hung a curve to Robinson, another to Freese, but got away with them both.

"We should hit those pitches," I said. "Willey's too good a pitcher to make many mistakes."

"Nah," said Whisenant. "He's a .500 pitcher *because* he makes those pitches too often."

In the fifth inning, Jay scored the only run of the game sliding bumpily over the plate as the throw from the outfield bounced away from the catcher.

"They could hear you score clear up in Milwaukee, Joe!" O'Toole said, shaking Jay's hand.

The Braves, who had already been beaten three times in 1961 by Jay, did not threaten to score until the eighth inning. Then, with two out, Chrisley and Maye singled. Henry warmed up hurriedly in the bullpen as Bob Boyd batted for McMillan.

"Mathews is the next hitter, Gab," I said as we both started to throw hard. "If Boyd gets on you're probably in there. Mathews can't hit you, y'know."

Henry nodded. Jay threw three balls to Boyd, then two straight strikes.

"Come all the way back and get him, Joe," Henry muttered.

Boyd rapped a ground ball to the mound and Jay jumped happily into the air as Coleman took his throw for the third out.

In the ninth Mathews and Aaron lined out to put Jay one pitch from his first twenty-game year, and the first for any Cincinnati pitcher in fourteen years.

Adcock hit a long drive to right field and Robinson ran back to the fence as the ball headed for the bleacher seats.

"The wind's got it!" I yelled as the ball slowed down. Robinson took one step forward and grabbed it. Jay, who had frozen in a stiff crouch as the ball took off from the bat, threw his hands up over his head as the entire club rushed out to congratulate him.

In the clubhouse the photographers asked Jay to kiss Pinson because Vada had driven in the only run of the game.

"I'll *do* it!" Jay said, laughing.

Personally, I'd kiss his ear to win twenty games.

While the Reds rested for two days and pretended there really wasn't a pot of gold two weeks away at the end of the season, the Dodgers won two games in the Coliseum. They trailed us by four and a half games, but were definitely not out of the race yet. The clutching cold fingers of pessimism occasionally gripped my tired old nerves. I felt certain pangs of fatigue in the arm that had never held me up in so high a position for so long during a major league season.

If I still had *my* doubts, the Red front office was gleefully optimistic. The practical necessities of preparing for a World Series demanded it. Tickets had to be printed, Crosley Field had to be painted and decorated, and a World Series program had to be prepared.

A photographer was hired to shoot a series of color pictures of the twenty-five-player roster that might represent the Reds in the Series. Howie Nunn, who had returned from the disabled list on September 1, was barred, by league rules, from the group that posed in left field three hours before our September 16 game with Philadelphia. Howie spit bitter gobs of saliva onto the bullpen floor while he watched us smile like pennant winners. His disappointment was a rankling burr in a generally happy scene.

"I deserved it more than some guys on this club!" Nunn said later as we started batting practice. "Don't you think so, Broz?"

"You're damn right, Rooms."

"Well, give me a chew. I might as well get really sick. Those twenty-five martinis last night damn near killed me!"

"Nobody can drink twenty-five martinis in one night," I said.

"Howie can," said Zimmerman.

Nunn didn't look it until we started running. The sloshing sound of his legs and arms stirring pregame adrenalin secretions accented my own ludicrous efforts to get loose. At the end of any season it becomes harder and harder to snap all the muscles into game condition. An usher in the stands giggled audibly at Nunn's effort to catch a fly ball.

"Why don't you pitch batting practice, Rooms, and let it all hang out," I suggested. "Really let 'em have it!"

"Better save it," he said. "I might pitch winter ball after the Series."

"Hutch is probably gonna use Whole Staff in every game from now on, I imagine," said Zimmerman.

Although the Phillies scored just two runs in the game, they threatened repeatedly, and Hutch had to use five pitchers to get a 3-2 win. Ken Johnson was batted out in the fourth, and Maloney walked four men in the fourth and fifth innings before he left without giving up a run. Henry pitched to six batters, and O'Toole worked a scoreless seventh inning. When we came to bat in the last of the seventh—"our part of the game," as Lynch assured us—we trailed 2-0.

Kasko singled and Pinson was safe on Demeter's error. That was all the encouragement Lynch needed. He doubled home two runs and scored the third one when Post, batting for O'Toole, singled to left. That gave us a one-run lead and put me on the mound.

I had been so engrossed in Sherman Jones's tale of his Army life that I'd missed hearing that the Cincinnati pitcher was batting eighth, not ninth in the order. Usually a relief pitcher knows to the minute how much time he has to warm up, but I had assumed, carelessly, that the catcher would hit before O'Toole and I had not yet started to throw hard when Post was announced as a pinch-hitter. Fortunately, Post's single gave me a little extra time to get hot—and to ponder Roadblock's travail.

"I had it made in the Army," Jones had concluded in his monologue of military life. "There, the less you say, the less you do, the less you're seen, the better off you are. But here, in this game, you gotta work to get ahead."

Ready or not, I had to work for two innings. I hadn't had a save for a month, and my chances to have it made in the near future depended on my ability to take advantage of every chance at present success. My present chances against the Phillies depended on my slider and I knew I couldn't make it without a good hard one. That conviction sustained me even after the first two batters singled. The next six men waved weakly at what Darrell Johnson called "a good, hard one. That's the way to shove it up their old giggies, Broz!"

That's one way to make it, Road.

Avery Robbins took over the clubhouse meeting before the game the next day, and outlined the prospective ticket situation for the World Series.

"We're not in it yet, I know, but we have to talk about it now. We will have ten tickets for each game at Crosley Field for each player, and five tickets for each game in New York for each player. I know that won't be nearly enough for any of you but that's all there is. Bring your checkbooks—you know that there are no passes, of course. Every seat in the Series has to be paid for. Now, for Christ's sake, win it, will ya?"

The Phillies, losers of nineteen of twenty-one games with us, proved to be stumbling blocks rather than stepping stones when we played the concluding game of our 1961 season series. Sleeping dogs should lie still when their masters so desire, but the Phillies were frisky and unmanageable for nine innings. Compared with our tensely nervous hitters the Phillies exuded pennant-contending confidence.

"Every man on our club goes up to bat looking like he's got an olive in his throat—a big, green one!" said Joey Jay, sarcastically. "Reminds me of '59, when the Braves won the pennant. Fred Haney didn't manage the club. He sat in one corner of the dugout, gulping down pills and saying to Crandall, 'What should we do, Del?' "

"Hutch isn't exactly loose as a goose," I said. "It's tougher on the managers in some ways than it is on the players, I guess, when you get right down to it. We sure as hell could use a laugher one of these games."

Whisenant grabbed O'Toole by the ears, mimed the act of decapitating O'Toole's head, and pretended to punt it into the stands.

236

"Damn it! Root for Purkey, Tootie," Pete said. "He roots for you."

O'Toole clapped his hands together and yelled, "Hang in there, Purk!"

Purkey was having little luck on the mound. A walk, two bloops, and a misjudged fly ball gave Philadelphia three runs in the third inning, and we couldn't get anything started against Mahaffey.

"I knew in the fourth we weren't gonna score today," said Purkey morosely when Hutch sent Post in to hit for him in the seventh. "Sometimes you get a premonition on the mound." Purkey picked up his glove, buttoned his jacket, and walked back to the clubhouse as Post struck out.

Although I had no particular desire to mop up in a losing cause, I realized some satisfaction, knowing I was in my fiftieth game of the season. That satisfaction disappeared quickly when Smith beat out a bunt and scored on a broken-bat single by Smith. (The Phillies, miserable as they were, probably craved anonymity. They had several Smiths on their roster and they were difficult to tell apart.) I cursed them both noisily, for an earned run annoys me more than bad breath.

Art Mahaffey, the Philly pitcher, had thrown seven straight bad balls to the first two batters he faced in the game, and the bases were loaded before he retired the side in the first inning. But from then on, the bases were empty, except for various Philly runners.

Mahaffey himself reached first safely, but he regretted it three minutes later. I had a 3-2 count on Malkmus, and could see Mahaffey take off for second on the pitch that Malkmus grounded to Blasingame. Blazer threw to Kasko at second, forcing Mahaffey, but when Art forgot to duck the relay to first, the ball hit him in the face and bounced halfway to the left field wall.

Mahaffey fell groaning, and while I personally couldn't stand to look at the damage at that moment, Peanuts Lowrey ran from his coaching position at third base to offer condolences. Lowrey also waved to Malkmus to come on to second as Lynch fielded the ball and threw it back to the infield. The ball beat Malkmus to the bag, but the gathering crowd prevented Kasko from making a play.

Mahaffey was carried from the field and Hutchinson protested the game, declaring that Lowrey was out of bounds and interfering in orthodox, orderly play of the game. The umpires maintained that there was nothing illegal about Lowrey's movements, and wasn't it too bad about Mahaffey?

"To hell with him!" I said. "What if a coach ran on the field every time a close play came up? You guys got some stupid rules! That might cost me a run!"

"There, there, Jimmy," said Jackowski, who had made the original call. "You got better stuff than that!"

I managed to get out of the inning with no further damage to my ego, and Sullivan preserved Mahaffey's shutout. Blasingame raced from the field into the clubhouse, and was sitting with a half-smile on his face when I reached my locker.

"If they had batted any longer in that ninth inning, I'da had to call time," he said. "I've got diarrhea!"

He wasn't the only one who looked sick.

"Broz," said Blasingame, two days later when Pittsburgh came to town for their last appearance in Cincinnati, "I'm reading the same book you are."

He pointed at a copy of *The Interns* lying in my locker. "In fact, I just checked where you left off reading and it's the same page I stopped on last night. How about that?"

"That's what I call the first good sign of the day," I said. "Togetherness. That's what's winning for us. Now, if you guys would just score about ten runs tonight I'd feel really buddy-buddy."

"That's all you pitchers talk about—runs, runs, runs!"

Nothing makes a pitcher feel more secure than the sight of his teammates circling the bases during a ball game. We had won six out of our last seven games on a total of twenty-three runs, which is hardly enough to glow about. The Dodgers had stayed with us, picking up a game and a half when we were idle. (The Braves had assured us that, after leaving Cincinnati, they would fly to the Coast, rack L.A. up three times, and hand us the flag. But then they'd blown all three games to the Dodgers and tightened the race once more.)

Friend and O'Toole matched each other perfectly for three innings as our string of scoreless innings increased to eleven straight.

"Go shake up those bats, Broz," said Whisenant as O'Toole shut the Pirates out in the fourth.

"Snap out of it," I yelled at the bat rack, scaring the box seat customers who sat next to our dugout. Kicking several bats in the lower slots, I giggled embarrassedly at my own foolishness.

But Friend blew up in the last of the fourth, and Tootie went back to work with a seven-run lead.

"That's the biggest inning we've had all year, Whiz!" I crowed happily.

"It came just in time," he said. "Look at the heavy bat."

The aluminum bat which our batters used to loosen up with in the on-deck circle had split halfway up the handle.

"Hutch do that?" I asked, awe-stricken.

"He *says* the batboy dropped it," said Whisenant. "But I don't know. Remind me not to argue with him . . . ever!"

In the seventh inning Gene Freese poled a long fly ball over the left field screen, ten feet foul. It was the forty-second time Freese had hit a ball out of the park foul during the season. Two pitches later, he hit his twenty-sixth fair home run, ten feet inside the line.

"If they moved that foul line thirty feet to the left I'd make 'em forget Babe Ruth," Freese said, flexing his muscles on the bench.

"You scare 'em to death, anyway, Augie," said Lynch.

The Pirates changed pitchers, but the game was in O'Toole's bag. He'd won six in a row as we came down the stretch. When the Cubs beat the Dodgers at L.A., 5-3, we had our five-game lead back and the magic number was down to five. Any combination of Red wins and Dodger losses that added up to five would give us the pennant.

Ten runs a game would make it easy on all of us.

"See how much fun this game is when you guys score

runs?" I said to Blasingame in the clubhouse.

"Beautiful," he agreed. "Just beautiful."

The Pirates, dethroned as National League champions, looked sadly bedraggled as they took a listless batting practice before the game the next night. The last ten ball games of the season are torturous exercises for those players whose high hopes for the season have been irredeemably squashed. The Pirates had four .300 hitters in their lineup and that means *beaucoup* runs in a 154-game schedule; but for this season that wasn't enough.

Don Hoak, whose early-season prediction that Cincinnati couldn't win the pennant hadn't come true, had more hopeful prophecies for the Reds' chances in the Series.

"You guys can beat the Yankees, 'cause you get the pitching to do it," he said to the Cincinnati reporters who had congregated in the Cincinnati dugout.

"And another thing," Hoak continued, turning to Wally Post. "Tonight, Post, you won't—I repeat, *won't*—hit a ball by me!"

Post, who had carried the club with his bat while Robinson slumped at the plate, laughed confidently. "I hope I get one pitch inside that I can handle," he said.

Two innings passed before Post had a chance to test Hoak's boastful confidence. With one out, Post lined a shot in the hole between third and short. Hoak dove for the ball, missed it, pounded his glove on the ground, and shook his fist at Post, who stood on first with a smile on his face.

Cardenas and Gernert singled Post around to third and, on Darrell Johnson's short fly ball to left, Post scored as Skinner's throw bounced high at the plate, preventing the catcher from making the tag.

"Nice bounce," said O'Toole on the bench.

"Breaks goin' our way, boys," I said.

"Breaks hell," said Whisenant. "That ball should have been a double! Skinner picks a bare spot in left field and never moves off it all night! He should have been in left center with Darrell hitting."

The fans along the third base line booed lustily when Hoak batted in the third inning. They booed again when Hoak took his position at the end of the inning. The heckling didn't affect his fielding but it ruined his disposition. Finally Hoak called time and walked over to have a word with his critics. Several fans, who didn't believe ballplayers could talk back, covered their ears in protest against this indelicate outrage. Jocko Conlan, the third base umpire, joined Hoak at the box seat railing, called a cease-fire to the verbal skirmish, and escorted Hoak back to his position.

Joey Jay shut the Pirates out until the eighth, when four singles produced two runs and a one-run lead for Pittsburgh. But in the last half of the inning, Post hit a ball *over* Hoak, over the left field wall, and even over the high screen atop the wall. Pinson was on base at the time, so Jay had his lead back.

In the ninth inning, Hoak batted with two out. The boos that greeted his appearance proved too much for him, especially when they turned into a shower of stones and other projectiles that kicked up dust on and around him. Again Hoak called time, put his bat down, walked over to the P.A. man, and asked that the crowd be enjoined from throwing at him. Mollified, he then returned to bat and popped up to end the game.

The fans beat a happy, if hasty, retreat from the stands behind third base, and the Pirate plane, carrying a somewhat disillusioned Don Hoak, flew home to Pittsburgh.

Since most 1961 minor league teams had completed their schedules, some of those ballplayers who lived in Cincinnati during the winter came down to the Crosley Field clubhouses on September 22 to review past glories and renew old friendships. When I arrived at the park for our game with the Giants, Jim Bolger, who had hit over .300 at San Diego in the Pacific Coast League, was showing Pete Whisenant, an old teammate of Bolger's, how he'd swung the bat all season.

"Can you imagine a bench with both Bolger and Whisenant on it?" asked Post. "They'd kill you!"

Whisenant, whose daily bat-swinging tours up and down

the dugout were an ever-present danger to benchwarmers, had nothing on Bolger when it came to taking practice swings, no matter how small the space or how large the crowd around him. Bolger had, in one memorable clubhouse instance, struck a Philadelphia sportswriter squarely on the chest with his bat.

"Man," Bolger had said, "Did you see that? First time I popped my wrists all year! I almost ran it out!"

The writer recovered, although he received little or no sympathy for having gotten in the way of Bolger's bat. As coincidence would have it, the same writer had been assigned to cover the Reds in 1961 until we cinched the pennant. He blanched at the sight of Bolger and his swinging bat, but side-stepped him and continued to dig for a story. Philadelphia sportswriters work at their job with diligent, sometimes irritating perseverance.

"What do all good relief pitchers have in common?" he asked me as I tied the laces on my spikes.

"Ulcers," I said, quickly. His question sounded like a riddle.

"Seriously," he said.

"One good pitch, good control, and a lot of nerve," I said. "Any pitcher who goes out there sixty times a season thinking he can get everybody out has to be lacking in practical good sense."

"How long are you going to keep it up?" he continued.

"One more game. Every day I say I'll try it one more game."

"Hurry up and cinch this thing. I'd like to go home to visit my family."

The reports from the team's physician and trainer made it seem unlikely that we could field a ball club. Kasko had a case of suspected diabetes; Freese and Edwards had severe ankle sprains; Pinson had a sprained wrist; Coleman and Jay had such bad skin rashes they could hardly wear jockstraps; Robinson was in the worst slump of his career. Various pennant pressure syndromes resulted in gratuitous offers of bad advice from the coaches and wild second guesses from the press and radiomen.

"Why doesn't it rain one time?" groaned Zimmerman.

"Swing the bat!" said Henry.

"O'Dell works fast," Whisenant repeated to each hitter. "Step out once in a while. Make him wait."

O'Dell, the Giant pitcher of the day, was in no mood to wait. Whichever Red batters appeared at the plate O'Dell retired with almost unbroken regularity. Purkey, pitching for us, voiced no premonitions about our chances of being shut out. As a matter of fact, after the third inning, Purkey retired to the clubhouse, showered, and went home.

San Francisco won 6-0, and did it so quickly that the final score of the Dodger game at St. Louis was not announced until I'd drunk my third can of beer, sitting before my locker, contemplating my navel. (The Dodgers won and reduced our lead to four games.)

"What's the magic number again, Broz?" Nunn asked.

"Two-two-one-six. My hotel room. I think I'll sleep tonight for a change."

"You must be sick," he concluded.

"We're the best team in the league right now," said a San Francisco ballplayer the next afternoon. "The Reds aren't even third best. Right now!"

Such a salty quotation was enough to fire up the boiling pot of ire in every editorial columnist who had rooted the Reds home for the last two months. It might even have riled the sensitivities of some Red ballplayers if the Saturday weather hadn't turned out to be so damned hot.

The temperature on the field before the game was ninety-five degrees. Whoever the grossly confident Giant mortal was that spoke disparagingly of the Reds, he did not even bother to take batting practice. Nor did any of his teammates. The Giants stayed in their clubhouse, either overweeningly arrogant or blushfully embarrassed. As the truth would have it, the *Giants* would be lucky to finish third.

Having taken an inordinate time to shave cleanly and dress neatly, as befitted a would-be pennant winner, I missed my bus and was late getting to the clubhouse. Pete Whisenant stood at the doorway, fungo bat in hand, looking like a coach, wearing the frown of a manager, staring at his watch like an about-to-be-damned fool.

"You're five minutes late, Broz," he said accusingly.

"That's right, honey," I retorted. "But I might have to play today."

Assuming a crushed, coachlike mien, Whisenant stalked from the clubhouse, muttering, "Get serious, Brosnan."

Jim Turner, standing behind the batting practice pitcher, welcomed me as I came down the ramp to the field.

"Nice of you to show up, Captain. Why don't you chase some ground balls now, just to get loose?"

He grinned, I grinned back, and we both knew I wouldn't take him seriously. Whisenant stood at the batting cage, fungo at the ready, waiting to chase me back and forth on the infield.

"Forget it, Colonel," I said and walked out to the scoreboard, half-fearing a line drive off Pete's fungo. Coaches *can* be pushed too far. I couldn't have picked a better time to see how far.

Whisenant had a definite "To hell with you, Broz" look about him just before game time, so I went out to the bullpen when the lineups were announced. The Giants had picked a rookie to pitch against us and help them prove their alleged superiority.

The rookie didn't last long. He gave up two home runs to Gordy Coleman, the first home runs that Bubbles had hit in over a month. San Francisco infielders chipped in some third-place efforts to give us three more runs; and Ed Bailey contrived, almost desperately, to help us win.

Bailey allowed two foul fly balls to drop to the ground, and in each case had to bluff a Giant infielder out of a routine catch. Later in the game he forced a runner at second base, then left first base and trotted to the dugout in mistaken assumption that he, too, was out. Giggling happily, O'Toole, on the mound, threw the ball to first, where Coleman waited for Bailey to return to the bag and be tagged out. Instead, Bailey stood at the edge of the Giant dugout in shocked embarrassment and was called out for delaying the game or something.

244

O'Toole breezed into the eighth inning but the heat hit him at the same time as the Giant batters started to swing, and Hutch excused O'Toole for the day. I relieved, fully conscious that I could get no save for the day's work. The scoreboard already had listed the score in St. Louis—Dodgers 8, Cardinals 5. We *did* need a win, so there was absolutely no excuse for me to hang two sliders in a row.

Alou hit one to the scoreboard, where Pinson made a leaping catch. That fly ball drove in a run from third, and Cepeda hit the next hanger over the center field fence—*far* over the center field fence.

From our dugout came a chorus of advice, Whisenant's voice distinctly audible.

"For Christ's sake, make some pitches!"

Fortunately, I had a couple left over from July.

After the game I called home to tell my wife that it looked inevitable.

"We'll cinch it in Chicago on Tuesday. Order champagne, break the seal on the Napoleon brandy, ol' Dad's bringin' home the bacon, baby!"

For our final regularly scheduled game of the season at Crosley Field September 24, the S.R.O. sign was hung up early in the day. Avery Robbins chalked a notice on the clubhouse bulletin board that "Family Passes Only" would be honored by the front office.

"Who in hell drew the fans all year?"

"On the last game of the year?"

"How chintzy can they get?"

Indignant outcries, widespread if not unanimous, could have been expected. Their malevolence on this last day of the season would have tainted the air at a harpies' bazaar. The telephone lines buzzed as apologetic explanations were made to expectant free-loaders all over the city.

"I not only can't get you a ticket to the World Series; I can't even get you a pass to today's game! It's ridiculous."

Bizarre requests for World Series tickets had to be rejected each day by each player on the Reds. They came by mail, by telegram, by long-distance phone call. They made brotherly love worth analyzing, and rudeness necessary. They came from relatives and close friends whose disappointment rankled; they came from long-forgotten friends whose merrily explicit memories made the suppressed feeling of passing years a graphic fact; and they even came, occasionally, from an acquaintance who, you suspected, wouldn't give you the shirt off his back even if it were yours and he'd borrowed it a month before.

And they all had to be refused, for there were no tickets available.

Joey Jay limped about the clubhouse before the game, his pained expression only partly dulled by the pills that Doc Rohde had given him for his skin rash.

"I don't know what town I'm in even," said Jay. "Doc gave me two more pills to counteract the opium or whatever it was I took last night. I'd rather itch. At least I'd feel like I'm alive."

The Giants' hitters obviously wished him ill, and in the fourth inning knocked him out of the box. Ken Johnson relieved, unwillingly.

"Boy, I just can't pitch relief, Rooms," he had told me before the game. "It's different from starting a game."

Johnson walked two batters on ten pitches, then threw a fat slider to Orlando Cepeda. The Baby Bull banged it over the scoreboard halfway up the light tower, for a grand-slam home run.

"That should set the record for long ball of the year," I said to Nunn in the bullpen. "Howie, *you* may even get into this contest!"

"No chance," he said. "We're not far enough behind yet. I tell you, though. I'd throw strikes."

"Don't get on my roomie, Johnson, Rooms," I said.

While the Giants scored most of the runs in the 12-5 win the packed house found something to cheer about each inning as the Cardinal-Dodger game was posted on the scoreboard. By the sixth inning St. Louis led 6-0; in the seventh the score read 6-5; in the eighth inning it was 8-5. The gut-pleasing roar that would have greeted the final St. Louis win was denied our ears because our game ended too quickly.

When the final score of 8-7 reached me I was halfway to the airport on my way to Chicago. The knowledge was no less sweet. We only needed a win from the Cubs while Pittsburgh beat L.A. either on Monday or Tuesday.

I wondered, then, just what my wife *would* wear to the World Series.

Chicago — September 26

"WHEN this season is over I'm going to tear this thing out of the wall!" my wife said as she jerked the phone from its cradle and half-shouted: "Hello! Yes, he's here! You've got five minutes to talk with him. Then I get a chance! Please?"

The well-wishing congratulations of a dozen friends was a bit premature. The Dodger-Pirate game scheduled for Monday, the twenty-fifth, had been rained out, and even if we beat the Cubs on this twenty-sixth day of September we still needed one win by the Pirates in their twi-night doubleheader in Pittsburgh.

"Even when you're home I don't see you," my wife grumbled. "Pitch three good innings today and win, and tell Hutch you need the rest of the week off. I'll be waiting."

"You're not going to watch us cinch it?"

"I couldn't stand it!" she insisted.

There were fewer fans in the Wrigley Field stands than there were photographers and reporters on the field before the game.

"Do we play well before crowds of reporters, Joey?" I asked Jay.

"They *still* can't believe we could win it," he said. "Experts. Ha!"

"Poor babies!"

The Cubs started off like Dodger-helpers, scoring a run in the first inning on a pop fly that fell between Lynch and Pinson and a long double by George Altman, the best hitter in baseball according to Cincinnati's pitching charts for 1961.

Bob Purkey's luck continued to run bad. In the five innings

he pitched the Cubs scored three runs, none of them rightly earned, and two of them blatant gifts from the Red infield. Meanwhile the Cincinnati bats were virtually hitless.

"Fine time for Purkey to get snake-bit!" moaned Nunn. "When are we gonna score some runs? Shake yourselves, you hitters!"

Little Howie's irritated, needling squawk added a last straw to the burden of guilt that their own defensive faults had piled on the Red hitters.

John Edwards, who hadn't hit a home run since the day he broke in against the Cubs in July, stroked one in the sixth inning, and Robinson hit a two-run homer in the seventh to tie the score. Despite the fact that the Cubs' lineup was loaded with left-handed hitters Hutch called me in to pitch.

"Go get 'em, Broz," Henry said as I started in from the bull-pen.

"My God, I could lose *three* games to these guys!" I thought.

For once, however, I knew I had good stuff. My slider was fast and sharp, the best I'd had all year. The Cubs went down in order.

With two out in our half of the eighth Pinson walked. Lynch, who had promised Whisenant, "Don't worry, Pete. I'll get one. Hit it on the fists or something," ran the count to 2-2. Whisenant yelled from the bench, "Hit for yourself, Jerry! Hit what you see!" and Lynch swung.

"He did it! He did it!" Whisenant shouted. "Look at it go!"

The ball sailed far over the right field bleachers, giving us a two-run lead.

"You're something else, Lynch," I murmured to myself.

"Go get 'em now, Broz!" Lynch urged me when he returned to the bench.

"Right man in the right spot, Broz!" said Whisenant.

The more strikes I threw, the better I felt as the Cubs swung through, under, and over the slider. Three of the last four Cub batters struck out and little goose bumps broke out on the back of my neck, ran down my spine, and popped out on my right arm.

"Nice going, big man," said Hutch, gripping my hand firmly after the third out. "That should do it."

The bus ride to the airport was a swinging, beer-swigging, song fest. Halfway to Cincinnati our plane's pilot informed us that L.A. had won the first game from Pittsburgh 5-3. Hutchinson shrugged it off and said, "Tonight I'm giving a party at the Netherland Hilton. Pittsburgh is going to win that second game, so let's celebrate!"

A noisy, cheering crowd greeted us at the airport. Fans, gathered at intersections along the ten-mile route to downtown Cincinnati, waved Red pennants and Halloween noisemakers. Children from an orphanage near the airport squealed as the bus carrying the players crawled by in a caravan of horn-honking cars.

Fountain Square in the heart of town was jammed with thirty thousand people who listened to a broadcast of the Pirate game from loudspeakers set up at both ends of the square. They roared when Pittsburgh scored five runs in the third inning. They cheered each Dodger out, and shouted encouragement to each Pirate batter. When Bob Skinner caught a fly ball for the last Dodger out, bedlam broke loose.

Bands played, sirens wailed, fans hugged each other and danced in the street. Hutchinson was carried about on the shoulders of the crowd that rocked the Red bus as it inched its way toward the hotel.

The desk clerk greeted me with a grin and a handshake.

"We've got a convention here," he said. "For you guys we have rooms. For anybody else, no. We're jammed. They're having a tough time finding a room for your party. Hutch is looking for one now."

He found one.

FINAL NATIONAL LEAGUE STANDINGS

	WON	LOST	PCTGE.
Cincinnati	93	61	.604
Los Angeles	89	65	.578
San Francisco	85	69	.552
Milwaukee	83	71	.539
St. Louis	80	74	.519
Pittsburgh	75	79	.487
Chicago	64	90	.416
Philadelphia	47	107	.305

CINCINNATI REDS 1961 PITCHING RECORDS

	GAMES	WON	LOST	INNINGS	STRIKE-OUTS	E.R.A.	SAVES
Brosnan	53	10	4	80	40	3.04	16
Henry	47	2	1	53	52	2.20	16
Hook	22	1	3	62	36	7.71	0
Hunt	29	9	10	136	75	3.97	0
Jay	34	21	10	247	157	3.57	0
Johnson	15	6	2	83	42	3.14	
Jones	24	1	1	55	32	4.42	3
Maloney	27	6	7	94	57	4.26	2
Nunn	24	2	1	38	25	3.55	0
O'Toole	39	19	9	252	176	3.11	2
Purkey	36	16	12	246	116	3.77	1

CINCINNATI REDS BATTING RECORDS—1961

	AVG.	GAMES	AT BATS	RUNS	HITS	DOUBLES	TRIPLES	HOME RUNS	R.B.I.
Bell	.255	101	235	27	60	10	1	3	33
Blasingame	.222	123	450	60	100	18	4	1	21
Cardenas	.308	79	198	23	61	18	1	5	24
Chacon	.250	61	132	26	35	4	2	2	5
Coleman	.283	150	520	63	149	27	4	26	87
Edwards	.186	51	145	14	27	5	0	2	14
Freese	.276	152	575	78	159	27	2	26	87
Gernert	.306	40	62	4	19	1	0	0	7
Johnson	.315	20	54	3	17	2	0	1	6
Kasko	.271	126	469	63	127	22	1	2	27
Lynch	.315	95	181	33	57	13	2	13	50
Pinson	.343	154	607	101	208	33	8	16	87
Post	.295	98	282	44	83	15	3	20	57
Robinson	.323	153	545	117	176	32	7	37	124
Zimmerman	.206	75	204	8	42	5	0	0	10